NEGRO CHILD WELFARE
IN NORTH CAROLINA

NEGRO CHILD WELFARE
IN NORTH CAROLINA

A ROSENWALD STUDY

DIRECTED BY

WILEY BRITTON SANDERS, Ph.D.
ASSOCIATE PROFESSOR OF SOCIOLOGY
THE UNIVERSITY OF NORTH CAROLINA

———

UNDER THE JOINT AUSPICES OF
THE NORTH CAROLINA STATE BOARD OF CHARITIES
AND PUBLIC WELFARE
AND
THE SCHOOL OF PUBLIC WELFARE, THE UNIVERSITY OF
NORTH CAROLINA

———

PUBLISHED FOR THE NORTH CAROLINA STATE BOARD OF
CHARITIES AND PUBLIC WELFARE BY
THE UNIVERSITY OF NORTH CAROLINA PRESS
CHAPEL HILL
1933

INTRODUCTION

ALTHOUGH THE North Carolina State Board of Charities and Public Welfare is interested in the welfare of every citizen in the State, its peculiar responsibility is the individual underprivileged or handicapped through physical or mental defect or social maladjustment. Because those drafting the articles for the government of our State believed "one of the first duties of a civilized and Christian State" to be "beneficent provision for the poor, the unfortunate and orphan," they wrote a constitutional mandate[1] charging the General Assembly "at its first session to appoint and define the duties of a Board of Public Charities." This Board of Public Charities has realized that its responsibility for the poor, the unfortunate, and the orphan was not circumscribed by race or creed but included all such members of all groups within the borders of the State. As the work of the Board expanded and developed, a Division of Work among Negroes was created in 1925 in the Board. North Carolina, therefore, was the first state in the Union to establish a Division of Work among Negroes. The chief function of this Division has been the organizing of the leaders of this race in both state and county so that through their ability they may aid the poor, the unfortunate, and the orphan of their race, thus protecting both the individual and the group or society.

From its beginning Lieutenant Lawrence A. Oxley has been the Director of this Division. Many interesting articles on his work have been published, and it was through reading some of these articles on the program for public welfare work for Negroes in North Carolina that Mr. Julius Rosenwald became interested in this field of service. Through Mr. N. C. Newbold of the State Department of Public Instruction, with whom he

---

[1] *Constitution of the State of North Carolina* (1868), Art XI, Sec. 7.

had long been associated in educational work, he made a tentative offer of help to this public welfare program, expressing his desire "to find out just what is being done of a substantial nature and whether they have sufficient money to carry on the work." He also asked for suggestions as to a basis of cooperation. Mr. Newbold in turn referred Mr. Rosenwald's offer and inquiry, not revealing from whom it came, to Mrs. Kate Burr Johnson, then State Commissioner of Public Welfare, suggesting that a small sum of money might be contributed and requesting that she give a detailed plan as to what she thought should be done with it. Mrs. Johnson first suggested a case-work study of 200 Negro children with reference to: (1) home and housing conditions, (2) community conditions, (3) manner of spending leisure time, (4) school record, and (5) whether compulsory school attendance and child labor laws really function for Negro children. Such a study would have been similar to one made six years before of 200 white children. It was thought that the results of this study would (1) show how well social institutions of North Carolina function for the protection and development of the Negro child and (2) foster a more thorough, systematic and intelligent care of the Negro child of the future. It was estimated that a minimum of $10,000 was needed to finance the project and that at least a year's time would be necessary for completing, compiling, and preparing the study for publication. Soon after this tentative plan was submitted to Mr. Rosenwald, he offered to give $5,000 toward a study if the State Board could raise a like sum. Since all State Board funds are appropriated by the General Assembly for specific purposes, the State's share had to be raised from private sources. This was in the spring of 1927. Soon North Carolina had raised $3,000 of its $5,000. Of the $3,000, $2,500 was pledged in service by the School of Public Welfare and the Institute for Research in Social Science of the University of North Carolina. The remaining $2,000 was more difficult to secure. But it came in gradually in gifts, ranging from pennies of Negro school children to $100 checks from organizations and citizens of both races. To Mr. Rosenwald, who

made the study possible by his generous gift, we feel most
indebted. But next we should pay tribute to the Negro school
child and his parents who, in giving what they could through
self-denial and in great faith rather than in understanding
as to what this project might mean, demonstrated how eager
they were to do their share toward helping. Knowing Mr.
Rosenwald's understanding and sympathy, we know that he,
too, appreciated the spirit of this gift. As it was necessary
to have the full $10,000 actually available before beginning
the investigation or the field work for the study and since
the funds were slow in accumulating, it was not until the
summer of 1929 that the project was really launched and
workers were in the field.

Meantime there had been ample opportunity for contempla-
tion and discussion of the study with the result that as the
plan was formulated it became more comprehensive. In October, 1928, the Committee consisting of the Commissioner,
the Director of Work among Negroes, and the Director of
Child Welfare, all of the State Board, and the Director of the
Study, Dr. Wiley B. Sanders, of the School of Public Welfare
of the University of North Carolina, outlined the study as
follows:

"Objectives:

1. To secure such information as will enable the public welfare
system in all its branches to function more successfully in extending its services to the Negro population of the State.

2. To help the institutions now caring for delinquent, dependent,
neglected and defective Negro children to understand their problem in relation to the whole field of Negro child welfare and to
persuade each institution to make such changes in its institutional
program as will enable that institution to make more successfully
its own distinct and original contribution to a unified State program
of child-care and protection.

3. To work out a State-wide program for the care of the
feeble-minded Negro children in North Carolina."

In planning the field work for this study it was agreed by the
members of the Committee that one of the most valuable sources

of information relating to delinquent, neglected, dependent and defective Negro children in North Carolina was to be found in the juvenile court docket books of the city and county juvenile courts throughout the State. These records covered the history of juvenile court cases for the first decade of juvenile court work, namely, from 1919 to 1929. Since there was no uniform system of reporting juvenile court cases to any State authority, these records were largely buried in the county courthouses and city halls, and little was known definitely about the nature and extent of juvenile court cases on a State-wide scale. In spite of the formidable nature of the task of collecting this information, it was planned to have members of the staff of the State Board and special workers to visit every county and city juvenile court in the State, and to make transcripts on cards of all the juvenile court cases recorded in the docket books, or otherwise recorded by the juvenile court, for both white and Negro children. Incidentally, it was planned that each worker in visiting the county courthouse for the purpose of transcribing the juvenile court records should talk informally with various courthouse officials, chiefly the clerk of court, the superintendent of schools, and the welfare officer, with regard to their attitude toward Negro welfare work, educational facilities for Negroes, and, in general, the place of the Negro in the life of the State. It was felt that such a study of attitudes would indicate what would be the principal obstacles (mainly prejudices) that had to be overcome before there could be worked out a comprehensive welfare program for Negroes in North Carolina.

To supplement the juvenile court statistics, and also to contrast the various types of social data, the research program also included a study of the children, white and Negro, who had been committed to the State's Prison as far back as adequate records were available. In addition to the statistical data, intensive case studies were planned both of Negro children handled by the juvenile courts, and those cared for in the various institutions.

Another major phase of the study agreed upon by the Committee was a survey, to be made by a nationally recognized child welfare agency, of every Negro child-caring institution in North Carolina, with reference to equipment, methods, and needs of these institutions. These institutions were:

(1) Morrison Training School for Delinquent Negro Boys, Hoffman.

(2) State Industrial Training School for Negro Girls, Efland.

(3) Memorial Orphanage, Winston-Salem.

(4) Colored Orphanage, Oxford.

(5) Ward for Feebleminded, State Hospital for Insane, Goldsboro.

(6) Ward for Negro Children, State Orthopedic Hospital, Gastonia.

(7) Ward for Negro Children, N. C. State Sanatorium for Tuberculosis.

(8) State School for Negro Deaf and Blind, Raleigh.

With minor modifications, and some additions, the plan as outlined above has been carried to completion. During the summer of 1929 four field workers: Miss Janet Quinlan, who had just completed her Master's degree in the University of North Carolina, Miss Zoe Marshall, a young Negro woman social worker from the New York School of Social Work, and two regular members of the State Board staff, Miss Lois Dosher and Lieutenant L. A. Oxley—collected statistics from the county juvenile courts throughout the State. A little later, Miss Marshall collected the social data for the case studies of the Negro delinquent children, while Lieutenant Oxley and Mr. R. Eugene Brown secured the statistical data on the Negro children in the State's Prison. Early in 1930, Miss Mary Irene Atkinson, Director of Department of Institutional Care of the Child Welfare League of America, made an institutional survey of Morrison Training School, State Industrial School for Negro Girls, Memorial Orphanage, and Oxford Colored Orphanage, while the material on the other Negro child-caring institutions was contributed by the superintendents of those institutions and members of the staff of the State Board of Charities and Public Welfare.

The study of the race attitudes of the county officials in thirty-seven counties covered by a member of the State Board staff proved most enlightening, but, it was felt by a number of the influential leaders in educational and public welfare work that it would serve no useful purpose to publish the results, and might lead to misunderstanding and criticism. This phase of the study, therefore, has been omitted in the published report, but the results as tabulated and written by the director are on file in the office of the State Board.

The first part of the study dealing with the history and present status of Negro welfare work in North Carolina was contributed by Lieutenant Lawrence A. Oxley, Director of the Division of Work among Negroes, of the State Board, while Miss Lily E. Mitchell, Director of the Division of Child Welfare, wrote the chapter on the care of dependent Negro children through Mother's Aid and in Placement in Foster Homes.

Other chapters, not included in the original plan, but added later to make the study more comprehensive, are "The Negro Unmarried Mother and Her Child" (embracing material already available but hitherto unpublished, and relating chiefly to Orange County), written by Miss Janet Quinlan, graduate student in the University, and Mr. George H. Lawrence, Superintendent of Public Welfare of Orange County, N. C.; "Negro Schools in North Carolina," written by Mr. N. C. Newbold of the State Department of Public Instruction; and "Health Work for Negro Children," contributed by Dr. G. M. Cooper, Director of Division of Preventive Medicine, of the State Board of Health.

Valuable advice in planning the study was received from Dr. C. C. Carstens, and Miss Emma Lundberg of the Child Welfare League of America, while Dr. T. J. Woofter, Jr., of the Institute for Reseach in Social Science of the University of North Carolina, generously gave technical assistance in the preparation and arrangement of the tables relating to the juvenile courts.

In its complete form, therefore, this child welfare study represents the work of nearly a score of social workers, both white and Negro. The institutional expert from the Child Welfare League of America, the young Negro woman case worker, and another field agent employed for a short time, were the only workers receiving their salaries from the Rosenwald grant. The remainder of the workers, including the director of the study, received their salaries from other sources, and their contributions to the study were, for the most part, what they were able to do in their spare time, as it were, while presumably employed on a full-time basis in another capacity. These facts may explain to some extent why the different chapters were written at different times, why the report has been so long in being completed, and may account, likewise, for the relatively loose arrangement of material, for inconsistencies, and for differences in point of view.

Begun under the administration of Mrs. Kate Burr Johnson, this study was completed under the administration of Mrs. W. T. Bost, as State Commissioner of Public Welfare.

TABLE OF CONTENTS

NEGRO CHILD WELFARE
IN NORTH CAROLINA

PART I

HISTORY AND PRESENT STATUS OF NEGRO WELFARE WORK IN NORTH CAROLINA

CHAPTER I

THE DEVELOPMENT OF NEGRO WELFARE WORK IN NORTH CAROLINA

ALTHOUGH THE Negro composes only twenty-nine per cent of the total population of North Carolina,[1] he furnishes approximately sixty per cent of the dependent population, and sixty-six per cent of the case-load of public and private social agencies throughout the state. Such concentration of poverty and dependency in a racial group representing less than one-third of the state's population would indicate the urgent need for a study of the causes of this condition. This study seeks to find the solution to this problem, and those intimately related to it, by finding out what becomes of the defective, delinquent, and dependent Negro children of North Carolina.

At the outset it should be pointed out that the Negro population of North Carolina is very unevenly distributed. In the extreme western border of mountain counties the Negroes make up less than ten per cent of the population. On the other hand, there are two Black Belts where the Negroes compose from fifty to seventy-five per cent of the population. One of these areas lies in the east north central part of the state,

---

[1] The total population of North Carolina in 1920 was 2,559,123. Of this number 1,783,779 were white, and 763,407 were Negro. The Negro population made up 29.8 per cent of the state's total population. In 1930, the total population of the state was 3,170,276, of which 2,234,948 were white and 918,647 were Negro. In this census the Negroes represented 28.9 per cent of the state's total population. During this ten-year period the white population increased 25.5 per cent, while the Negro population increased only 20.3 per cent. This decrease in proportion of Negroes in the total population of the state is probably due to the northward migration of Negroes seeking better industrial opportunities. (*Statistical Abstract of the U. S., 1931*, pp. 12-13).

and embraces the counties, Warren, Halifax, Northampton, Hertford, Bertie, and Edgecombe. The other Black Belt area lies in the south central portion, and comprises the counties, Anson, Richmond, Scotland, and Hoke. Just east of the mountains the Negroes make up from ten to twenty-five per cent of the population, while in the remainder of the state they represent from twenty-five to fifty per cent of the total population. Three-fourths of North Carolina's Negro population live in rural agricultural sections. With the possible exception of Durham, Winston-Salem, and Reidsville, few Negroes are found employed in manufacturing plants. Each year during the tobacco market season of approximately four months' duration, many local Negroes and large numbers of migrant Negroes from South Carolina, Virginia, and Georgia find employment in the cities of Wilson, Rocky Mount, Greenville, Kinston, Tarboro, Smithfield, and other eastern North Carolina tobacco market cities. Negro farmers in Eastern Carolina are principally tenant farmers, suffering all the ills that such a system of tenant farming entails.

Ever since its creation in 1869, the North Carolina State Board of Charities and Public Welfare has endeavored to extend the benefits of the State's social welfare program to whites and Negroes alike, but lack of funds and perhaps a more or less indifferent attitude on the part of county and city officials prevented the development of any specialized effort in the field of Negro welfare. On January 1, 1925, however, through funds made available from the Laura Spelman Rockefeller Memorial to the State Board of Charities and Public Welfare and the School of Public Welfare of the University of North Carolina for a Four County Demonstration of rural social work possibilities, there was created in the State Board a new division relating to Negro welfare work, under the direction of Lieut. L. A. Oxley. The original grant from the Memorial expired June 30, 1927, and in recognition of the accomplishments and progress made by the state in this pioneer field an additional grant of $16,600 was made to the state to continue and extend the benefits of the Negro welfare program to other counties in the state. The new grant was to run for four years, ending June 30, 1931. In establishing the Division of Work among Negroes, it was the hope of the State Board that a demonstration program could be promoted with the ultimate view of developing a state-wide program of public welfare for the Negro.

During the past seven years the major emphasis has been placed on the theory that the only practical approach to the Negro community lies through the machinery the Negroes themselves have set up; and that in every activity planned to build a healthier and happier social order, the primary purpose must continue to be to train the Negro to help himself. The original wise policy adopted by the State Board of inviting the Negro to have a voice in the planning of the program has been consistently followed. A program of social welfare work which has for its objective the improvement of Negro community life through the creating and promoting of constructive family standards must have as a prerequisite an intelligent knowledge and understanding of the social assets and liabilities of Negro family and communal life in North Carolina at the present time. Scientific study of the Negro family and community is still so rare that accurate and fruitful comparisons of social problems within this group are practically impossible. Ignorance, poverty, crime, vice, disease, misuse of leisure, bad housing, and many other social ills do not respect race or color, nor are they different in character when found in a Negro community. Human depravity, mental defectiveness, broken families, illegitimacy, increased morbidity and mortality, and many other social liabilities of the Negro community are found in direct ratio to the lack of a community consciousness on the part of the masses of Negroes. The first step in a welfare program for Negroes, therefore, is to find out the facts about the social conditions and the social needs of the Negro, and to acquaint the Negroes themselves with those conditions and needs. Education must precede organization. The Rosenwald Study of Negro Child Welfare in North Carolina is a direct and logical outgrowth of this policy.

The major objectives of the Division of Work among Negroes are community organization or the organization of

Negro social forces; placement of trained Negro social workers; promotion of institutes of public welfare—providing supplementary training for Negro social workers; social studies of the Negro family and community; school attendance; race relations; and coöperation with the Executive Counsel's office in connection with its duties relating to pardon and parole.

When the program of the Division of Work among Negroes was launched, January 1, 1925, a survey of social agencies and other forces for Negro betterment would have shown one Negro social worker employed by a county welfare department; no Negro community organized for social welfare; no state provision for the care and training of delinquent Negro boys and girls; no program of hospitalization for Negro children with orthopedic defects; no facilities for training feebleminded Negro children; no provision at the State Hospital for Negro Insane for segregating children and other inmates according to mental types; flogging of prisoners quite common in county prison camps of North Carolina—with Negro prisoners usually the victims of the lash; no facilities available within the state for the training of Negroes in the technique of social work; and no state-wide organization of Parent-Teacher or Community League Associations.

COMMUNITY ORGANIZATION

Seven years later, January 1, 1932, social welfare as it relates to the Negro in North Carolina presents a different picture. It has been the desire of the State Board that the plan of community organization for Negroes be of greatest value to the entire state. Consequently, each step in the program has been carefully studied in conference with a large number of people in cities and counties which have had experience pioneering in this virgin field. The outline has been gone over carefully in individual and group conferences, with members of the staff of the State Board of Charities and Public Welfare, with faculty members of the School of Public Welfare of the University of North Carolina, and with a large number of representative Negro men and women throughout the country. It is felt, therefore, that the North Carolina plan

for organizing the social forces in Negro Communities represents a composite opinion of a large number of people who
are engaged in various phases of community organization activities. Starting in 1925, the State Board of Charities and
Public Welfare, in coöperation with county officials, under-
took a survey of Negro organizations in Wake County. A
county-wide social welfare program for Negroes soon followed.
From this beginning in Wake County we find now thirty-eight
counties in North Carolina where a definite program of welfare
work for Negroes is in various stages of development. Many
Negro communities have a considerable number of local organizations, particularly fraternal, and the lines of cleavage are
often marked. These groups are apt to become self-centered,
lacking community spirit; consequently, they may have no
feeling of responsibility for the general welfare of the whole
group. It has seemed wise, in initiating work in Negro communities, to endeavor to unite existing groups for work rather
than to form new machinery.

PLACEMENT OF WORKERS

Improvement is noted in the placement of trained Negro
social workers. Twenty-five trained Negro social workers are
now employed in North Carolina: twelve listed with county and
city welfare departments; eight listed with associated charities;
one listed with a bureau of social service; two listed with a
juvenile welfare commission; one listed with a juvenile court
as probation officer; and one listed with a recorder's court
as a probation officer. In addition to these workers, there are
eight trained Negro social workers employed by church social
service departments. One of the most difficult problems facing
the Division of Work among Negroes has been that of securing
trained Negro social workers. There is a growing demand for
educated social workers in the South. This demand for an
educated leadership is part of the larger demand for the best
leadership among Negroes in other fields. A study of the educational qualifications of the twenty-five Negro welfare workers now serving with city and county welfare departments,
associated charities, and juvenile courts, brings to light the

following facts: Eight have completed four years of college work plus two years of special training at schools of social work; six have finished two years of college work, and three of this number have pursued special courses in social work; two are graduates of accredited high schools and have taken a special course in social work and have had six years of experience with social work organizations; and nine are graduates of accredited high schools and have had at least five years of experience with accredited social agencies. Twenty workers are women, and five workers are men. In order to give supplementary training for Negro social workers, seven annual institutes of public welfare have been conducted under the direction of the Division of Work among Negroes, with a total attendance of 702 workers and leaders in social work among Negroes. These institutes have been held in the following cities: Winston-Salem (two), Raleigh (two), Greensboro, Durham, and Fayetteville. There are only two schools of social work in the South for the exclusive training of Negro social workers: namely, the Atlanta School of Social Work, Atlanta, Georgia, and the Bishop Tuttle Training School, Raleigh, North Carolina. There have been twenty-five graduates of the Bishop Tuttle School since the school opened in 1925. Every one of the graduates of the Bishop Tuttle School has been placed, and the same is the case at the Atlanta School of Social Work, and there continues to be a demand for trained Negro social workers. All of the graduates of these two schools had completed at least two years of college work or their equivalent before starting the course at either of the schools mentioned. The Atlanta School and the Bishop Tuttle School are rendering an invaluable and most effective service in training Negro workers for the several fields of social work.

INSTITUTIONAL DEVELOPMENT

During the month of February, 1925, the Morrison Training School for delinquent and under-privileged Negro boys was opened. During the past seven years the North Carolina General Assembly has made appropriations totalling approximately $150,000 for permanent improvements at the Morrison Training School. The original population capacity of this institution was 88; its present capacity is 200. Because of the lack of capacity during the past year, 280 applications for admission were denied.

Through a generous gift of $40,000 made by Mr. B. N. Duke, a permanent ward for the treatment of Negro crippled children is available at the North Carolina Orthopedic Hospital at Gastonia. Negro children needing orthopedic treatment are received in all clinics throughout the state; and those needing hospitalization are admitted to the Orthopedic Hospital in the order of their application. The Negro ward has a capacity of 50 beds.

The story of the development of the Negro welfare program in North Carolina would be incomplete without some mention of the efforts made to extend to the delinquent Negro girl the advantages of a training school of a reformative nature. Deeply conscious of the seriousness of the problem of the maladjusted Negro girl, and appreciative of the urgent need for a constructive program which would provide the proper care, treatment, and training for her, and realizing also that genuine interest in any project is best demonstrated by individuals first helping themselves, the North Carolina Federation of Colored Women's Clubs purchased three hundred acres of farm land in Orange County near Efland, and, as a nucleus for a training school, they erected a modern frame building. The Federation of Colored Women's Clubs has invested about $25,000 in this project—an investment that may be well termed "a venture of faith."

The Negro club women have offered the school to the State as a gift, upon the condition that the State maintain it as a State institution. Several legislatures have failed to accept the responsibility of the school, but since 1927 the State has appropriated $2,000 annually for its maintenance. North Carolina's institutional program for delinquent youth will not have been completed until it has provided adequately for the delinquent Negro girl. We find many instances in which maladjusted Negro girls drift into delinquency, crime, and disease when early treatment in a training school might have saved them to society.

The opening of the Memorial Industrial School at Winston-Salem, an institution caring for dependent Negro children; the providing of more buildings and equipment at the Oxford Colored Orphanage; provision for the care and treatment of tuberculous Negro children at the State Sanatorium; and the segregation of children at the State Hospital for Negro Insane represent other outstanding achievements in the field of Negro welfare in North Carolina.

During the past four years the Division of Work among Negroes has coöperated with the Governor's Council in matters relating to the investigation of applications for paroles and pardons made by Negro prisoners.

STUDY OF CAPITAL PUNISHMENT IN NORTH CAROLINA

A part of the second grant from the Laura Spelman Rockefeller Memorial was used to finance the completion of a study of capital punishment in North Carolina,[2] which was begun by the Director of the Division of Work among Negroes early in 1926. Quoting from the introduction to this bulletin, "The primary object of the study of capital punishment is to present to the people of North Carolina, and to the state's judicial and penal officers and social workers, material which hitherto has not been conveniently available, and which it is hoped, they will find valuable in its bearing on the grave problem of capital crime and the state's method of dealing with those offenders who are guilty of it. The facts presented are eloquent in themselves, and strongly suggest the necessity of further serious study of the subject of capital punishment and other related social problems, especially that of mental deficiency."

FOLLOW-UP PROGRAM

In addition to the activities directly relating to the organization of Negro welfare programs for community better-

---

[2] N. C. State Board of Charities and Public Welfare, *Capital Punishment in North Carolina*, Bulletin No. 10 (1929), p. 173.

ment, the Division of Work among Negroes has had the direct responsibility for the follow-up work in the thirty-eight counties of North Carolina where Negro welfare work has been started. Systematic follow-up work constitutes a major activity of the Negro division and is of vital importance in the successful promotion of the state-wide program. Follow-up work entailed individual and group conferences with superintendents of public welfare, county commissioners, members of county welfare boards, members of the city and county Negro advisory welfare boards, and officials of state, county and city institutions for Negro defectives, delinquents, and dependents. Many community, social, individual and racial problems have been discussed, differences ironed out, and an understanding reached.

CASE WORK

Inter-state and intra-state case work among Negroes has formed a part of the Division's responsibilities and program. With an increase in the placement of trained Negro social workers, it becomes possible for the Division to render a more efficient service to those agencies handling Negro case work of an inter-county and inter-state nature.

NEGRO CO-OPERATION

Whatever progress has been made and results obtained are due in large measure to the hearty response and splendid cooperation that have come from Negro leaders and organizations throughout North Carolina. Among the many helpful organizations in promoting the program of Negro welfare particular mention must be made of the Parent-Teacher Association work among Negroes in North Carolina. As far back as 1915, several communities, realizing the need for greater coöperation between families and teachers, home and school, formed groups and clubs, somewhat similar to the pastor's aid, church aid and other clubs that are doing such splendid work in the churches. This movement was started by the teachers themselves in order that the splendid work begun in the school room, might not be destroyed in the home.

Parents were shown how they could do much to lessen the burdens of the teacher, improve school attendance, relieve crowded conditions, and in many instances build new attractive and commodious school houses as well as lengthen the term of the short term schools. These groups were called community clubs, betterment associations, and community leagues.

In 1923-24 this work was definitely organized and linked up with the general movement known throughout the country as the Parent-Teacher Association work. Immediately the work took on a deeper meaning. The school house became the social center of the community along with the church. Programs and socials were held, money was raised, patrons developed greater interest in the schools, and students and teachers alike showed increased pleasure in the work of the schools. These groups plan and work during the summer months when schools are closed to enlarge the buildings, to put up teachers' homes, and to provide other much needed additions to the program of the school. In 1927 this movement in North Carolina had developed to the place where twenty-six city and twenty county units, composed of seven hundred and seventy associations, with a total membership of 10,117, were represented at a meeting to perfect a state organization. Reports at this meeting showed that $65,513.97 had been raised and expended for school betterment by the association. The accomplishments of these associations cover a wide range of activities, such as purchasing land for Rosenwald Schools, helping to build Rosenwald schools, purchase of school furniture and equipment, purchase of playground equipment, purchase of pianos, sewing machines, victrolas, libraries, radios, office equipment, auditorium fittings, and providing hot lunches.

In many instances also school terms have been lengthened, busses purchased and operated, and teachers' salaries supplemented. No statement of Negro welfare work in North Carolina could be made without special mention of the Jeanes supervisors and their fine coöperation in its development and progress. These splendid workers have organized local groups, held meetings, mapped out programs of activities, and traveled about their districts lecturing at churches and giving encouragement to the movement.

Many Negro public health nurses, also farm and home demonstration agents in the several cities and counties of North Carolina, have played no small part in developing a better and more wholesome Negro family and community life. Day by day these Negro workers in the fields of health and home and farm activities carry a gospel of better living to thousands of underprivileged Negroes scattered throughout the state.

The 1931 North Carolina General Assembly, duly recognizing the constructive results obtained in the field of Negro welfare, included in the state budget an item providing for the state's assuming full financial responsibility for the continuance of the program that had been initiated as an integral part of the State Board of Charities and Public Welfare, after the expiration of the second Memorial grant. The gratitude and appreciation of North Carolina is due the trustees of the Laura Spelman Rockefeller Memorial for financing what has resulted in a successful demonstration of social engineering in the field of Negro welfare.

PART II

INSTITUTIONS CARING FOR NEGRO CHILDREN IN NORTH CAROLINA

CHAPTER II

MORRISON TRAINING SCHOOL FOR NEGRO BOYS
HOFFMAN, NORTH CAROLINA

PURPOSE

THE MORRISON TRAINING SCHOOL cares for delinquent Negro boys under the age of sixteen years committed by any juvenile, State or other court "having jurisdiction over such boy." The Board of Trustees may, upon the request of a court of proper jurisdiction, receive a boy over the age of 16 if within its discretion these are special reasons which make such acceptance desirable.

CAPACITY AND POPULATION

The institution has a bed capacity for 150 children exclusive of the new cottage which at the time of the study was not completed. At times the population has exceeded this number. On February 20, 1930, the population was 150. The maintenance appropriation for the biennium 1929-1931 was figured on the basis of a population of 160 children during the first half of the period and 200 during the last half. The new cottage has a capacity for 50 children. The average population for the period ending December 31, 1928, was 134. The distribution of population by counties in February, 1930, was as follows:

Alamance County	1	Caldwell County	3
Anson County	2	Chowan County	3
Beaufort County	5	Catawba County	1
Bertie County	1	Cleveland County	1
Brunswick County	4	Cumberland County	3
Buncombe County	3	Craven County	3
Cabarrus County	1	Davie County	4

2

Davidson County	1	Onslow County	1
Durham County	5	Orange County	1
Edgecombe County	3	Pamlico County	3
Forsyth County	2	Pasquotank County	1
Franklin County	2	Pender County	2
Gaston County	5	Pitt County	7
Granville County	2	Randolph County	3
Guilford County	13	Richmond County	6
Haywood County	1	Robeson County	4
Halifax County	2	Rockingham County	1
Harnett County	1	Sampson County	2
Henderson County	2	Scotland County	1
Jones County	3	Stanly County	1
Johnston County	4	Union County	2
Lenoir County	1	Vance County	1
McDowell County	2	Wake County	5
Mecklenburg County	11	Warren County	2
Montgomery County	2	Wayne County	1
Moore County	3	Wilson County	4
Nash County	2		

The age grouping of boys under care was as follows:

Age	Number of boys
8 to 10 years, inclusive	12
11 to 13 years, inclusive	29
14 to 16 years, inclusive	65
16 and up	44
Total	150

ORGANIZATION

The law provides for the appointment of eight trustees by the governor of the state, five of whom shall serve for four years and three for a term of three years.

Thus, five members serve for terms coexistent with that of the governor and three members carry over from one administration to another. Six members of the present board are white and two are Negroes.

Board meetings are held quarterly as a matter of routine and additional meetings are arranged on call if necessary.

The superintendent meets with the Board. Matters of general policy, of parole, of special admissions, etcetera, are discussed and plans are made for important undertakings.

FINANCES

The Morrison Training School is maintained by state appropriation which for the year 1929-1930 is $25,000 and for 1930-1931 is $32,000. However, some reduction in these amounts will be made because of the unusual economic conditions which prevail in North Carolina at this time.

Estimated receipts for the first period of the biennium are $4,700 and for the second period $5,300. These receipts are from sale of farm produce and the labor of the boys who work for the farmers in the neighborhood.

The law provides that in admitting children the trustees shall "distribute such admissions as near as may be in relation to the Negro population of the several counties until all the maintenance appropriation from the state is exhausted. If after such maintenance fund is exhausted it be found possible to provide housing space and control for additional inmates, then the trustees may receive such additional number of inmates as can be cared for upon the payment by private persons or municipal or county authorities of the actual cost of the maintenance of such inmates."

At the time of the study a few children were being boarded by counties but the number was negligible on the basis of ratio to the entire population. Complete outfits of clothing had in some cases been requested from the counties by the superintendent as one of the conditions of admission in order to conserve the maintenance appropriation as much as possible.

The annual per capita for the year 1929 out of the state appropriation was $155. The estimated per capita for the biennium 1929-1931 is $160. Adding the estimated earnings the per capita for the first and second periods of the biennium would be approximately $185 and $186.50 respectively. These cost figures are considerably under the per capita costs of similar institutions elsewhere.

STAFF

The present superintendent, who was educated at Tuskegee and is a minister, has been in charge of the Morrison Training School since it opened early in 1925. He had had teaching experience prior to coming to the School. The superintendent has also had some technical vocational training which is a valuable asset in his present position. He receives a salary of $225 per month.

When the School was first opened the business administration was in the hands of a white manager who lived at some distance from the institution. The superintendent was responsible for the care, discipline, education and general training of the children but had nothing to do with the purchase of supplies and the general operation of the farm.

It soon became evident that the work of the School would never develop as it should under divided authority. Finally, the Board of Trustees decided to make the superintendent the executive of the entire enterprise on a more or less experimental basis. If he succeeded the arrangement was to continue and if he failed he would be expected to withdraw so that some other plan might be devised.

The present superintendent has been able to demonstrate to the entire satisfaction of his Board and interested state officials his ability to carry executive responsibility and the School has moved forward under his leadership.

The wife of the superintendent who is a college woman is employed as subsistence supervisor. She supervises the store room, plans the menus and directs the boys who work in the kitchens and dining rooms. She receives $75 per month.

The supervisor of the boys, who is called the commandant, has been on the staff of the School for three years. He was previously employed in an orphanage caring for dependent Negro children. He is responsible for the athletic program, supervises work squads, and is in charge of the boys' building. During the absence of the superintendent he is responsible for such administrative details as the superintendent's wife does not carry. He receives $115 per month.

The other employees include the following, all of whom receive maintenance:

Administration Department

1 Secretary ....$ 85

Instruction (8 months)

Director $100

Teacher and band master.....................................95

Teacher (1) 90

Teachers (3) 80

Custodial Care

1 Farm Supervisor..$ 75

Operation of Plant

1 Supervisor of building and grounds.......................$ 85

One of the women teachers has been at the School three years and two of them have been on the staff for two years.

Persons on the staff the entire year receive ten days vacation with pay. This does not apply to the teachers who are employed for eight months. They receive only the usual legal holidays which occur during the school year.

Staff meetings are held once a month at which time the superintendent and other workers discuss the various problems which have arisen and make plans for future activities.

The actual ratio of children to workers for 1927-1928 was 13.4. The estimated ratio for 1929-1930 is 13.3. The estimated ratio at the Stonewall Jackson Training School for 1929-1930 is 9.1.

COMMENTS AND RECOMMENDATIONS ON STAFF

The capacity for leadership which the superintendent possesses has enabled him to carry his staff with him in developing the program of the Morrison Training School. He has the ability to interpret his ideals of accomplishment to his associates in such a way that he enlists their whole-hearted coöperation. The superintendent has not had specialized training in the field of institutional administration and social welfare. However, his training in allied fields and his intelligent understanding of people together with his inherent integrity and strong personality compensate to a considerable extent for the lack of specific training.

An effort has been made to secure workers who by the examples which they set and through the influence of their own personalities are able to contribute to the remotivation and retraining of the boys.

The teachers in the School all hold certificates. Most of them have previously taught in public schools. The wife of the superintendent, who supervises the subsistence department, has had technical training in this field.

The ratio of workers to children shows that the School is being operated with a much smaller staff than industrial training schools ordinarily require. This means that the boys themselves are given important assignments and carry a considerable amount of responsibility. This policy will be discussed in detail in a later section of this report.

When the trades building is equipped there will have to be certain additions to the vocational training staff. The final decisions as to the equipment to be installed will determine the selection of additional teachers. The resources of the community and of the state should be utilized to the fullest extent as through such coöperation supplementary service may often be secured without cost to the School.

The opening of the new cottage will necessitate certain reassignments of staff on the basis of combinations of service which the superintendent will work out.

In the section of this report in which medical service is discussed, the need for adding a nurse to the staff as the population increases will be pointed out.

The following recommendations on staff are presented for consideration:

1. If there are not too many practical difficulties in the way, the superintendent should arrange to spend three or four weeks in observation and consultation at the New Jersey Training School for Boys at Jamesburg, New Jersey. Mr. Calvin Derrick, the superintendent of the New Jersey Training School, is one of the outstanding executives in the country. He and his associates are carrying on scientific experimenta-

tion continually in order to arrive at decisions as to what works and what does not work in the organization of the regime of the School and why. If the superintendent of the Morrison Training School could spend enough time at Jamesburg to acquaint himself particularly with the academic and vocational aspects of the program, it would aid him materially in the further development of his own plans for Morrison.

2.   Additional teaching staff will be needed when the trades building is equipped. The extension departments of the state universities, the State Departments of Education and of Agriculture, the State Board of Charities and Public Welfare, and groups interested in vocational and trade training should be consulted in order to determine to what extent the services of the regularly employed staff of the training school can be supplemented by outside persons.

3.   A nurse should be added to the staff as soon as funds are available.

PLANT AND EQUIPMENT

The Morrison Training School is located in the pine and sand district of North Carolina on a tract of land containing something over three hundred acres. The School is about three miles from Hoffman and seven or eight miles from Rockingham, the county seat of Richmond County. This region is in the peach growing district and there are many orchards of large acreage in the territory adjacent to the School.

A considerable portion of the land has been cleared and a large supply of food stuffs is raised. It is necessary to fertilize the fields each year which adds to the cost of production. Fruit trees have been set out and berry patches started.

The plant includes an administration building containing administrative offices and living quarters for the superintendent; the boys' building which has a wing containing rooms for the teachers; the school building which contains the combined gymnasium and auditorium, the school rooms, and a basement which has been used as a vocational department; a wooden structure which contains the dining room and kitchen, the laundry, store room and refrigeration plant; a new cottage for 50 boys, not yet occupied; a one story trades building which as yet is not equipped; and a number of frame out-buildings and dairy barns.

All of the buildings except the commissary department are of brick construction. The large main building with boys' quarters on each floor has a central unit and two wings. One of these wings contains rooms for the teachers. The new cottage is a two-story brick building having dormitory and toilet facilities, clothes rooms, closets, two large well-lighted living rooms, and four staff bed rooms.

The new trades building which cost approximately $7,000 is large enough to house a variety of vocational shops. The floor plan and the lighting are such as to make it possible to place the equipment advantageously. This building is a splendid addition to the institutional plant.

The original building in which all of the boys now live has space only for dormitories and toilet facilities. Thus the boys have no place in which to congregate during their leisure hours in the cold weather except in their sleeping quarters. This building must have been poorly constructed as it has deteriorated greatly in the short time it has been in use. Apparently this has not been due to lack of care as the defects which are most noticeable are structural rather than merely in the finish of the building.

Double-decker beds are used in all the dormitories, presumably for the purpose of conserving floor space. Standard requirements call for 500 cubic feet of air space and 50 feet of floor space per child. The following table gives the number of children in each dormitory and the number for which there is adequate air space and floor space on the basis of the standard requirement for institutions.

TABLE I

Ward	No. of beds in ward	No. of boys in ward	Capacity on basis of floor space	Capacity on basis of air space
"A"	15	30	27.4	28.8
No. 2 "A"........	13	25	20.3	21.3
"B"	18	30	24.7	22.2
"C"	16	30	24.7	22.2
Junior "A"	6	8	8.6	7.7
Junior "B"	7	8	8.8	7.9
Junior "C"	6	8	8.6	7.7
Junior "D"	6	8	8.8	7.9

From the above table it appears that the maximum capacity of four of the dormitories has been somewhat exceeded.

There are no facilities for isolation of sick children or newly admitted boys. In an institution caring for a large number of children and located at some distance from a hospital the lack of even simple hospital quarters is a handicap.

COMMENTS ON PLANT AND EQUIPMENT

Without going into further detail regarding the plant and equipment the following comments and suggestions are presented for consideration:

1. The poorest facilities of the institution are those of the building unit in which are located the kitchen, dining room, store room, refrigeration plant and the laundry. In the section of this report on training, reference will be made to the desirability of providing special training in cooking, serving, general cleaning, etcetera. Such training, however, ought to be preponderantly practical rather than too highly theoretical. It should also be integrated with the daily routine of the institution. For this reason it is recommended that in replacing the present commissary department the building and equipment be so planned that it would be well adapted not only for the cooking and serving of the meals for the boys and the

staff, but also for training purposes. In a training school for
girls it is essential that the household administration department be set up on a small unit basis and that the girls be given
an opportunity to do their practice work on the basis of family
units. However, in organizing training of this type for boys
it should be borne in mind that for the most part those who
later enter this vocational field will be working in kitchens in
which food for a large number of people is prepared daily.
The present building has outlived its usefulness. It is difficult
to keep it in a sanitary condition. The equipment in the kitchen
is of the most elementary type and does not furnish an opportunity to acquaint the boys with the various utensils and
mechanical apparatus found in modern hotel kitchens.

2.   As already indicated the institution is seriously handicapped by the lack of any hospital or isolation facilities. The
size of the population is large enough to warrant a small
hospital unit. It is suggested that consideration be given to
using one of the dormitories in the new cottage for isolation
and hospital purposes temporarily. Another alternative would
be to use one of the small dormitories in the main building for
this purpose when the new cottage is occupied. Eventually
a small one-story cottage should be provided for isolation and
emergency hospital purposes. The State Department of Health
should be asked to furnish figures on the number of hospital
beds required for emergency care and the temporary isolation
of newly admitted boys in an institution of this size.

3.   Because of the poor construction of the main building
certain repairs are needed. As a matter of economy these repairs should be made as soon as possible in order to prevent
further deterioration.

4.   Some of the toilet facilities in the boys' building did
not meet accepted institutional standards at the time of the
study. With a small expenditure these facilities could probably
be made satisfactory.

5.   Whenever practicable some rearrangement should be
made in the boys' building whereby one of the rooms on the
first floor used for dormitory purposes may be converted into
a living room. Fortunately, the new cottage will have living

room facilities. It is true that during the major portion of the year the children can play out-of-doors practically all of the time. However, when they are not in school or at work or on the playground, the only places in which they can congregate are the dormitories. This is not a satisfactory arrangement for a variety of reasons. As part of an adequate training program there should be some place which can be used for playing table games, for reading and for various group activities which do not require the facilities of the gymnasium. It may be argued that the majority of children come to the training school from homes in which the standards of living are so low that by comparison the present facilities of the school are quite superior to what they have previously known. This is probably true. However, the task of the school is to give children better standards of conduct and of living than they had when they came. The environment provided contributes a great deal to the retraining process if properly used. Thus in urging that the Training School have a simply furnished living room equipped with plain, substantial chairs and tables, one or two good pictures, some book shelves, and some shelves or cupboards in which each boy may keep minor personal belongings the main objective is to provide a setting which will furnish additional opportunities to teach children to respect property; to consider the comfort and happiness of others; and to make social adjustments which are essential if we are ever to "live in peace and love."

6.   Equipment for the new trades building is needed immediately as the vocational program cannot be fully developed until necessary machinery is installed. The state appropriation was largely used for the construction of the building which is well planned; and was economically built. The sum left is not sufficient to equip more than one or two of the departments requiring the most inexpensive tools and machines. It is recommended that every effort be made to secure proper equipment for the trades building either through additional appropriation from the state or from private sources as this is one of the most pressing needs of the School.

7.   The Trustees and executive of the Morrison Training

School will continually face the problem of having more applications for admission than they are able to accept. In the long run, the School will serve its purpose best by limiting its intake to the number of children it can properly care for. To disregard standards of sanitation in order to give a poor quality of care to a large number of children cannot be defended from any standpoint.

8. The present provisions for fire protection should be rechecked in order to be sure that every precaution has been taken. Fire drills should be given at frequent intervals and some drills should be at night in order to be sure that every boy would know what to do if he were suddenly awakened.

LIFE OF THE CHILDREN

While the boys sent to the Morrison Training School have been committed as delinquents, the program of the institution is set up on the basis of training rather than of punishment. As far as the work of the School has been developed, it has gone in the direction of retraining and rehabilitation rather than of confinement and punishment. The result is that the atmosphere at Morrison is not that of a jail. In so far as it can be done an effort has been made to provide the setting and the atmosphere of a real school.

At the time[1] the study of the Morrison Training School was made the daily schedule was as follows:

6:00 a.m.	Rising hour
6:30- 7:00.	Breakfast.
7:00- 8:00.	Morning chores.
8:00-12:00.	School and work for alternating groups.
12:00- 1:00.	Dinner and noon chores.
1:00- 5:00.	School and work.
5:30.	Supper—Free play period for half hour after supper on campus.
6:30.	Free periods in dormitories.
8:30.	Bed time.

At 10 o'clock in the morning and 2 in the afternoon, 30 minutes for recreation were given. There were also deviations

---

[1] February, 1930.

from this schedule for athletic practice and games, for band practice and for various other reasons. Some shift is also made as the weather changes.

Education.—All of the boys are in school every other day, the schedule being arranged so that they are in school one day and at work another. During the past year there were classes through the eighth grade. The work on the odd day includes assignments in the fields, in the institution and in the shop.

It was stated that the farm manager, under whose supervision the boys work in the fields, appreciated the importance of using an educational approach. No plan has as yet been developed, however, for coördinating some simple theoretical instruction in agriculture with the assignments made by the farm manager.

The training given in the shops includes shoe repairing, for which there is no modern equipment at present; brick masonry; the making of cement blocks; wood working; and painting. These activities, together with the work on the farm, the care of the dairy herd, and the practical instruction given in the cooking and serving of food, the cleaning of the institution, etc., constitute the vocational training available.

All of the teachers have either Grade A or Grade B certificates. Some of the teachers have attended Summer School. Others plan to attend during the coming summer in order to secure a higher classification.

Cultural and recreational facilities.—A music teacher had been on the staff most of the year up until just a few weeks previous to the study, when she became ill and had to leave. The manual training teacher gives instruction to the band, and the boys have been greatly interested in qualifying for band training. The institution has been handicapped by the lack of an adequate number of instruments, but some additional equipment has been provided during the past year.

There is a moving picture machine in the auditorium, but it has not been used this year because of lack of funds for films.

The boys put on special programs of one sort or another,

particularly at holiday time. Occasional parties are held in the dining room and it was stated that these events were eagerly looked forward to.

The commandant is also the athletic director. Football, basketball, baseball and boxing are taught. Recently it has been possible to arrange games with outside teams, and during certain seasons of the year one game a week has been played. The commandant also trains the boys to drill using infantry regulations.

There is a swimming pool, and during the summer definite periods in the day's routine are set aside for swimming.

Discipline.—The school is organized around a modified military system. The limited number of adults on the staff makes it necessary to give the boys considerable responsibility and authority. Undoubtedly one of the most effective ways of doing this with any degree of success is to approximate a military system of control. The commandant is responsible for the immediate supervision of the disciplinary system. The boys are classified as privates, corporals, second lieutenants, lieutenants, and captains. These various ranks must be attained through good behavior. A captain, with a couple of lieutenants to assist him, is considered eligible to take a group of boys out on a work assignment. When a boy violates the confidence placed in him, he is demoted in rank and denied other privileges. Ranking officers are not permitted to administer corporal punishment. When such discipline is necessary it is given by the superintendent. Since there is no inclination to make fear the motivation for proper conduct at Morrison, corporal punishment does not play a large part in the scheme of things. There is one room which is used for the temporary isolation of boys who have given serious trouble and who are not amenable to other forms of discipline. The use of this room is resorted to only when necessary in order to preserve the morale of the School.

Work.—In addition to the work which the boys do at the institution, groups of them also go out to work during the spring and summer seasons for farmers in the neighborhood. In formulating the budget for the Morrison Training

School, an estimate is made as to the probable income from the sale of farm products and from the labor of the boys. The money which they earn, therefore, goes into the contribution to the general fund and is not available for use by the institution for some particular project. Neither do the boys receive any part of the money earned for personal use.

The farms on which the boys are employed are located near the institution so that they return to the school for lunch and a rest period at noon. The commandant acquaints himself with the conditions under which the boys work, and while he does not stay all day with each group, he appears during their employment period in order that he may know how the boys are getting along and whether unreasonable demands are made upon them.

Religious training.—Devotions are held on Sunday morning, and formal religious services take place each Sunday in the Auditorium. The superintendent of the institution usually conducts the formal services. In addition to the religious services, emphasis is placed on the teaching of ethics. The fact that the teachers and other members of the staff at Morrison Training School try to apply their ethical standards in their daily contact with the boys probably influences the attitudes of the children to a much greater extent than the formal instruction does.

COMMENTS ON LIFE OF THE CHILDREN

In discussing the daily schedule with the administration it was stated that certain changes were made from time to time in order to allow other unscheduled activities to be carried out and to make allowance for variations for the group of children from eight to thirteen years of age, inclusive, of whom there were 41 at the time the study was made. It would seem that the hours of work might be fairly long if the boys worked through the entire period at top speed. It was explained, however, that there were rest periods and that care was taken not to overtax any child.

The point which has been raised earlier in this report regarding living room facilities comes up again in considering the daily schedule. During certain seasons of the year the boys come in off the campus at 6:30 o'clock and must spend the time between then and bed time in the dormitories on the nights when there are no special activities in the gymnasium. The difficulty in trying to provide wholesome leisure time outlets for a group of 150 children will be readily appreciated by anyone who has had institutional experience. To reconcile the interests of the boy who wishes to study, the one who wishes to read, those who wish to play table games of various sorts, and those who wish to play outside is a problem of major proportions. Providing an environment in which children may exercise some choice as to their leisure time pursuits is an essential part of a training program as the making of choices has a distinct value in the development of personality and of ethical standards.

Most institutions for the training of delinquent boys and girls schedule their programs so that the children have formal instruction for half a day and are assigned to shop work, work on the farm and routine tasks the other half of the day. The policy at the Morrison Training School of having each boy go to school for an entire day and then work an entire day raises the question as to which plan is preferable. We know that any child does better work if he is not kept at one task for too long a period. The newer schools of progressive education develop their schedules around the principle that a child should be permitted to work at a particular project when the peak of his interest is at such height as to insure successful performance. It would seem that it might be worth while to experiment again with the plan of a half day of school and a half day of vocational activities and labor. The superintendent's argument is that it takes a boy a considerable length of time to adjust himself either to a day in school or a day at work; therefore, he considers that the amount of adjustment necessary is reduced by giving a whole day to one type of activity. It may be, however, that the adjustment period to the day's routine would be materially reduced if the opening session of school were given over to a subject of special interest; and if the schedules for work and shop training were so systematized that the boys would know beforehand where they were expected to be and what they were expected to do at a definite period. It is suggested that the superintendent and his staff discuss the advantages and disadvantages of both plans and check results with sufficient care to determine which system seems better suited to the special needs of Morrison Training School.

The superintendent appears to have an appreciation of the desirability of seeing school, vocational training, work, play, and personal relationships as a composite whole through which boys may be retrained and remotivated. In other words, he tries to avoid isolating the various aspects of the training program from each other. An effort is also made to integrate the things the boys are being taught with the day by day living in the school environment. While stress is doubtless placed upon the future with the hope of stimulating a boy's efforts to make good, there was an understanding of a child's natural tendency to live in the present rather than in the past or in the future. If a boy is to develop in such a way that he will be able to meet adult responsibilities successfully, he needs to experience the stimulation which comes through living in a wholesome and satisfying present. In some training schools there is too much stress on projecting a child ahead to the time when he goes back into the community. Training for such readjustment into family and community life should be a major feature of the institution's program. But it should not be so over-emphasized that both the staff and the children lose sight of the importance of having the present make some contribution to a boy's happiness and well being.

The new trades building to which reference has already been made, will provide a splendid setting for a variety of vocational training enterprises. In deciding upon the kinds of equipment to be purchased, there must be kept in mind the probable capabilities of the boys coming to the institution and the vocational fields which will be open to them. While there are certain kinds of shop equipment which it might be desirable to have as a means of further vocational experimentation, it would seem that any funds available for equipment at

Morrison in the near future should be used only for such things as will equip the boys for future employment in fields that are open to them.

It does not lie within the scope of this report to make specific recommendations on shop equipment, as this can be done only by persons having technical training in the field of vocational education and familiar with the peculiar problems of industrial training schools. It is urged, however, that when equipment is purchased it be real equipment such as a boy will have to work with when he seeks employment in a particular field after leaving the institution. Delinquent boys who have already exhibited anti-social tendencies and who have in many instances gotten into difficulties because they were idle, do not need play-toy equipment. They need to become skilled in some particular line of endeavor so that under normal economic conditions there will be something for them to do in their local communities. It is advisable also for major and minor interests to be developed to avoid having a boy get the idea that he is justified in remaining idle if he cannot find the particular sort of work for which he has had intensive training at the school.

The superintendent and the Board of the institution have given considerable thought to the reorganization of the vocational program as the new trades building has neared completion. They have recognized the possibilities for training in agriculture, shoe repairing, wood turning and carpentry, printing, brick and concrete masonry, barbering, auto mechanics, and blacksmithing. They have also recognized the value of some training in domestic science with particular emphasis upon the cooking and serving of foods, the cleaning of houses, and the care of standard plumbing and heating equipment. Most of the vocational fields listed herein undoubtedly offer opportunities for the employment of Negro boys. However, unless the equipment provided is such that the training will be practical and that a boy will be able to go from the shoe repairing shop at Morrison, for example, into a shoe repairing shop in Raleigh, investment in it will not yield the returns sought.

A number of training schools no longer consider printing as it is taught in most institutions of a great deal of value, since the linotype machines are so generally used in the printing offices throughout the country.

The New Jersey State Home for Boys at Jamesburg has found out through job analysis that it takes a twelve-year-old intelligence to become a successful typesetter under Union conditions. About the simplest grade of work in a printing establishment is that done by the typesetter. In the north, training schools have found that it is almost useless to train Negro boys to be printers because the printing trade is so highly unionized that it would be practically impossible to place them in industry. On the other hand, a type of instruction similar to that found in Junior High School vocational courses would be a means of general laboratory activities for young boys which would help them with their spelling, sentence construction, composition, and general informational topics. The superintendent of the New Jersey State Home for Boys from whom information was sought regarding the introduction of printing, and who furnished the data in the previous paragraphs, makes this definite statement: "Therefore, I would advocate printing only as one of several rather elementary exploratory shop courses for younger boys, offering an occasional opportunity for an older and mentally well-equipped boy as a helper on advanced work. The linotype machine has no place in this scheme."

Economic conditions in North Carolina are different from those in New Jersey and New York and the above opinions may be of little value in connection with the Morrison Training School program. It seems desirable to include these opinions in this report, however, in order that the objections raised and the limitation of opportunity for employment pointed out may be considered before decisions are reached concerning the purchase of equipment.

When the trades building is equipped, there will be two rooms in the basement of the school building available for other purposes. These rooms would be well adapted for class rooms in which to teach theoretical courses in domestic science.

A properly equipped institution kitchen and dining rooms, however, as previously indicated would provide laboratory facilities for the practical side of such a course without investment in special equipment.

In view of the exceedingly poor facilities of the commissary department and the great need for a new unit which will be modern as to floor plan, equipment, sanitation, plumbing, storage facilities, etc., we do not believe money should be spent for equipping a special domestic science department similar to that found in an ordinary high school. Instead, whatever funds are available either from the State or from private sources should be spent in the construction and equipment of the type of service unit which will provide adequate facilities both for the institution as such and for practical teaching purposes. Only a very small sum would be necessary to provide enough classroom equipment for one of the rooms in the basement of the school building to enable a teacher to give the required theoretical instruction.

Not every person qualified by training and previous experience to teach domestic science courses in schools would be able to swing a project in which the teaching was to be closely integrated with the daily regime of a large institution. It is urged, therefore, that when the training school is provided with proper equipment to undertake specialized training in the domestic science field, adequate funds will be made available to secure a teacher competent to make the most effective use of the facilities in terms of the training of the boys.

Games and athletic sports of various kinds and the opportunities for vocal and instrumental music provided enrich the recreational program. An athletic field, swimming pool, a band, and group singing are all important adjuncts in keeping the Morrison regime from going stale and in giving the boys proper outlets for the play instinct which is universal.

Additional band instruments would give a larger number of boys an opportunity to participate in this particular activity. If harmonicas were supplied there could be several harmonica bands organized among the remainder of the children who otherwise might feel more or less left out.

In organizing the recreation of an institution, it is important to make sure that every child has an opportunity to participate. The boy who has a capacity for leadership will usually find his place in the program but the less confident child may become a chronic observer instead of a participant unless the supervisor sees to it that he is drawn into some form of activity.

It would require further study of the training school to determine whether every boy has a chance to participate in the varied recreational activities. The question is raised, however, in order that the administration may test the present program on this score as it is an important factor in the training process. Interest in a wide range of wholesome leisure-time activities will do much to safeguard boys against getting into trouble when they leave the institution.

Boxing appears to be both an athletic activity and a means of settling disputes at the school. Boys are taught how to box for the sake of the sport as such. However, it is also used as a means of settling differences of opinion which might otherwise be settled with less sportsmanship and grace. When two boys appear to be having serious personal difficulties, they are given gloves and with proper attention to the formalities of boxing, encouraged to determine which is the "better man" on the basis of boxing skill.

An institution caring for a group of previously undisciplined boys must maintain a reasonable degree of order if it is to accomplish anything worth while. This requires that a form of discipline be developed which will exert the greatest influence on the largest number of boys. Various plans are carried out in different training schools throughout the country. Some schools have what is termed a student government plan based on more or less elaborate forms of organized municipal, state, or federal governmental systems. In other schools there is a strict military discipline which depends for its success upon mass treatment and mass control. In still other institutions, there is no particular system and a variety of methods is used to maintain order and to carry out disciplinary measures. Flaws can be found with any of these systems. No one has as yet discovered a perfect plan.

To a large extent the success of a training program depends upon the leadership and personality of the executive; the caliber of the personnel with which he surrounds himself; and the richness of content of the institutional program. When children participate in a varied and stimulating daily routine directed by persons in whom they have confidence and for whom they have respect, the negative aspects of a disciplinary system are reduced to a minimum.

The ratio between adults and children at the Morrison Training School indicate that if the work of the institution is to go on and any semblance of order is to be maintained in an environment which has no suggestion of a jail, the adult staff must be supplemented by the older boys able to carry a certain degree of responsibility. One of the usual methods of utilizing the service of the children is an adaptation of army control. We have seen systems of such control in operation which seemed indefensible from every standpoint. In the regime at the Morrison Training School, however, it would seem that many of the objectionable features of such a plan had been overcome. For one thing, there appeared to be an intangible sort of gaiety and spontaneity which cannot be found in schools where there is abnormal repression or a lot of bullying. Captains, first lieutenants, second lieutenants and other officers seemed to be striving diligently to achieve the bearing ascribed to "an officer and a gentleman." It is true that boys were not seen in action in the fields or far removed from adult supervision. Thus it is possible to record only impressions of the system and not to present factual data on concrete results.

In the hands of a less skillful and dynamic executive and in a larger school there would be grave hazards in the present set-up. The dangers in the plan are the abuse of authority; the chance for older boys to bully children under them; the opportunity which the plan offers for the older boys to make demands upon the younger ones in order to avoid being reported; the risk that the boy who is a natural leader will be in the limelight too much and the backward child will not have a chance to develop such capacities for leadership as he may have; and the temptation to keep boys who have become competent workers in the institution too long. Some of these inherent dangers are probably eliminated because of the fact that the school is still sufficiently small to enable the superintendent to know the boys personally. It is highly improbable that a boy would suffer very long from the brutality or bullying of an officer without having it found out by the superintendent, the commandant or farm supervisor. The student officers are not permitted to administer corporal punishment which is, of course, an additional safeguard.

There is no formal plan for student government as such. It was stated that certain situations are sometimes discussed with the boys in order to get their point of view as to what should be done. Since student government plans in schools for delinquent children are always more or less artificial, the development of a formal plan of this sort would not add a great deal to the effectiveness of the school routine. On the other hand, there should be opportunities for a boy to make decisions which will affect him and his group. Student participation in the affairs of a school is a desirable method of giving children such experience. The superintendent of the Training School has recognized the value of treating the boys as partners and the informality of his approach is probably more effective than a cut-and-dried so-called student government scheme would be. To give children opportunities to make decisions and choices involves more hazards for the administration than a plan of control which eliminates all chances for doing either. However, the way in which a boy reacts to situations involving choice is the test of what a training program is doing for him.

To sum up, the extent to which the boys carry responsibility for the discipline and industry of the group is considerably larger than that usually found in schools of this character. The system at the Morrison Training School would probably not work in any other school in the country. Its success depends largely upon the unique interplay of the personalities of the executive, the staff and the boys. This involves intangible elements which can be sensed but not described.

In spite of the lack of penal atmosphere, there is no "milk and water" quality in the relationship between staff and boys. No one doubts that the administration runs the school. To continue with a plan which thus far has proved to be successful, to face its dangers honestly, and to check its continued usefulness by its effectiveness in terms of development of character and wholesome personality seems to be a logical procedure.

It is reasonable to expect that a boy sent to the training school should be taught habits of industry and that he should assist with all of the routine tasks of the institution. Neither is there serious objection to having groups of older boys go out to work for neighboring farmers occasionally if the conditions under which they work are satisfactory. Proper precautions for safeguarding the boys against exploitation seems to have been taken by the administration.

However, it would seem that one valuable by-product of the employment plan has been overlooked, namely, the opportunity it affords for providing some economic training. If we were living in a civilization based on the principle of common ownership, then the plan of having the returns from the outside work of the group go into a common fund could not be questioned. In the economic system in which we live it would seem more desirable to let the boys benefit personally from their individual efforts. Boys who are old enough probably understand that for the time being the state is responsible for their support and that it is right for them to assist with the work of the institution in return for their maintenance even though they did not come to the school upon their own initiative. When they go out to work, however, the situation is somewhat different. If there were any way in which it could legally be done, there would be considerable advantage in giving the boys in a special work squad a small per cent of the wages received. Planning what to do with money they have earned by their own labor will be helpful to the boys in various ways.

Many children coming to an institution have little idea as to what clothing, food and other materials cost and no interest in saving any part of what they have. The small amount of the boys' earnings which it would take to enable them to experience the personal satisfaction which comes from getting some return for honest effort would not reduce the income sufficiently to embarrass the State of North Carolina financially. The practical difficulties of letting children in a correctional institution have money are overcome by having a special "store day" once or twice a month in which a good imitation of a real store is set-up and the boys who merit such distinction are delegated as managers.

MEDICAL SERVICE

When a boy is sent to the Morrison Training School, a medical certificate filled out by the physician in the community from which he comes is sent with him. In some instances, laboratory tests have been required, but this is not a routine procedure. The form used asks for a statement as to symptoms of tuberculosis and venereal diseases and of hookworm, pellegra, and malaria. The condition of the lungs, throat, teeth, eyes, and ears are noted. This blank, however, does not call for recommendations and is a medical inspection blank rather than a report on an intensive examination. As there are no isolation facilities, a boy is assigned immediately to the building in which the other children live after he has been bathed and given clean clothing.

A Negro physician from Rockingham comes to the institution once a week. He receives $25 per month. There is no nurse on the staff nor is there any public health nursing service available.

At the time of the routine visit the physician sees any children who have been admitted since his previous visit. If he suspects venereal diseases or tuberculosis from clinical evidences, tests are made. Otherwise this is not done as a matter of routine. The institution has no facilities for taking care of active venereal diseases. If cases are discovered, they are returned to the county from which they came.

Through the assistance of the State Sanatorium for Tuberculosis, the boys were examined in the spring of 1929 and twelve or fourteen were found to be tuberculosis suspects. They were taken to the Sanatorium for X-ray and were put on a special diet and a rest regime. Reports on their weights were sent to the physician every ten days.

All of the boys in the school in 1929 were vaccinated. There have not been routine immunizations against diphtheria and typhoid fever.

When hospital service is necessary, children are taken to Hamlet, where there are hospital facilities for Negroes. Two cases of appendicitis were cared for there during the past year.

A dentist who receives $20 a month comes to the institution once a week to take care of the children's teeth. The equipment is limited and for certain treatments boys have to go to his office.

Detailed medical records giving the findings of the physician following the admission of the children and the corrective service provided thereafter, are not kept. There is no way, therefore, in which to estimate the amount of preventive and corrective work done. The routine already established indicates an appreciation of the importance of safeguarding the health of the children and of using the period of residence in the institution as an opportunity to correct remediable defects. The medical service, however, is not complete and should be supplemented as follows:

1. As the population increases, nursing service should be provided, preferably through adding a nurse to the regular institution staff. The need for bedside care alone would not justify employing a nurse as the policy of using the hospital at Hamlet for serious illnesses should be continued. There is a need, however, for regular public health nursing service which is invaluable in keeping children well and in reducing the dangers of infection and contagion which exist in group life.

If there is public health nursing service for Negroes available through the county health unit in the county in which the school is located, it might be possible to secure a limited amount of service from such a source. The State Department of Health might be able to suggest some plan for obtaining at least part-time public health nursing service for the school. A nurse would be able to conserve the time of the physician and could do many things which it is not possible for him to include in his general routine, such as the keeping of complete records; the weighing and measuring of the children; sorting out cases for examination by the physician; following up on recommendations made by the physician regarding correction of defects; and teaching personal hygiene.

2. Since it is possible to have laboratory tests made by the state without cost, every boy should be given a Wasserman test either before admission or immediately afterwards. In view of the surroundings from which most of these children come it is essential that this be done.

3. Tests for determining tuberculosis should be included as part of the admission routine. The coöperation worked out in the spring of 1929 between the Morrison Training School and the State Sanatorium has demonstrated the possibility of supplementing the general medical service by means of specialized service made available through other state units.

4. Reference has previously been made to the importance of not over-crowding the institution. We wish to repeat at this point that the first responsibility of the institution is to safeguard the health of the children accepted. The prevalence of tuberculosis among Negroes makes it especially important that the dormitories are not over-crowded. The location of the Morrison Training School offers distinct advantages for the proper building-up of children with tubercular tendencies and these should not be sacrificed by exceeding the normal capacity of the institution.

5. It is important that complete records be kept of the initial findings of the physician at the time a boy is admitted and of all subsequent corrections and treatments. Such a record is of value in making the work assignments of the children. If the medical record is consulted by the person who is responsible for work and school assignments, it will be possible to avoid placing children at tasks which for physical reasons they should not be doing. While an honest effort is undoubt-

edly made to schedule the work of the children in accordance with their physical condition, there must occasionally be certain slips in the assignments due to the lack of intensive data on health conditions.

PSYCHOLOGICAL AND PSYCHIATRIC SERVICE

At the present time the Morrison Training School lacks the necessary facilities for psychological and psychiatric services. If through the resources of other State institutions or of universities a definite amount of such service could be made available to the Training School, it would contribute a great deal to the development of the program. Instead of depending so largely upon a trial and error method to determine what capacities a boy has and what training will be most valuable to him it is possible on the basis of tests and analyses to make much more accurate judgments. The Intelligence Quotient arrived at through psychometric tests is not, of course, an infallible guide as to whether a boy will be a success or a failure. Certain children having a fairly low Intelligence Quotient but considerable emotional stability can be taught to do many useful things and to lead a satisfactory life in their communities. It is important, however, for those planning the academic and vocational training for such children to recognize their mental limitations in order that demands will not be made upon them which are quite beyond their capacities. Every boy coming to the training school needs to experience success in some field of endeavor as the stimulation which results from successful achievement is a constructive force in the retraining process. Unless the superintendent knows what it is reasonable to expect from the children, he is handicapped in formulating courses of study, and in making school and work assignments.

In any discussion of programs for the prevention of crime, the importance of the early discovery of criminal tendencies is stressed. Most of the boys who come to Morrison Training School have been guilty of minor offences such as truancy, pilfering, breaking and entering, etc. With better facilities in the respective counties for checking on school attendance and for adapting educational programs to the capabilities and interests of children, the number of children sent to the institution merely for truancy should decrease. With improved methods of family case work, the number of normal children who drift into delinquency primarily because they are neglected should also be reduced. Wholesome recreation and directed play activities are also important factors in preventing juvenile delinquency.

While any detailed discussion of the prevention of delinquency cannot be included in this report it is important that the administration of a training school does not lose sight of these broader aspects of the problem. In its efforts to reduce juvenile delinquency the state of North Carolina will gradually reshape its social program so that those services which bear a definite relation to the prevention of delinquency will be increasingly provided.

The Morrison Training School is in a position to play an important part in the development of such a program. If through coöperation with other units of service or through the addition of workers to its own staff the institution is able to classify the children committed, instead of paroling boys who are so defective mentally or so psychopathic that they cannot possibly get along in the community, it will see that they are transferred to custodial institutions. Experience elsewhere has shown that a certain per cent of boys sent to industrial training schools later go to reformatories and penitentiaries. In many instances these are the children of psychopathic tendencies and low mentality who cannot stand up under the strain and stress of modern civilization.

Early discovery and proper treatment with continued custodial care, if necessary, will ultimately reduce the number of juvenile "repeaters" who are delinquent because they are defective. More emphasis upon making public school systems sufficiently flexible to meet the needs of all children, upon conserving and improving family life and upon providing adequate recreational opportunities should affect the number of normal children for whom institutional care is needed.

The Board of Trustees and the superintendent of the Training School have already seen the need for psychological and psychiatric service and in a few cases have sought the assistance of specialists. It is urged that the possibilities of securing more adequate service from other state institutions be canvassed and that a definite plan of coöperation be developed if at all practicable.

DIET

The wife of the superintendent, who is the subsistence supervisor, is responsible for planning the meals and for supervising the cooking and serving of the food. A great deal of truck farming is done, and during the spring and summer seasons there is an abundance of vegetables. In the winter season the supply is less adequate. A dairy herd is kept but as yet the milk supply is not as large as could be used. The supervisor, who has had technical training, tries to plan the meals so that the boys are given the foods necessary for growth and development. Those who are under-weight or for whom a special diet is recommended are given more milk and an attempt is made to carry out the complete diet recommended by the physician. A yearly food per capita of $100 is considered a minimum average for food costs in institutions in the United States.

SOCIAL POLICIES

When a boy is committed to the Morrison Training School, the institution is given a copy of the judgment and commitment. On the information blanks sent in at the same time are data regarding a boy's family and his personal habits, secured usually by the county superintendents of public welfare. There is also a health certificate, to which reference has already been made. The information blank in some instances is filled out completely, and in other cases, only a few of the items called for are given in any detail. In some of the records checked not a great deal of discrimination was used in the comments made on the habits of the boys. For example, in one boy's record it was indicated that he was very industrious and also "that he was totally lacking in ambition." These two statements were somewhat conflicting.

Following admission to the institution, the superintendent usually has a conversation with the boy in order to get his slant on the circumstances leading up to the commitment to the institution. These interviews are not usually written up. In a few of the records notations had been made which were of considerable value as they supplemented materially the meager facts sent in by the courts or the superintendents of public welfare.

The Board of the institution passes upon all cases of parole, the superintendent reporting to the members on a boy's progress and making recommendations for or against parole. Presumably the superintendents of public welfare in the respective counties look after the boys paroled from the institution. But some of the counties are without full time superintendents of public welfare and in others the work is so heavy that the supervision of paroled children cannot be undertaken with any degree of thoroughness. The result is that the parole service for the Morrison Training School is practically nil since the institution itself has no parole department.

In a separate section of this report the importance of supplementing institutional service with proper parole service is discussed and will, therefore, not be repeated at this point.

The institution has started a proper record system with a card file and folders for all the records and correspondence pertaining to a particular case. The following suggestions are made for improving the record system:

1. Since the superintendent is already interviewing the boys at the time of admission the information which he secures should be used as the beginning of a case record on each boy. From time to time either the superintendent or his assistant should incorporate into the record some comment as to the progress each boy is making in school, in the shop, at work, and in his general conduct and social relationships with the other boys and the staff.

2. At the time of commitment, the superintendents of public welfare and the courts should supplement the facts called for on the blank with a more complete statement of the circumstances leading up to commitment to the school. When psycho-

logical and psychiatric services are available it will be necessary to have more social data than the present records contain.

3. The medical records, to which reference has previously been made, are more easily accessible if they are kept in a looseleaf notebook during the time a boy remains at the school and transferred to the individual file when he leaves the institution. If a nurse is added to the staff, the keeping of the medical records would be her responsibility but they should be available for the use of the superintendent and such of his associates as have anything to do with the school and work assignments.

Summary

1. The superintendent should be given an opportunity to spend some time at the New Jersey Training School for Boys in order to gain practical experience in a well organized school which will aid him in developing the vocational program at the Morrison Training School.

2. The trades building should be equipped with the necessary machinery for teaching practical vocational courses as soon as possible. The teaching staff will necessarily need to be increased when the trades building is completely equipped.

3. The present commissary department should be replaced by a modern unit so equipped that it may be used for practical training in domestic sciences.

4. Simple living room facilities should be provided in the boys' main building so that the dormitories do not have to be used for all indoor activities.

5. Facilities for fire protection should be tested and checked at frequent intervals. Fire drills should be given both in the daytime and at night.

6. Acceptance of children should be governed by (1) the standard capacity of the buildings and (2) the adequacy of the maintenance fund.

7. Every resource should be explored in order to supplement the teaching, nursing, medical, psychological and psychiatric services which the school itself can provide from its

own funds until such time as the state can make more adequate provision for these specialized services which are important adjuncts to the complete development of any training school program.

CHAPTER III

THE NORTH CAROLINA INDUSTRIAL SCHOOL FOR NEGRO GIRLS

Historical Background of Industrial Schools

THE FIRST SCHOOLS in the United States for delinquent boys and girls cared for both sexes and, in the north, for both white and Negro children. In the south the first training schools were for white children. Institutions for the training of delinquent Negro girls have been established only in comparatively recent years. At the present time there are ten training schools for Negro delinquents, some being state institutions and others being operated under private auspices with or without public subsidy. These ten schools are as follows:

Name of School[1]	Date Founded	Type of Control
Industrial Home for Colored Girls, Melvale, Maryland	1882	*Private
Industrial Home for Negro Girls, Tipton, Missouri...	1909	Public
Virginia Industrial School for Colored Girls, Peaks Turnout, Virginia	1914	Public
Dorcas Home, Houston, Texas	1914	Private
Fairwold Industrial School for Colored Girls, Columbia, S. C.	1919	Private
Industrial School for Colored Girls, Marshallton, Del.	1920	Public
Oklahoma Industrial School for Colored Girls, Taft, Oklahoma	1920	Public
Florida Industrial Home for Colored Girls, Ocala, Fla.	1921	Private
Girls' Rescue Home, Mt. Meigs, Alabama	1921	Private
North Carolina Industrial School for Negro Girls, Efland, North Carolina	1925	†Private

* Receives state and city subsidy.   † State grant.

[1] Margaret Reeves, *Training Schools for Delinquent Girls*, Russell Sage Foundation, 1929.

PURPOSE

The North Carolina Industrial School for Negro Girls accepts delinquent girls between the ages of fourteen and sixteen, who have been committed to the institution by the Juvenile Court of the counties in which they have legal residence. There is no other provision in North Carolina for the special care and training of delinquent Negro girls.

CAPACITY AND POPULATION

The institution has a capacity for from fifteen to eighteen girls. There are, however, beds for twenty children. At the time of the study there were eighteen girls in care. From November, 1929, to February, 1930, three girls had been admitted. The girls under care at the time of the study came from the following counties: Carteret, Buncombe, Mecklenburg, Vance, Forsyth, Durham, Robeson, Guilford, Wake, and Pasquotank. The largest number of girls came from Durham County, there being five under care from Durham on February 10, 1930. Some deviation from the rule about age limits is made from time to time. There was one girl at the school who was eleven years old and four girls who were twelve. The others ranged in age from fourteen to seventeen years.

ORGANIZATION

The North Carolina Industrial School for Negro Girls has been made possible through the efforts of the Federation of Negro Women's Clubs of North Carolina. These women raised the necessary funds for the purchase of the farm where the institution is located and have made themselves responsible for the maintenance and support of the institution. A board of eight trustees appointed by the Federation is responsible for the administration of the school. The chairman of the board is a white woman, but the other members of the board of trustees are Negroes.

The leaders in the Federation have never anticipated continuing the operation of the training school as a private enterprise. Since the beginning the idea has been that ultimately

the state should take it over. But the women themselves were
willing to do everything possible to increase the value of the
property in order that their efforts and sacrifice would demonstrate to the state officials their earnestness of purpose and
their willingness to do their part in providing facilities for
the retraining and education of delinquent girls. Thus far the
attempts to have the legislature accept the school and operate
it as a state institution have not been successful. The various
state organizations composed of white women have given their
support to the efforts of the Negro Women's Clubs in this
direction.

FINANCES

The General Assembly of 1927 appropriated $2,000 to sup-
plement the annual maintenance fund raised by the Club
Women and this amount has been granted each year since
1927. The state money is used chiefly to pay the salaries of the
workers. The amount remaining is used for supplies. In a
few instances counties have paid board for girls committed but
the amounts collected from the counties have been thus far
negligible. The Federation of Negro Women's Clubs makes itself
responsible for all financial obligations incurred. The Club
members also donate clothing and household supplies. The
total amount spent for the maintenance of the institution in
1929 was $7,622.12.

The remaining indebtedness on the property is in the form
of notes held by private individuals to the amount of $2,000.
The mortgage was taken up in order to offer the property to
the state without encumbrance.

STAFF

The superintendent in charge of the institution at the time
of the study came to the school in December, 1929. She is a
woman who has been interested in club work and in the promotion of work with girls by the churches. She had no special
training in social work nor any previous experience in the
administration of an institution for delinquents. She took
charge following the resignation of the previous superintendent

and apparently has been striving to keep things going until such time as other arrangements might be made. Her practical common sense and her poise have made it possible for her to render valuable service in a new and difficult field. She receives a salary of $65 a month and maintenance.

The assistant received her education at Scotia Seminary. She has had teaching experience and is carrying the responsibility for the school work of the girls at Efland. She not only teaches academic classes, which she has arranged more or less on the plan of an ungraded school but also has done a limited amount of teaching of elementary home economics. The assistant had been at the school previous to her present term of service which began in November, 1929. She receives $40 a month and maintenance.

A farm hand who lives in the neighborhood comes in by the day. He is paid $50 a month.

PLANT AND EQUIPMENT

The institution is located on a tract of approximately 150 acres of land located about two miles from Efland in Orange County. A one story frame cottage is the only building which has thus far been constructed. It contains a fairly large school and living room combined; a smaller dining room; a fair sized kitchen and pantry; one bathroom, containing two toilets, one tub, one shower and one lavatory; four dormitories, one having nine beds, one five beds, and two rooms having three beds each; one small room used for disciplinary purposes; one room used as an office and sewing room; and a matrons' room occupied by both members of the staff.

The school and living room has built-in desks which constitute practically all the furnishings of this room except for a broken victrola and a couple of chairs.* Until recently there were practically no school books but through the interest of the faculty of North Carolina University books have now been provided.

The dormitories are equipped with single iron beds. Some

* Since the time this study was made a piano has been given to the school.

of the mattresses are worn and the filling is so thin that it is difficult for the girls to keep warm in the cold weather. The assistant has been making straw ticks of the sacks in which provisions come, and has put these ticks under the mattresses. There is inadequate space for personal belongings of the girls and in some instances they conceal clothing and other articles in their beds for safe keeping.

The dining room contains two oilcloth covered tables, a chair for each girl and a sink for washing dishes. The table service consists of plates, forks, spoons and some glass jars in which mustard and pickle and other foodstuff have been purchased. At the time of the study there were no cups and saucers, no bowls for cereal, practically no serving dishes, and only three or four knives for a population of eighteen girls. The supply of cooking utensils was also meager. There were no napkins and no table cloths, even for special occasions. The relationship between this lack of equipment and proper training of the girls will be discussed in a later section of the report.

The institution depends for its water supply upon a drilled well. The electric power is furnished by a Delco Light System although the school is so located that it is now possible to secure power and light from the Carolina Power and Light Company. A septic tank is provided for sewage disposal. There is a pipeless furnace in the house but as the cottage is located on land which has the lowest elevation in the entire tract there is so much water in the cellar that at times the furnace cannot be used. On the day of the visit to the institution there was a fire in the cook stove and a small fire in the matrons' room but none in the furnace.

The institution is without a telephone so that in the event of any special difficulty, such as illness or a general riot on the part of the girls, it would not be possible to communicate with the outside world except by going into Efland or to the home of a neighbor.

The tract of land belonging to the school is not entirely cleared but enough of it is tillable so that it is possible to raise a considerable amount of vegetables and food stuffs. A few fruit trees were set out several years ago and in the spring of 1930 students from the University of North Carolina set out an additional seventy-five fruit trees and twenty-five grape vines donated by Lindley Nurseries. Pigs, chickens and a cow are kept.

THE REGIME OF THE GIRLS

As has been indicated earlier, the assistant conducts a school which is organized largely on the basis of an ungraded one room country school. The routine for the school session is varied somewhat with the seasons. During the winter classes are held both morning and afternoon as there was only a small amount of outside work to be done. It was stated that when the garden work began school would be held for a shorter period. Sometimes after the girls have worked out of doors in the afternoon a school session is held in the evening.

The majority of the girls coming to the school have had very little education. Frequently truancy has been one of the contributing factors to their delinquency. In view of the differences in the amount of schooling which the children have had previously, their ages, and the size of the population, an ungraded school plan is undoubtedly the most effective one to follow.

An attempt is made to give the girls training in Home Economics, in order that they may have something of an educational approach to the household tasks to which they are assigned. The assistant appears to be competent to do some rather formal teaching along this line if she had minimum essentials in the way of equipment. In addition to their work in the house, the girls work in the gardens, take care of the animals, and cut most of the wood used.

There is one sewing machine and the girls are taught to make their own clothes. They have also done a considerable amount of hand sewing during the past winter. Handkerchiefs, sofa pillows, a quilt, and other articles have been made with creditable skill.

A pastor comes in from the outside every second Sunday for religious services and the superintendent and her assistant conduct services at other times.

An effort is made to discipline the girls by talking to them and by denying them privileges which other girls have, if they are wilfully disobedient. There is a room opening off the bathroom which is used as a place of confinement for girls who have violated the rules of the school and who have not been amenable to other forms of punishment. This room, which is practically unfurnished, has one heavily screened window.

No special recreational program is carried out but the girls have time for free play and games. Special holidays are marked by some form of entertainment which the children themselves arrange.

MEDICAL SERVICE

Prior to commitment to Efland a medical inspection of each girl is required in the county from which she is committed. This is supposed to include tests for venereal disease. However, in order to be sure that there are proper safeguards, each new girl is referred to the Lincoln Hospital in Durham for examination for venereal disease. If treatment is needed the hospital provides it without cost to the school. When a girl is no longer in an infectious stage she is returned to Efland and then brought back to the hospital at intervals for reëxamination and treatment if necessary. Greater emphasis is naturally placed upon detecting and providing treatment for venereal disease than upon any other physical condition. There are no medical records kept at the school except the blanks which are filled out at the time a girl is committed.

DIET

During the winter it was stated only two meals a day were served but when the outdoor work began three meals were provided. Breakfast usually consisted of hash, grits and bread. For the heavy meal, white beans, bacon and corn bread had been served on the day the institution was visited. Prunes were being used on an average of once a week. Canned tomatoes and macaroni were substituted on certain days for beans. At the time of the study no butter, milk, eggs or fresh fruit were being used.

SOCIAL POLICIES AND RECORDS

Children are accepted only by commitment of the Juvenile Court as has been indicated previously. The information which accompanies the commitment is merely identifying data and in none of the cases checked were there case records which would give a comprehensive picture of the circumstances surrounding a girl prior to her admission. The superintendent in charge of the school prior to December, 1929, made an effort to place some of the girls who were old enough and who had been in the institution for a considerable period, in family homes, at service. The report of the North Carolina State Board of Charities and Public Welfare, for the biennial period July 1, 1926, to June 30, 1928, shows that during that time one girl was placed in a family home; three girls were returned to parents and relatives; and seven girls ran away. Since that time, however, additional placements have been made. The number of runaways in proportion to the number of children formally discharged appears to have been large. Recently there has been less difficulty in this regard.

There has been no definite plan worked out for the placement and subsequent supervision of the girls whose response to the training of the school apparently justifies parole. Presumably the superintendents of public welfare in the various counties undertake to give such service but as yet there has been little attempt to integrate the work of the school with the social service programs of the counties.

The commitment and identifying family history for each girl together with the medical blank filled out by a physician from the community from which she comes are kept in the envelope in which they are received. In addition there is a paper covered notebook in which are recorded admissions and discharges, together with the age, date of admission and residence of each girl. No other records are kept.

DISCUSSION AND RECOMMENDATIONS REGARDING FUTURE DEVELOPMENT

Throughout the United States the theory that the care and re-training of delinquent boys and girls is a function of the State is generally accepted. That North Carolina has acted upon this theory is proven by the fact that it owns and maintains four such schools at the present time, namely, the Stonewall Jackson Manual Training and Industrial School, the State Home and Industrial School for Girls, Eastern Carolina Training School, and the Morrison Training School for Negro Boys. The State is also subsidizing the school at Efland to the extent of $2,000 per year, as has already been stated.

In any line of social endeavor there will always be a periphery of individuals and situations which will remain untouched by the service available. For example, there are few communities in which the public health programs are as yet completely inclusive. In spite of the services provided, some people still die from preventable diseases. Within the past twelve months a mother killed her three children and herself because, regardless of the multiplicity of social agencies in the city in which she lived, her economic and physical burdens had made her desperate.

During the war the Federal Government granted some $427,000 to 43 institutions for women and girls. This amount was matched by states or local communities. "The major purpose of federal assistance," says Margaret Reeves in her book, *Training Schools for Delinquent Girls*, "was to develop quickly a program for the protection of soldiers and sailors against venereal disease by aiding in the enlargement of facilities to care for and treat infected women and girls."

It cannot be assumed that the government had any idea the entire problem of the care of delinquent girls could be solved even with federal assistance. The importance of recognizing the need for such service, however, and for meeting at least a segment of the need undoubtedly stimulated both public and private efforts toward the prevention and treatment of delinquency.

In North Carolina there is a population of approximately 800,000 Negroes. A training school for 20 delinquent girls does not, in itself, materially affect the sum total of delinquency among Negroes in the State. It does, however, demonstrate the value of and the possibilities for the re-training of delinquent girls; and it stimulates greater interest in correcting community conditions which tend to produce delinquency.

In the social field as in the field of health, we find ourselves affected in a variety of ways by those whose social and economic status is far removed from our own. We are usually quick to see this when our property rights are violated. We believe that the State should make provision for those minors who take liberties with our material possessions. We are, however, less inclined to try to salvage the girls who overstep established moral codes although many of them are going to drift in and out of our own homes, hotels, restaurants, mills, shops, laundries, etc. If social and humanitarian reasons do not stimulate our interest in attempting to cope with the problem of delinquency among girls, our interest in protection against disease and in securing competent and well trained workers in various fields should enlist our support.

In the past there was a general acceptance of the theory that there are sharp lines of demarcation between dependency, neglect and delinquency. Today it is more clearly recognized that delinquency often has its roots in neglect and in the social and economic dependency of the families from which delinquent children come. This newer approach to the problem has changed our conception of what training schools are for. Instead of regarding them as places in which children are confined for punishment we now regard them as instruments through which delinquents may be retrained for purposeful living.

Training schools for delinquent colored girls in other parts of the country have demonstrated that it is possible to do constructive work with delinquent Negro girls. The Virginia

Industrial School for Colored Girls, particularly, has shown what can be done in a southern state. Not every girl has made good following her training but the percentage of successes is sufficiently large to justify the investment made in the school by the State of Virginia.

Other sections of the study of Negro Child Welfare in North Carolina will give definite data regarding the number of Negro girls coming to the attention of the Juvenile Courts throughout the State in a given period. These data will show to what extent the delinquency of Negro girls constitutes a social problem of major importance. The recommendations made herein regarding the further development of the school at Efland are based on the following premises:

1. The function of a training school is not to punish youthful offenders. It is to retrain the girls sent to it and to give them certain ideals and skills which will enable them later to live useful and satisfying lives in the community.

2. The objectives of a training school can be reached only when the personnel consists of individuals qualified by training, experience and personality for the difficult task of working with delinquent girls.

3. The plant and equipment should meet proper standards of sanitation; and should furnish a satisfactory medium on which to carry out a modern program of ethical and vocational training.

4. Health and medical facilities should be such as to safeguard the health of all the children.

5. At least a minimum amount of psychological and psychiatric service should be provided in order to avoid (1) accepting non-educable children for training and (2) returning to the community those girls who are so deficient mentally or so unstable emotionally that permanent custodial care should be provided through transfer to an institution for mental defectives or to a hospital for the psychopathic and insane.

6. Every training school for delinquents should have a social service program in order that home conditions may be determined as soon as a girl is received and constructive work done with the family while she is in the school; that suitable

wage homes and jobs may be found for girls ready for parole and the length of stay in the institution thereby shortened; and that proper supervision may be provided subsequent to parole.

7. A training school for girls, whether they be white or Negro, cannot possibly care for every girl who shows anti-social tendencies. It should be regarded, therefore, as a demonstration of what can be accomplished under given conditions; and as a means of stimulating interest in developing those community resources which will be of value in the prevention of delinquency.

8. The care and training of minors who have been declared delinquent is the responsibility of the state.

At the time of the study of the Negro Child Welfare in North Carolina the school for girls at Efland was doing little more than providing the barest minimum of the service regarded as essential in a well-organized training school. The acting superintendent who had carried on very well was not, however, qualified by training or experience to assume full responsibility for developing a complete program for the re-training of delinquent girls.

There was no supervision of the academic and vocational classes by any outside agency such as the State Department of Education or the County school authorities. Through the interest of some of the faculty members at the University of North Carolina school books had recently been provided, but for a time the school was without a supply of textbooks.

The limited equipment in the kitchen and dining room made it difficult to teach the most simple processes in home economics in such a way that a girl would become sufficiently skillful to go into a home and render service of much value. For example, the teacher indicated that she could not teach the girls how to lay a table properly because there was no table linen and the table service was so limited. Thus, girls placed at service would be handicapped because of their lack of training. The few cooking utensils available were so large that it was practically impossible to teach girls how to cook on the basis of serving an average size family. In pointing out the desirability of having necessary equipment for the dining room and kitchen, the idea is not to surround the girls with unnecessary luxuries but to teach them to work with the kind of tools which they will have to use if they go into a family home of average standards.

Furthermore if children are to profit from any kind of training there must be something in that training which will stimulate and interest them. We seriously doubt whether a girl would find much incentive for putting her best efforts into learning something about household management unless better equipment were available than that which the institution provided during the study.

The work which the girls do in the garden and the assistance which they give in caring for the chickens and hogs is necessary in order to get the work done and to keep them occupied. There is, as yet, no plan to approach these tasks from the basis of training in horticulture, poultry raising and animal husbandry. There is no quarrel with the policy of having the girls do a reasonable amount of work. However, there should be injected into the program certain training aspects which are now non-existent and which can only come with the development of additional facilities for both vocational and academic teaching.

The medical routine of an institution caring for delinquent girls and the provision for training in personal hygiene are important phases of the program. As the work of the school is amplified, the generalized medical service should be more intensive and the period in the institution should be regarded as an opportunity to put a girl in such physical condition that when she is paroled she will not be a physical menace to her community. It is important, therefore, that the girls coming to the training school are examined carefully enough to determine the presence of incipient tuberculosis, pellagra, heart conditions and malnutrition as well as of venereal diseases. Records should be kept on the findings at the time of initial examination and of all corrective services rendered or treatments given during the time a girl is under care. Such record is of vital importance in planning work assignments and school routine, and also for determining the type of placement to be made when girls are ready for parole. If the physician is in a position to make a definite statement regarding a girl's physical condition it will often be possible to make a much better placement than would otherwise be the case. The facilities provided by the State through the Department of Health and by the county through the local health unit, and by Lincoln Hospital should be utilized to the fullest extent.

The food supply at the time of the study and the planning of the meals would not be regarded as satisfactory by a dietitian. Three meals a day should be served throughout the year. Less starchy food and more vegetables, milk, eggs and fruit would provide a better balanced diet.

The importance of a well organized system of parole will be discussed in a separate section of the report on Negro Child Welfare in North Carolina. Therefore, no further reference will be made to it at this point.

To sum up, there is no question but what an institution for the retraining and education of delinquent Negro girls in North Carolina is an essential part of the well-coördinated state-wide social program. What has been done thus far at Efland is a mere beginning in the right direction. It is consistent both with practical experience and accepted social theory to urge the further development of the North Carolina Industrial School for Negro Girls.

The following questions enter into any consideration of developmental projects:

(1) Shall the Federation of Women's Clubs, through its own efforts and with $2,000 per year subsidy granted by the State, continue to operate the institution as it has been managed up to now with the hope that ultimately the State will take it over and develop the program?

(2) Shall an effort be made to secure financial assistance from private sources in order to proceed as soon as possible with the logical steps in the development of a modern program?

(3) Shall an effort be made to secure the coöperation of the

State and of private individuals or groups in order that through joint effort adequate resources for expansion of service may be provided in the near future?

(4) Assuming that funds were available, what are the next steps to take in order to perfect an up-to-date training school program?

The purpose of this report is to point out what needs to be done, from a social point of view, to improve the work of the school at Efland, rather than to discuss possible methods of financing which must remain a state and organization problem. The fourth question, therefore, will be considered further at this point.

As more of the counties in North Carolina equip themselves to meet their social needs there will be increased demands for specialized forms of social service. There are at present 26 counties in which definite programs of welfare work for Negroes are in various stages of development and in which Negro workers are employed. It seems particularly important, therefore, that a definite, state-wide policy relative to the care and training of delinquent girls be formulated under skilled leadership at as early a date as possible. Many mistakes in programs for delinquents have been made in the past from which the State of North Carolina can well profit and which it should not have to repeat.

One of the most effective ways in which to influence social attitudes toward and treatment of delinquents in local communities is through demonstration by the State. This is possible only when there is well-organized training school and adequate social service through which the facilities of the school itself will be supplemented by the careful placement and supervision of paroled girls. For this reason, it seems highly desirable that the program at Efland go forward rather than merely mark time. Disregarding all questions of how the cost of further development at this time may be underwritten, the following suggestions are made regarding what seem to be the logical next steps:

(1) It is urged that in developing the Efland project, emphasis be placed upon qualitative rather than quantitative considerations. No definite recommendation can be now made as to what the future capacity of the institution should be. However, a small institutional unit which provides high-grade service and thereby justifies the investment by the quality of its accomplishments will, in the long run, affect the whole problem of delinquency much more effectively than a large institution which does little more than feed, clothe and shelter three or four hundred children.

(2) As the first step in improving the facilities of the Industrial School it is recommended that two new cottages each having a capacity for fifteen girls should be constructed. These cottages should be complete units in order that they may serve both as living quarters for the girls and also as training centers in which practical courses in household administration may be given. A few single rooms and dormitories for three or four girls should be provided in order to make some classification possible. Ideally each girl should have a single room. The advice of the engineer and architect should be sought as to site as additional cottages should not be located on the lowest corner on the entire tract of land where the first cottage was placed.

(3) The old cottage should be used for school and administration purposes. With a few changes, one room in this cottage could probably be set aside for isolation of new girls. Facilities for this purpose are essential in an institution for delinquent girls.

(4) In addition to the building of the cottages, provision would have to be made for proper sewerage, an adequate water supply, better drainage and light and power. These facilities should be adequate to meet the needs as additional cottages are constructed.

(5) Roughly speaking, cottages can be built for $1,000 per individual. Thus a cottage for fifteen girls would probably cost approximately $15,000. An estimate as to the cost of

providing an adequate water supply, proper sewage disposal, etcetera, could be made only by an engineer familiar with local conditions.

(6) An executive with training and experience which will qualify her to exercise leadership in the development of a training school program should be secured as soon as possible. This will require some increase in the maintenance budget as the $2,000 which the State appropriates and the $2,000 to $3,000 which the Women's Clubs raise would be inadequate for the operation of a properly staffed school for thirty girls. The average yearly per capita for training schools for delinquent girls in the United States is around $500. Without suitable personnel, however, improved plan and equipment would be of little consequence. An executive of the caliber indicated would acquaint herself with the various local and state resources which might be used to supplement the services which the school itself can furnish. Medical and psychological services, additional vocational training resources and broader cultural and recreational opportunities could undoubtedly be discovered by a person accustomed to integrating the work of an institution with extra-mural facilities. Detailed recommendations as to vocational training, discipline, medical service, recreation, diet, opportunities for self-expression, social records, etcetera, are not included herein as until better equipment is provided and a properly trained executive is secured, radical changes in the present regime cannot be effected.

(7) With the buildings and equipment which have been suggested and a competent, well-trained staff, it would then be possible to formulate a well-rounded program which would individualize each girl and give her new avenues for constructive self-expression. The practical achievements of schools for delinquent girls in other parts of the country have demonstrated that these are attainable ideals.

(8) North Carolina is in a strategic position to influence the development in the South of training projects in the field of social welfare. A number of its universities and colleges are particularly interested in applied social sciences. It would seem, therefore, that the potential opportunities for practical

training in institutional service should not be lost sight of in considering the expansion of the Industrial School program. The New York School of Social Work and Western Reserve University have demonstrated the practicability of coöperation between schools of social work and institutions. As an adjunct to theoretical training in the care and training of delinquent girls, work in an institution under supervision of a skilled person is invaluable. Only recently have we come to see the necessity for training persons who will later go into the field of institutional service. In the specialized field of training Negro workers for institutional positions, there has been practically nothing done as yet. There is reason to believe that North Carolina could initiate a program which would not only serve the Negro girls of the State who are committed to the institution, but would also make a splendid contribution to the field of adult education. While this would naturally be a much later development of the program it is something which should be kept in mind in planning new buildings; securing new equipment; and in selecting the staff. If an executive is secured who has the training and leadership which will enable her to make a real contribution to the professional training of the workers on her staff, it will be possible to attract a much higher type of subordinate worker than might otherwise be secured for the salaries available.

Conclusion

The North Carolina Industrial School for Negro Girls is remarkable, not for what it has accomplished thus far, but for the fact that it exists. Its one nondescript, poorly furnished cottage and the patch of clearing with its fringe of brier-tangled, wooded acres are a monument to the Negro woman's faith in her sex and in her race. The dimes and quarters of working women as well as the larger contributions of those in more favorable circumstances have given substance to the dream. In spite of sweeping generalizations to the contrary, the thinking Negro woman believes that if given a chance a fair percentage of girls who have violated accepted codes may still become useful members of society.

The Federation of Negro Women's Clubs, having demonstrated its faith by its works, has reached the point where it must have help if the potentialities of the program it has initiated are to be fully developed. Either the State, private philanthropy, or both, should now undertake the task of making the school at Efland a center for the scientific retraining and education of juvenile delinquents.

SUMMARY

1. North Carolina, in accordance with established precedents, should ultimately accept full responsibility for the maintenance and necessary expansion of the Industrial Training School for Negro Girls.

2. As the counties in North Carolina undertake broader programs of social welfare, there will be a greater recognition of the need for facilities for the prevention and treatment of delinquency. It is important, therefore, that the development of the school at Efland be undertaken as soon as possible; and that both institutional care and social service be provided in order that the institutional plant may serve a maximum number of children in a given period. Two complete cottage units for fifteen girls each should be constructed as soon as funds either from public or private sources, or from both, are available.

3. Provision for general utilities and sanitation should be made in such a way that a gradual increase in the number of cottages will not require additional facilities.

4. The present cottage should be used for school and administration purposes, and if practicable, for the temporary isolation of new girls.

5. An executive, qualified by training and experience for the position should be employed as the first step in the further development of the program.

6. Through coöperation with North Carolina universities and colleges offering courses in applied social sciences, the North Carolina Industrial School for Girls should be used as a

training center for institutional workers when its personnel and regime warrant its entrance into the field of adult education.

CHAPTER IV

THE COLORED ORPHANAGE OF NORTH CAROLINA, AT OXFORD

PURPOSE

THE COLORED ORPHANAGE cares for dependent and neglected Negro children of both sexes having legal residence in the State of North Carolina. Children over two years of age who are not known to be physically or mentally handicapped are accepted. In a few instances children under two years have been received for special reasons.

CAPACITY AND POPULATION

The bed capacity of the institution is given as 250. As small single beds are not provided in all the rooms this capacity is based on the present practice of having two children, or in some cases when they are small, three children sleep in one double bed. The population in February 1930, was 248. The distribution of these children by counties was as follows:

Counties 46	Number of children 248	Counties 46	Number of children 248
Alexander	2	Durham	19
Buncombe	8	Edgecombe	7
Beaufort	2	Franklin	7
Bertie	3	Forsyth	8
Burke	2	Guilford	11
Columbus	2	Gates	1
Caldwell	1	Gaston	4
Cabarrus	6	Granville	14
Catawba	5	Hoke	6
Cumberland	9	Halifax	1
Davidson	1	Harnett	5

Counties 46	Number of children 248	Counties 46	Number of children 248
Iredell	2	Person	3
Johnston	5	Pasquotank	3
Lenoir	9	Randolph	8
Lee	1	Robeson	3
Moore	2	Rowan	3
Mecklenburg	10	Richmond	2
Northampton	3	Sampson	1
New Hanover	2	Stanly	2
Orange	5	Wake	20
Pitt	11	Wayne	10
Pender	5	Wilson	6
Pamlico	1	Warren	7

For the year ending December 31, 1929, 297 different children were cared for. During the same period 34 new children were admitted; 48 were discharged; one died; and 1 ran away.

Parental status of the 297 children and age grouping were as follows:

Parental status	Number of children
Both parents dead	137
Father dead	83
Mother dead	61
Both parents living	16
Total	297

Age	Number of children
Under 2 years	3
2-5 years	60
6-12 years	164
Over 12 years	70
Total	297

Organization

The Colored Orphanage Asylum was incorporated under the laws of North Carolina in 1887. The first Board of Directors was selected from the group of fourteen men who were the incorporators, and they were given power to appoint a Board of Trustees "who should perform such duties as assigned to them by the Board of Directors." The trustees are subject to removal at the pleasure of the Board of Directors.

The present board of trustees and special committees consist of sixteen members all of whom are men. The executive committee of five members, of which the superintendent of the instituiton is a member, is composed of two white men and three Negroes, all of whom live in Oxford. There are two members on the Board of Audit, both of whom are white, and both of whom live in Oxford. The budget officer and bookkeeper is white and is a resident of Oxford. Exclusive of the superintendent, of the persons serving either as special officers or as members of the board, ten are residents of Oxford and six are from Warrenton, Elbron, Kittrell, Wake Forest, Raleigh, and Virginia, respectively.

There is an annual meeting of the board of directors on June 30 and occasionally there is a second meeting held sometime during the year. The executive committee, all of whose members live in Oxford, meets two or three times a year for the transaction of business. The board of audit meets quarterly.

In 1909 the Legislature passed an act increasing the appropriation of the State fund to the institution with the provision that the Governor of the State appoint three men on the board as an auditing committee. The board, with the exception of the members of the auditing committee, is a self-perpetuating body. When there is a vacancy by death or resignation, the remaining members of the board select a new member.

Comments on Organization

The population of the institution at the present time represents 46 counties of North Carolina. The legislature appropriated $27,500 for annual maintenance for the biennium, 1929-1931 which is approximately 80 per cent of the total budget.

In view of the state-wide service which the institution is giving and the amount of money received from the state it would seem that the governor should appoint half the members of the board of trustees for definite terms of office and the other half continue to be appointed by the board of directors of the corporation for definite periods. Since the State is bearing such a large share of the support of the institution the question is raised as to whether it should not also bear a proportionate amount of responsibility for the administration.

It is desirable that there be several women board members appointed since the institution is caring for young children of both sexes. In a normal family setting, fathers and mothers participate in the task of bringing up children. The interest and critical judgment of both men and women are also needed in formulating policies for the operation of an institution caring for dependent boys and girls of all ages.

When the Colored Orphanage was organized women were not participating in public affairs as they are today. As other changes have been made by the institution in order to keep pace with a changing world, it is urged that the policy of appointing only men as members of the board of trustees also be changed in order to enlist the intelligent interest of several qualified women in the important service which the orphanage is giving.

It is usually found that board members are more active in the work of a social enterprise if they meet frequently enough to acquaint themselves with some of the more important administrative problems. The entire board of an institution caring for over 200 children ought to meet quarterly and the executive committee monthly. Unless persons are sufficiently concerned to give this amount of time they cannot contribute a great deal to the progress of the institution.

The following recommendations on organization are presented:

    1. The membership of the board of trustees should be more

representative of the entire state; and consideration should be given to determining what legislative changes would be required to enable the governor to appoint half of the members of the orphanage board.

2. Two women and preferably three should be appointed as members of the board of trustees, and at least one of these members should serve on the executive committee. It would be advisable to select women members living in or near Oxford in order that they might keep in close personal touch with the institution.

3. The entire board of trustees should meet quarterly and the executive committee monthly.

The above recommendations are based upon what is usually regarded as a proper form of organization and not upon any specific criticism of the way in which the present board has discharged its duties. Because of the increasing volume of service the institution is rendering and its relation to the State, the existing form of organization and the way in which its functions appear to be somewhat unsatisfactory.

FINANCES

In 1928 the State appropriation to the Colored Orphanage was $25,000. In addition to this amount, the Duke Endowment gave a grant of $5,769. Something over $500 was donated by church groups, and other gifts amounting to $512 were received. The State appropriation represented 78.6 per cent of the total maintenance budget. The last general assembly increased the appropriation to $27,500 per year. The per capita for 1928 was $117.05. The income from the labor of the children employed by farmers in the neighborhood amounted to approximately $2,000 during 1929. This money was put into the maintenance fund of the institution.

The financial forms worked out by the Duke Endowment are being used by the institution and one of the members of the Board is designated as budget officer and bookkeeper.

As will appear later, many important services have not been provided and thus the low per capita cost should not be regarded with too much complacency.

STAFF

The present superintendent of the institution who receives a salary of $2,500 per year has been in charge of the Colored Orphanage for about twenty-seven years. He also was a leading factor in the organization of the orphanage. He states that as a young student he became interested in dependent and neglected colored children and that he was working unceasingly to provide proper care for them. The superintendent has the distinction of being the only Negro living Ex-Congressman ever representing North Carolina at Washington and is one of the three living Negro Ex-Congressmen. He is devoted to the institution and can stimulate the interest and sympathy of others when he discusses the work of the Orphanage.

The wife of the superintendent is chief matron of the institution. She gives particular attention to the supervision of the kitchen and dining-room and to the girls' cottage. She also does a large part of the clerical work and record keeping. She has a fairly good educational background and considerable native ability. She receives a salary of $55 per month.

The other members of the staff include the following persons:

One girls' matron.....................$ 40 per month and maintenance
One boys' matron.....................$ 35 per month and maintenance
One head cook and dining room
    supervisor........................$ 40 per month and maintenance
One kitchen assistant.................$ 35 per month and maintenance
One head farmer.....................$ 60 per month and maintenance
One farm assistant...................$ 50 per month and maintenance
One farm assistant...................$ 25 per month and maintenance
One janitor (8 months in year).......$ 30 per month and maintenance

               (The janitor sleeps on the second floor of boys' cottage and supervises children at night.)

Six teachers...........................$ 60 per month each

               (Note: only one of the teachers lives in the institution.)

Physician.............................$400 per year
Budget officer and bookkeeper........$ 33.33 per month
Two members of the auditing committee. $ 18.75 per quarter each

The matron in the girls' cottage has been connected with the institution for eighteen years. The boys' matron has served the institution for about ten years. Last year an additional teacher was employed for the home economics department but during the present year this position was not filled because of financial reasons.

COMMENTS ON STAFF

The ratio of children to matrons for the year 1928 was 86.7 to 1. In February, 1930, the matron in charge of each of the two cottages was caring for over 100 children. While the chief matron gave some assistance and the janitor supervised the older boys' dormitory at night, the two matrons were largely responsible for those forms of service which mothers render to children in family homes. It is obvious that such large groups make individual attention practically impossible and that the only alternative is mass treatment and control.

If only older children were cared for the lack of a larger staff would be less serious. During 1929, 21 per cent of all the children cared for were five years of age or under; and 55 per cent were from six to twelve years, inclusive. When one thinks what demands children of these age groups in families make upon the time and effort and understanding of the mother, it is clear that the two matrons would do well to keep their children washed and clothed and their houses in a fair condition of cleanliness and order with such help as the older children can give.

The matron or cottage mother is the parent-substitute in an institution. The executive, the teachers, the vocational supervisors and other members of the staff do not have the same opportunities for personal relationships with the children as the matrons have. The examples which they set in their contacts with the children and their attitudes toward them undoubtedly influence the boys and girls much more than any other phase of their institutional training. It is largely through the cottage mother, too, that children deprived of their own parents, seek those emotional satisfactions which are so essential in the development of personality and stability of character.

The plan of the buildings lends itself to large grouping and presents serious problems when one begins to consider practical methods of reducing the number of children under the care of one woman. However, as will be pointed out later, certain changes could be made which would greatly improve the present situation.

It is urged that the executive and members of the board give serious consideration to the need for additional house mothers and that as funds are available for this purpose an effort be made to get women properly qualified for this important division of institutional service.

PLANT AND EQUIPMENT

The Colored Orphanage is located on a tract of land about a mile and a half from the city limits of Oxford. There was originally something over 200 acres of land in this tract but in 1928 an additional parcel containing 157 acres was purchased which will add to the pasture land and make it possible to keep a larger dairy herd. The location of the institution is admirable in many ways since it is possible to have the advantages of rural life without the disadvantages of isolation from the community.

The superintendent lives in a family dwelling across the street from the institution. The offices are also located in this house. The institutional buildings consist of a boys' building which is a two-story building of brick construction; a girls' building also two stories and of brick; the administration building on the second floor of which is the chapel and on the first floor the dining-room, the kitchen and one room which was previously used as a classroom; and a large modern two-story school building which is called the Angier-Duke Memorial School and which was made possible through a special donation from the Duke family. This school building contains adequate facilities for the regular school classes, a room for library purposes and a well-equipped domestic science department.

A new laundry building has recently been constructed the

upper floor of which is used for a sewing room. No laundry equipment has been secured as yet.

A dairy barn has been built during the past two years and is located about 300 yards from the main part of the campus. It is stated that the requirements of the State Board of Health for the construction of such a building were complied with.

The institution has finally completed the installation of adequate toilet facilities in each of the cottages and the old outside toilets have been entirely done away with and the grounds cleared. Proper provision for sewage disposal has been made.

In the boys' building all of the children sleep in dormitories. An effort is made to separate the young children from the older ones who sleep on the second floor. There are two play rooms, one of which is used by the small boys and the other by the larger boys. The small boys' play room is used also as a general utility room. On the day of our visit some of the older girls were ironing in this room, heating their flat irons on the stove. The bath room containing the new equipment is on the first floor. It was in good condition and the facilities appeared to be adequate.

In the girls' cottage there is a large dormitory on the first floor that is used for the younger children. The older girls are on the second floor and have smaller rooms. In some of these rooms there was one double bed and in others there were one double bed and a cot, and in some instances two cots. The small bed rooms were neat and fairly attractive. Several of them contained dressers and the children had been permitted to arrange their small personal belongings as they wished.

There is a room on the second floor in the girls' cottage which has been used as an infirmary but due to a recent fire it was not equipped for use at the time the study was made.

There is a sitting room on the first floor quite well furnished, and it was stated that this room is used by the children when their parents come to see them. There is also play room which has very little equipment and is bare-looking and un-attractive.

The chief toilet facilities are on the first floor although there are additional facilities on the second floor for night use and for the use of the infirmary.

The chapel on the second floor of the administration building is said to be large enough to accommodate 500 to 600 people. There is a stage at the rear. The walls and floors are in splendid condition and it is one of the most attractive rooms in the institution.

The dining room and kitchen occupy the first floor of this building. While the kitchen equipment is not elaborate it seemed to be fairly adequate to meet the needs. The dining room is well lighted and can be properly ventilated as it has windows on the two long sides. There are twelve or thirteen long oilcloth covered tables used by the children and two smaller ones for the matrons and other workers. The table service consists of iron stone china, glasses and the necessary cutlery. The chief matron is to be commended for seeing that proper equipment is provided. There is not room enough for all of the children to eat at one time. The girls and the little boys eat first and then the older boys are served. This plan is not particularly satisfactory, but there seems to be no other way to meet the situation at present. The dining room was clean and orderly and the tables neatly set.

The water supply comes from drilled wells from which it is pumped into a storage tank. The steam heating plant in the girls' building is not used as it is out of order and has never been repaired. Stoves or heatrolas are used for heating purposes in both the boys' and girls' cottages and in the dining room. The school building is equipped with a steam heating plant and was warm and comfortable.

COMMENTS ON PLANT AND EQUIPMENT

The following comments and suggestions on plant and equipment are presented for consideration:

1. As soon as funds are available, the laundry building should be equipped with standard laundry machinery. However, in installing such equipment it should be borne in mind that unless funds are also allocated for the salary of a person

who knows how to operate such machinery, the investment cannot be properly safeguarded. Since the institution provides fairly long time care and an effort is made to provide some training, a properly equipped laundry operated under the direction of a skilled supervisor would offer additional facilities. While the older girls should be taught to do their personal laundry by hand, there would be some vocational value in working in a plant having modern equipment.

2.   As rapidly as possible the double beds should be replaced by single iron cots. The institution has from time to time had difficulties because of the health conditions of its children. Some time ago when the population was examined, a number of children were found who had venereal infections. The physician in charge of the medical program states that it is difficult to prevent the spread of scabies among the children. In such a large population there is undoubtedly a considerable number of children who have either been exposed to tuberculosis or who are predisposed to the disease because of previous neglect and poor environment. For these reasons as well as for others which need not be discussed, it is urged that the institution take definite steps to discontinue the use of double beds. It should be possible to rearrange one dormitory at a time throughout the institution until all the dormitories are so equipped that each child sleeps by himself. Iron cots which are smaller than an ordinary three-quarter bed would be entirely satisfactory. The rooms in the girls' cottage which now have double beds and cots would have room for three cots.

There is no reasonable argument for accepting groups of dependent and neglected children unless proper physical safeguards can be provided. Regardless of how many children the Colored Orphanage accepts in a year there will still be some Negro children in North Carolina who are being improperly cared for in their communities. The number accepted is in the final analysis less important than the quality of the service given to those who have been admitted. If proper habits of personal hygiene are formed while the children are in the institution and decent standards of living are taught, when children later establish homes for themselves they will have some incentive for trying to create a better environment than their parents were able to do. There is reason to believe that the administration of the Colored Orphanage would have the support of the citizens of North Carolina interested in public health measures if during the next two years it made a special effort to secure some additional funds for re-furnishing its dormitories. The number of beds in each dormitory should be limited to the accepted standard of 500 cubic feet of air space and 50 square feet of floor space per child. Upon this basis an accurate capacity figure could be set.

3. The question of providing separate quarters for the children under six which has already been considered by the administration should be regarded as an important and necessary development of the program of the Colored Orphanage. It is urged that when such construction is definitely decided upon, the Board of Directors consider building small one-story units in which not more than 15 children will be provided for. This would make it possible for one woman to be a real parent-substitute and to give habit training which at present is impossible. By having small children in a one-story building they can also get out of doors easily. It would be unfortunate for the institution to decide upon building a three-story structure for little children in a climate like that of North Carolina. The campus of the institution is large enough in scope to lend itself admirably to the one-story unit construction plan. Furthermore, this type of construction would not be prohibitive in cost.

4. The superintendent recognizes the disadvantages of having such a large number of children under the supervision of one matron. He has considered placing an additional matron in the girls' cottage but there have been difficulties which made such an arrangement impracticable at this time. Reference has already been made to the fact that the meals of the children have to be served in relays because the dining room is not large enough to seat them all at once. It is suggested that consideration be given to making the girls' cottage a complete unit, having dining room and kitchen facilities, and that two matrons be employed, one to be responsible for the cooking

6

and serving of food and the other to be responsible for the
training and discipline of the girls. Another alternative would
be to convert the girls' building into a duplex cottage containing two complete units, each to be in charge of one house
mother. This would mean that in addition to the training in
home economics which the girls get in school they would also
have opportunities for further practical training at home.
This cannot be given in a kitchen in which cooking for approximately 300 people is done each day as experience gained
in such a large kitchen does not have a great deal of value
when a girl goes into a family home.

5.   If additional cottages are provided for the little children,
they should be equipped with dining rooms and small kitchens.
While a considerable amount of the food could be cooked in
the main kitchen and conveyed to the cottages, there should
also be a minimum amount of equipment so that special diets
for the younger and more delicate children could be prepared
in the cottages.

6.   The boys' building in some respects would lend itself
advantageously to the group system plan, that is, dividing
the children into two groups and having a house mother in
charge of each group. The first and second floor dormitories
and the two play rooms would make a fair amount of separation possible. The success of such a plan would depend upon
the ability of the two house mothers to work together but
experience elsewhere has proven that this is not impossible.

7.   The present plan of heating the cottages is not entirely
satisfactory. The only way in which the isolation room in the
girls' cottage can be heated is by a small stove. The heatrolas
that are used in the dining room and in the girls' play room
and the play room for the older boys are much safer than
ordinary stoves. There seemed to be some hazards in the
type of a stove in the play room for small boys as it got very
hot.

8.   Both the boys' building and the girls' building have
living room facilities. The furnishings of these rooms are exceedingly meagre, and no attempt has been made to make them
attractive. If a home economics teacher is employed for the

next school year, it would seem that the decoration of the living rooms might be undertaken as a project by the older girls under her direction. Without a great deal of expenditure and with the help of the older children, these rooms could be made attractive. It may be that there are some old tables and chairs somewhere in the institution which might be repainted in bright colors and used, particularly in the living room for the girls.

9. The facilities for isolation are limited to one room on the second floor in the girls' building. In an institution as large as the Colored Orphanage, it is important that there be some provision for the isolation of new children until they have been examined and the reports on laboratory tests have been received; and for the care of sick children who should be separated from the group but who are not ill enough to need hospital care. It is suggested that a representative from the State Department of Health, the county health officer, the physician on the staff of the institution and the superintendent go over the institution to determine whether there is any way in which more adequate isolation facilities may be provided through some rearrangement of the dormitories or other departments.

10. The board of trustees and executive should determine whether all necessary precautions against fire hazards have been taken and if fire drills are being held at frequent intervals. Some of the drills should be at night in order to make sure that both children and adults would know what to do in an emergency.

LIFE OF THE CHILDREN

Daily schedule.—The boys who are assigned to duties in the barn get up at 5 o'clock. The other children get up at six. The schedule for the day is as follows:

Breakfast for older boys......................................7 A.M.
Breakfast for girls and smaller boys.........................7:30 A.M.
Morning chores ....7:30 to 8:45
School ....8:45 to 12
Noon meal ....12 to 1
School ....1 to 3:30

From 3:30 to 5:30, which is the supper hour for the girls and smaller boys, the younger children have free play. The older children are assigned to various routine tasks from the time school is out until supper time. The older boys have their supper at 6 o'clock. After supper, the younger children play and the older children have some free time and a study hour. Nine o'clock is bed time.

Education.—The children attend school within the institution until they have completed the seventh grade. Those who have shown ability are then sent to the Mary Potter High School at Oxford. There are ten pupils attending this year.

The six teachers employed by the institution have elementary certificates. Some of them have had public school experience. The course of study followed is that used in the public schools although some deviations have to be made. The distribution by grades for the last fiscal year is as follows:

Grade	Boys	Girls	Total
Kindergarten	31	14	45
First	26	18	44
Second	23	14	37
Third	13	23	36
Fourth	11	13	24
Fifth	10	11	21
Sixth	5	18	23
Seventh	3	3	6
Total	122	114	236

The grades in which the largest numbers are enrolled are single grades taught by one teacher. In the higher grades there are combinations. While the term kindergarten is used in the above classification by grades there is no kindergarten training within the technical meaning of the term. Neither are there the Froebel gifts and other necessary equipment for such teaching.

A laboratory for the teaching of home economics is located on the second floor of the school building, the equipment for which was approved by the State Department of Education. During the past year it has not been used.

The superintendent of the institution serves as principal of the school. If he is not available when a decision must be made, one of the teachers who has been given the authority to do so acts in his place. There is no outside supervision of the school either from the County Superintendent of Schools or the State Department of Education.

There is no special equipment for manual training or other formal vocational work for the boys. The superintendent states that the boys learn to become fairly proficient with the use of tools by helping to do odd jobs about the institution and that a number of the boys have been taught to make and to lay brick. There is a plant at the Orphanage for brick manufacture and in the construction of some of the buildings the brick has been made there. Skilled workmen are employed when there are special jobs to be done, and the boys work under their direction. It was stated that a number of the boys have been able to get positions as brick masons after leaving the institution.

Religious services.—The older children are permitted to go into the village to attend church services. There are also religious services at the institution each Sunday. It was stated that people from the outside frequently participated in these services.

Recreation.—During the eight months' school year, the recreation of the children is largely under the direction of the teachers. The children play baseball and other games among themselves, but they do not play outside teams. There is no special direction of the recreational program.

Programs to celebrate special occasions are arranged at various times throughout the year. A great deal seems to be made of the school closing and there is usually an entertainment in the auditorium at that time. There is no special instruction in music other than what the teachers do in their classrooms.

Discipline.—It was stated that children were disciplined principally by being deprived of privileges. Some corporal punishment is administered usually by the superintendent, although occasionally a matron may punish a child. The disobedient child may also be asked to go without his meal until the other children have finished eating. The chief matron indicated that children are not deprived of food as a means of punishment.

Work.—The boys and girls who are old enough help with all the routine tasks of the institution. The washing which is done on wash boards in wooden tubs placed on a long bench in the laundry is done by the older girls. There are spigots at intervals so that the water does not have to be carried and the tubs can be emptied into a trough near the bench.

In addition to the work which the children do in the institution and on the farm of the institution, those who are old enough also go out to work for farmers in the neighborhood during the tobacco and cotton planting and harvesting season. The persons for whom the children work furnish them with at least one meal a day and sometimes with two. As indicated earlier the institution is paid for the services of the children. This money is turned into the general fund of the institution and is used for maintenance purposes.

COMMENTS ON LIFE OF THE CHILDREN

Because of the large population and the range in ages of the children from two years up and the limited number of supervisors, it is inevitable that the discipline and training are pretty largely on a mass treatment basis. The chief matron upon whom much of the responsibility for supervising the work in the cottages falls, recognizes that this is true. The effect of caring for such large groups in one unit is apparent in the reactions of the children. They are less spontaneous than children in institutions where there is more individualization.

The institution is to be commended for sending its older children out to public school as in addition to the broader educational opportunities this affords, there are social advantages in having institutional children participate in community activities.

An executive responsible for all the details of operation of a large institution cannot be expected to devote a great deal of time to planning and supervising the educational program. It would seem, therefore, that in the selection of teachers, one person qualified to serve as principal should be employed to whom the responsibility for the administration of the school would be delegated by the superintendent of the Orphanage. A principal having proper professional standards would seek the advice and assistance of the city or county superintendent of schools and of the State Department of Education in developing a school system especially adapted to the needs of institutional children.

With the fine equipment already provided it is unfortunate that the home economics department has not been used during the past year because of inadequate funds. Many of the girls in the institution will undoubtedly go out to service when they leave. The practical training which they receive in the Orphanage is based on a unit of service not comparable with an ordinary family home, and the emphasis necessarily is on getting the work done rather than on an educational approach. It is important that there be formal training in home economics to supplement what is learned in the ordinary day's routine.

Changes in industrial conditions and new conceptions of the functions of an institution for dependent children have had a definite influence upon vocational education for boys in institutions. More effort is made to provide opportunities for a variety of simple exploratory courses in manual arts and skills in order to discover special interests and aptitudes through which boys may later be guided into vocational pursuits for which they are best qualified.

The Colored Orphanage has utilized the resources which the routine of the institution has provided for the training of the boys but as yet has not been able to add any formal courses to the school curriculum. This should be regarded as an important next step in the development of the educational program.

At the time of the study all of the children of school age were enrolled in school. Some of the older children were dismissed for certain periods in order to assist in the various departments of the institution. The chief matron stated that she tried to plan the schedules in such a way that one child was not kept out continuously or at a period when he would lose some important part of his school work.

When the planting season comes on some of the children work on Saturdays and after school in the fields. On the basis of information given by the administration of the institution during this study, it would appear that children are not hired out to farmers at times when they should be in school.

It would be desirable if some plan could be devised whereby a small sum would be paid to each child who goes out to work so that he could learn to handle money and to save part of what he earns. As many of the children coming to the institution will later be thrown entirely on their own resources, it is important that while they are under the care of the institution they be given some chance for economic experience. The superintendent might be interested in acquainting himself with what other institutions have done in this regard. For example, the Presbyterian Orphanage at Barium Springs, North Carolina, has worked out a plan of payment for services rendered within the institution by the older children. Out of the money which they earn, they are expected to buy certain personal necessities for themselves. One of the hardest tasks that any institution has is to teach its children economic values as they are so far removed from the sources through which maintenance is secured.

All of the individuals interviewed in connection with the study of the institution stressed the advantages of having the children go out to work in order to learn habits of industry. It is urged that the institution go one step further and let the children experience the personal satisfaction which results from handling money earned by their own efforts.

No one can say except upon the basis of close observation where legitimate work assignments for children terminate and exploitation begins. Somewhere between these two points there is a twilight zone in which the one merges into the other.

The State of North Carolina presumably does not intend that dependent and neglected children, many of whom are without parents and must look to the State for protection, shall be subjected to any form of exploitation. Its child labor law sets twelve years as the minimum age for employment in certain industries when school is not in session. While the child labor laws do not prohibit farm labor it is assumed that an institution for dependent children would not permit the employment of children under 12 except for brief periods. The policy of group employment of dependent children, furthermore, is not consistent with accepted standards of child welfare in the United States. If because of peculiar local conditions the officials of the Colored Orphanage believe that the children should continue to go out to work it is urged that they determine the physical condition of each child prior to his employment; and that they safeguard the best interests of the children sufficiently to merit at all times the confidence which the State has placed in them as administrators of an important social enterprise.

The statement was made that the superintendent had the children under good control and that they were not lawless and troublesome to the community. Whether this satisfactory response is motivated by fear or is the result of the ethical training the children receive could only be determined by further study and observation.

In attempting to analyze the regime of the children the following points stand out most clearly:

1. The size of the buildings vastly increases the problem of individualizing the care and training of the children and of securing a properly qualified staff.

2. The ratio of children to house mothers is such that mass treatment is unavoidable and certain refinements of service cannot possibly be expected under existing conditions.

3. Children under six receive too little mothering; and there are no directed activities such as are provided in nursery schools and kindergartens. As behavior patterns and social attitudes are pretty well established by the time a child is six or seven years old, the training of the young children is an important part of an institutional program.

4. The work of the school in both the academic and voca-

tional departments would be strengthened if the major responsibility for its organization were turned over to a principal qualified by training and experience for such a task.

5.   The first step in bringing about needed changes is for the members of the board of trustees and the executive to map out a developmental program which will set definite objectives to be obtained during a five or ten year period. As soon as the administration itself develops a more critical insight into the condition of the institution progress in new directions can be made. The accomplishments of the past augur well for the future if there is the will to do.

MEDICAL SERVICE

With the admission blank sent to the institution by the Superintendents of Public Welfare at the time children are admitted, there is also a medical blank on which the physician in the community from which the child comes records his findings. This examination is usually a medical inspection and not an intensive, stripped, physical examination.

It was stated that in a number of instances children who the examining physican had said were mentally sound and free from contagious and infectious diseases had proven to be either feebleminded or suffering from some disease discovered after admission. Because of such experiences the physician employed by the institution is now called each time a new child is brought to the institution. If conditions are found which make the child a menace to other children, he is sent back to the community from which he came.

There are no routine laboratory tests nor does the physician record his findings. The only medical records which the institution has are those sent at the time of admission by the local physicians.

There is no nurse on the staff and as previously indicated the only facilities for isolation are on the second floor of the girls' building.

When hospital service is needed, children are sent to the hospital in Oxford. It was stated that the same medical board runs both the white and Negro hospital in Oxford and that the standard of service was satisfactory. The utilization of the existing hospital facilities is preferable to equipping a complete hospital within the institution.

From time to time the County Health Department has given service to the institution. Immunizations against small pox have been made by the Health Department and at one time Wassermann tests were given to a considerable number of the children and treatment provided for those having venereal disease. There is no definite arrangement between the institution and the County Health Department, however, as to how frequently the Department shall give service and just what may be expected from it.

PERSONAL HYGIENE

The chief matron stated that the children are bathed twice a week. The clothing of the older ones is also changed twice. That of the younger children is changed more frequently.

Each child has an outfit of play clothing, a set of school clothes, and an outfit of better clothes for special occasions.

There is no provision in the bath rooms for the care of individual toilet articles, and common towels are used throughout the institution except in the older girls' department. These girls take care of their towels and other toilet articles in their bedrooms.

COMMENTS ON MEDICAL SERVICE

The institution has apparently made an effort to safeguard the health of the children by employing a physician and by securing some assistance from the County Health Department. However, at present the plan of medical service does not include all of the essentials in a program of preventive and corrective health service designed to keep children well and to overcome remediable defects.

With the increased interest in public health service and a more general understanding of the relation between the neglect of physical defects in children and later economic dependency, the health and medical service of an institution has become one of the most important aspects of its program. It should include the following:

1. A complete physical examination at the time of admission with such laboratory tests as the pediatrician recommends.

2. Isolation of new children until reports on the laboratory tests have been received and the physician clears them for transfer to main buildings.

3. The careful recording of the initial findings of the physician, the reports on laboratory tests and the recommendations for treatment and corrections of defects.

4. The recording of all treatments given, all corrections made, and all illness, while the child remains in institution. A summary of this record should be given to the person taking the child from the institution in order that there may be adequate follow-up.

5. Regular recording of weights and heights. The underweight children should be weighed weekly, those who are of normal weight monthly or bi-monthly.

6. Both medical and nursing service should be provided. When an institution is small it is sometimes possible to arrange for some nursing service through coöperation with a local health department or visiting nurse association. When the population is large, however, it is more satisfactory for the nurse to be on the staff of the institution in order that she may follow up all the recommendations of the physician, keep the records, supervise the personal hygiene training, do bedside nursing in cases of minor illnesses when hospitalization is not necessary, sort out children whom the physician should see, etc.

7. Routine re-examination of all children at least annually. Frequent check-ups on those having defects and under treatment.

8. Routine dental examination and treatment.

If the present medical program of the Colored Orphanage is checked with the outline given above, it will be readily seen that while a start has been made in the right direction the services are inadequate.

The physician on the staff of the institution, who is a general practitioner, receives a salary of $400 per year. For a number of years he served the institution without any remuneration. He feels that he cannot afford to give more service than he is already giving for the salary he is paid.

The County Health Department in Granville County, of which Oxford is the county seat, has very limited resources, The Health Officer and one nurse do all of the work that is done in the county. The total budget is approximately $7,500. Of this amount $2,500 comes from the State of North Carolina and $1,250 from the Federal Government. The county furnishes the balance. The small amount of public health service available precludes the possibility of supplementing the institutional service through this source to any appreciable extent.

The starting point in reorganizing the health program is to find out the physical condition of the children. This cannot be revealed by a cursory examination nor by merely getting weights and measures. It requires the skilled services of a pediatrician who is interested primarily in health rather than in curative service.

Work assignments, school assignments and recreational activities cannot be intelligently planned without knowing a great deal more about the physical condition of children than was known about the population of the Colored Orphanage at the time of the study.

If accurate data were secured on the present population it would not be such a task to keep the service up-to-date as the number of admissions in a year is not large. It is suggested, therefore, that the chief of the medical staff and the superintendent consider ways and means whereby they may secure the coöperation of a pediatrician and such other specialists as may be needed to set up the necessary clinics for the complete examination of the entire population during the coming vacation. The State Department of Health, if requested, might assist with such a project on a child-health demonstration basis. The county health unit might also give some aid in such an undertaking.

In considering plans for the future two alternatives present themselves as possible methods for the further development of the medical service. Additional funds might be secured which would enable the institution to supplement the service now provided by employing a pediatrician who would make the intensive examinations and assist the physician in charge in such other ways as he might desire. The physician on the staff would be the family physician and the pediatrician the specialist. Other institutions have proven that such an arrangement can be made to work and that the cost is not prohibitive.[1]

The other alternative would be to secure additional routine service from the county health unit which would supplement what the institution itself is now doing.

This latter alternative is one that could only be carried out through the coöperation of the State Department of Health, Granville County and private philanthropy in developing the county unit of public health service; and in including the institution in its program as a demonstration of Negro child health service in a controlled environment.

Granville County is a small rural county in a section of North Carolina which has suffered heavily from crop failure and economic depression. It has both Negroes and white tenant farmers in its population. A survey of the county by persons in the public health field would, of course, be required in order to determine the need, the attitude of the county medical association, of county officials and other representative individuals and organizations.

The question of such a development is raised because in a small community institutions should not be regarded as isolated units. There should be a certain give and take between them and the other agencies in the community. If through recognition of the needs for better medical service for the children in the Colored Orphanage, better facilities are ultimately provided for all the children of the county, the institutions will have made an invaluable contribution to child health and protection in Granville County.

The following recommendations are presented for consideration:

---

[1] Thornwell Orphanage, Clinton, South Carolina, is one example.

1. During the vacation season all of the children in the institution should be given complete physical examinations which include laboratory tests as the first step in the reorganization of the health and medical service and as an important adjunct to intelligent school and work assignments. The chief of the medical staff and the superintendent should seek the assistance of the State Department of Health, the county health unit, and interested physicians in organizing the clinics needed for this purpose. The findings and recommendations of the physicians will furnish the beginning for an adequate system of medical records.

2. Through the alternatives suggested, or through others, the institution should include in its program the various services listed as essentials of health service in institutions. Complete acceptance of these essentials as desirable objectives to strive for is more important than the rate of progress which will have to be governed by practical considerations.

3. More attention should be paid to the teaching of personal hygiene as a means of controlling the spread of contagious and infectious diseases.

DIET

The chief matron of the institution is responsible for planning the menus, and for supervising the kitchen. For breakfast the children are given grits, oatmeal, corn flakes or some other kind of breakfast food. The cereals are served with milk. Sausage, bacon or beef hash is served for breakfast occasionally.

Dinner usually consists of corn bread, beans, collards cooked with meat, and on three days of the week some sort of dessert. The desserts are gingerbread, molasses pudding or pies, the pies being served on Sunday. Beef stew is occasionally the main dinner dish.

The supper served at the institution on a day in February consisted of hot biscuits, molasses and milk. It was stated that the youngest children had milk three times a day. The older ones have it less frequently. During the winter some butter

was made and it was served to the children once or twice a
week. Canned fruit, prunes, apricots or preserves of some
kind are served about three times a week. Apples are also
given the children from time to time.

As neither menus nor a meal book is kept, it is not possible
to make a definite statement as to food combinations and
variety of meals served in a given period. It is recommended
that a record of the food actually served to the children each
day be kept. Such a plan would make it possible to check over
what has been served and to note the adequacy or inadequacy
of green vegetables, fruit, milk, etc. It also makes it easier
to guard against serving the children a diet which includes
too much starch. An institution as large as the Colored Orphanage would undoubtedly profit by the service of a dietitian
but such a recommendation at this point in the institution's
development is not practicable. However, when there is a home
economics teacher on the staff again her assistance should be
sought in planning the meals even though she does not live in
the institution. If a nurse were available either on a full time
or part-time basis she also would be helpful in advising with
the chief matron concerning the meals.

The 1928 expenditures of the institution show that the food
cost was .1348 cents per day. We understand this figure includes the net cost of operating the farm, the dairy and the
garden. A minimum yearly food per capita for most institutions is $100. While there are some variations due to differ-
ences in locality this is considered a fair standard. On this
basis about 50 per cent of the standard minimum was spent
for food by the Colored Orphanage. Part of this difference
may be offset by the meals served to the children when they
are hired out to the farmers in the neighborhood. However,
unless they work out greatly in excess of what it is presumed
they do, these outside meals would not bring the total food
cost up to the minimum standard.

The surest way of determining the adequacy of the food is
by determining the physical condition of the children. This

cannot be done solely on the basis of heights and weights, as pointed out earlier in this report. In the absence of detailed records on menus and food served over a considerable period and of health and medical records, definite statements as to the adequacy or inadequacy of the food cannot be made. From the basis of cost it would seem that an entirely adequate diet for a population including so many young children who need a large amount of milk would not be possible.

As stated elsewhere in this report the dining room and kitchen were clean and in good condition. The one-story brick building used for food storage, however, is not well equipped for this purpose and it is difficult to keep it in a sanitary condition. Its location at some distance from the kitchen wastes the time of the cook and her assistant, as they have to make a considerable number of trips back and forth per day. When further repairs on the buildings are considered, provision for more sanitary storage of food supplies should be given attention as the present facilities are below minimum institutional standards.

SOCIAL POLICIES

In the past the institution has accepted children upon direct application from parents or other interested parties. At present, however, the superintendent states that he is accepting no children except those recommended for admission by the superintendents of public welfare in the counties in which the children have legal residence. This plan should be continued, as the institution itself is not equipped to make investigations and render other forms of case work service.

During the year ending December 31, 1929, there were 34 admissions to the institution. Forty-eight children were discharged. In a separate section of this report there will be further discussion regarding social service for child caring institutions. Therefore, no further comment will be made at this point.

The records sent by superintendents of public welfare at

the time of admission are filed. These are the only social histories available and are incomplete since for the most part they contain only identifying data.

CONCLUSION

The Colored Orphanage is the largest unit in North Carolina for the care of dependent and neglected children and therefore is an important factor in the development of a Negro child welfare program. Emphasis during the next five years should be placed upon raising the standards of care through certain changes in policy and an improved personnel. Even without the suggested changes in plant which have been mentioned but which cannot be made immediately, a more effective piece of children's work could be done if the board were reorganized as indicated and if the superintendent were able to supplement the present staff by the addition of several well qualified persons in strategic positions in the organization.

If the board and the executive of the Colored Orphanage recognize the importance of continually checking what they are able to do with accepted standards of service to children, which the forthcoming White House Conference on Child Health and Protection will crystalized in a new way, the institution should move forward into an era of greater usefulness than it has yet known. Dissatisfaction with the status quo has always been the route by which both individuals and groups have achieved progress.

SUMMARY

1. Half of the members of the board of trustees should be appointed by the Governor of North Carolina and half by the board of directors of the Colored Orphanage corporation for definite terms of office. Both men and women should serve on the board.

2. A definite policy of making gradual changes in the plant and equipment of the institution which will reduce the number of children under the care of one house mother should be adopted.

3. The girls' building should be made over into a complete

unit having dining room and kitchen facilities.

4. Separate quarters for children from two to six years of age should be constructed on a one-story unit basis. Fifteen should be the maximum capacity of each unit.

5. Modern laundry equipment should be installed in the new building as soon as resources are available. In order to use this unit for training purposes it should be operated by a skilled person.

6. The double beds should gradually be replaced by single beds so that each child may have a bed to himself.

7. The details of the administration of the department of academic and vocational education should be delegated to a principal of schools. The policy of sending the older children to public school should be continued.

8. The health and medical program should be reorganized to conform with accepted standards of the child health field. A complete physical examination of the entire population should be the first step in the reorganization plan.

CHAPTER V

MEMORIAL INDUSTRIAL SCHOOL

PURPOSE

THE MEMORIAL INDUSTRIAL SCHOOL, formerly known as the Colored Baptist Orphanage, was founded in 1900 by a Negro Baptist minister for the care of dependent and neglected Negro children of both sexes. It was incorporated in 1923 after the responsibility for financing and operating the institution had been taken over by a new Board. The name was changed at that time.

CAPACITY AND POPULATION

Each of the three cottages was built to care for 30 children. On February 11, 1930 there were 52 children in the institution ranging in age from 2 to 18 years. The age distribution was as follows:

Age	Number of children
2-5 years	9
6-9 years	20
10-12 years	10
13-15 years	9
16-18 years	4
Total	52

The parental status of the 52 children in the institution at the time of the study was as follows:

Parental status	Number of children
Both parents dead	19
Mother dead	17
Father dead	8
Parents living	8
Total	52

During 1929, 28 children were admitted to the institution and 8 dismissed.

The admissions of the entire population were as follows:

Year admitted	Number of children
1915	1
1916	1
1918	1
1919	5
1920	2
1923	11
1924	3
1928	2
1929	26
Total	52

ORGANIZATION

The board of the Memorial Industrial School consists of 16 persons of whom 14 are men and two are women. Three of the men are Negroes. The white members of the board are selected from the various luncheon clubs and from the woman's club of Winston-Salem. The Negroes are chosen to represent the Negro population.

The present form of organization was effected in 1923, when the affairs of the institution were in poor shape and it was necessary for some responsible control to be established if the work was to continue.

Meetings of the board are held at intervals but without regularity. There is a Receiving and Placing Committee which passes on intake and outgo, but which does not have regular formal meetings between board meetings. There are four other committees, namely, finance, administration, real estate and building. The main emphasis during the past few years has naturally been on getting the new institution ready for occupancy and on improving the farm.

COMMENTS AND RECOMMENDATIONS ON ORGANIZATION

There will be an increasing number of details regarding policies which will demand the attention of the Board of Trustees during the next two or three years. During the period of construction of the buildings and the development of the farm it was quite satisfactory for the Board to meet only when matters of major importance came up; and to depend upon one or two people to put through the building program. The stages of evolution through which the institution has passed would not have been possible without the type of leadership which was exercised. The modern and well equipped buildings and the productive farm are proof of the contribution which such leadership has made. However, now that the necessary material resources have been provided there will be certain advantages, perhaps, in some reorganization of the board. The following suggestions are presented for consideration:

1. As all of the board members live in Winston-Salem a regular schedule of monthly or bi-monthly board meetings at which the superintendent should be present to make his report and to confer with the members of the board upon important matters of policy should be adopted. An institution undertaking the kinds of service which will be indicated later would have enough matters of importance to merit monthly board meetings.

2. The members of the board should be expanded sufficiently to include a larger number of women. As young children

of both sexes are accepted by the institution, it seems important for both men and women to take an active part in the development of the program. There are a number of representative women in Winston-Salem who are particularly interested in the social welfare of Negroes, and it should not be difficult to interest them to serve on the Board which offers so many opportunities for service.

3. The Negroes elected to membership should be outstanding persons in the community as the institution should have the support and backing of the influential Negro group.

4. Members should be elected for definite terms of office which should be long enough to insure continuity of policy. If one-third of the board is chosen each year there will be two-thirds of the members familiar with the development which has come before. Such a plan insures continuity, and at the same time provides the stimulation of new members.

5. As there will be many problems involving technical knowledge in the educational and vocational funds it would be an advantage to have one or two board members from these fields who were also particularly interested in the training and education of Negro children.

6. The Receiving and Placing Committee should serve as a case committee to work closely with the social worker and to serve as a medium for social interpretation between the social case worker and the board, and the board and the public. If careful selection of women board members is made this will be one of the committees on which they can be most effective.

7. The work of the administration, real estate and building committees could all be done by an executive committee, thus reducing the five existing committees to three, namely, the executive committee, the finance committee and the case committee.

8. It might be desirable for the president to appoint a special educational committee for the period in which plans for

the school department are being made as there will be many details to be considered and the entire board may not be able to give the necessary time to the project.

FINANCES

The Memorial Industrial School receives a budget of approximately $12,000 from the Winston-Salem Community Fund. It also receives some support from the Duke Foundation —the amount for 1929 being $884. This will be slightly increased for 1930, as more children are being cared for. The total income for the year 1929 including Community Chest appropriation, Duke Endowment grant, direct gifts and income from the farm was $17,776.94. The expenses were $17,571.79. The estimated income and expenses for 1930 are $20,215. The investment in the farm and the buildings represent total assets of $236,833, according to the audit of 1929. The institution has at the present time a deficit of about $40,000; $25,000 of this indebtedness is being carried by a personal note given by a member of the board.

The yearly per capita for 1928 was $278.34. While this is higher than that of some of the other institutions for Negro children in the south it would be below the average cost of institutional care of dependent children in the United States. Furthermore, any comparison of per capita costs has little value unless there is a corresponding comparison of services rendered on a qualitative basis. There is every evidence that the maintenance funds available have been used with discretion.

STAFF

When the institution moved from the city to the country a new superintendent and matron were employed. The former superintendent who had founded the institution and his wife also went to the new plant, the idea being that they would continue to give such service as they could, but would not be held responsible for administrative details. This plan naturally

did not work out satisfactorily. After several months of trial
the arrangement was abandoned. At the time of the study
the staff included the following persons:

Superintendent.........................$1,500 per year and maintenance
Chief Matron (wife of superintendent)....$600 per year and maintenance
Supervisor of boys' cottage and teacher..$540 per year and maintenance
Supervisor of girls' cottage.......................$420 and maintenance
Supervisor of baby cottage........................$420 and maintenance
Engineer...$600 and maintenance
Farm superintendent.............................$1,500 and house rent
Two farm hands..$50 per month

The superintendent is a graduate of Tuskegee and has had
summer courses at the State Agricultural College, Ames, Iowa;
at Cornell, at the North Carolina A. and T. College; and at the
Kansas State Agricultural College. He has taught agriculture
and shop work in a number of schools and colleges. He holds
a special vocational teacher's class A certificate.

As less than a year has elapsed since the superintendent assumed his duties at the Memorial Industrial School it is hardly
fair to judge his ability on the basis of his accomplishments
thus far as there have been many problems to face. It would
seem, however, that with the background of training and experience which he has he should be able to render satisfactory
service when the institution is properly staffed and definite
policies are determined.

The superintendent of the institution takes no responsibility
for the management of the farm. His duties are confined to
the administration of the institution and the direction of the
staff and the supervision of the children. Boys who help with
the farm work are directed by the farm manager. The farm
manager is a graduate of the North Carolina A. and T. College
and has had two years additional training at Ohio State University. The board of the institution is to be commended
for employing persons with technical training for both executive
positions.

COMMENTS AND RECOMMENDATIONS ON STAFF

As will be pointed out later, the cottages are so planned that each is a complete unit in which the children may live on a family basis. As yet the institution has not been staffed in such a way that each cottage group could do its own cooking. All of the meals have been cooked in the boys' cottage and the boys and girls and staff have eaten in this cottage. The meals for the youngest children have been sent to their cottage most of the time although the cooking has been done in the boys' unit.

The plans regarding staff followed during the reorganization period have probably been as satisfactory as any which could be devised at the time. They are not consistent, however, with a modern institutional program in a well-designed plant such as the Memorial Industrial School has.

There is no other institution for Negro children in North Carolina, or probably in the south, built on the cottage plan. As soon as possible these units should be used on a family basis, one cottage mother and her children doing their own cooking, eating in their own dining room and planning many of their own activities.

The institutions in this country which are doing the best work are those which have recognized the importance of the cottage mother and the contribution which a properly qualified woman can make. Children who have been denied the care and protection of their natural parents must be provided with parent substitutes who will in some measure make up to them for the loss of their own fathers and mothers. Instead of assuming that any woman who is a fair housekeeper and who can look after the physical needs of children is equipped for a position in an institution it is now recognized that in addition she must be the type of person who understands both the physical and spiritual needs of children; and who by her own example and her personality will have something to contribute to the ethical training of children and to their emotional development. The qualities and training which we accept as prerequisites in a teacher are also essential in a cottage mother plus certain other attributes without which no one can be a successful parent substitute. Regardless of how well qualified an executive may be it is not possible for him to carry out his objectives in administration unless he has a staff which also has something to contribute to the lives of the children.

Suggestions regarding social service staff and teachers will be made later.

The following definite recommendations on staff for the care of the children in the cottages are presented for consideration:

1. As soon as practicable plans should be made for having a competent cottage mother in each cottage.

2. The woman now in charge of the cottage for younger children should remain in that cottage as a helper but the executive responsibility of the house should be taken over by a younger woman who has had some training in the care of young children and knows something about organization of play activities and how to carry out directions of a nursery school supervisor.

3. The cottage mothers in each house should operate their cottages as complete units. The wife of the superintendent who has had training in home economics should assist in planning the meals but the actual cooking should be done in each unit.

4. The salaries which will have to be paid to secure competent women will depend to large extent upon salaries paid Negro school teachers and other women competent to assume responsibility. Local persons who know conditions in North Carolina can best determine what the salary scale should be. However, if $50 and maintenance was set as a minimum for cottage mothers the expenditures for operation of the cottages would be as follows:

Cottage mother for girls' cottage.........................$50 per month
Cottage mother for boys' cottage.........................$50 per month
Cottage mother for young children's cottage..............$50 per month
Helper in young children's cottage.......................$35 per month

The amount budgeted for salaries in the cottages and for a cook in one kitchen to do cooking for all the cottages for 1930 was $1,800. The suggested set-up would require $2,200.

5. As the program of the institution develops there should be staff meetings at regular intervals in order that the school work, the vocational program, life in the cottages, the medical regime, and the social service program may be properly integrated; and each person on the staff may understand all phases of the institution's work.

6. No recommendation can be made regarding the present plan of administration by which the farm superintendent and the superintendent of the institution have a coördinate relationship to the board and neither is responsible to the other. Time and experience will tell whether the best interests of the institution can be satisfactorily served by such an arrangement; or whether one person should be made responsible for the entire enterprise. It is urged, however, that the problems which may arise from divided control be frankly faced and that decisions regarding future policy be based on those values which will contribute most to the well-being of the children for whom the institution was established.

PLANT AND EQUIPMENT

The Memorial Industrial School is located on a tract of approximately 425 acres of land about nine miles from Winston-Salem which is in the Piedmont section of North Carolina. Some of the peaks of the Sauertown range can be seen from the institution and the site is one of great beauty. The plot immediately surrounding the buildings is heavily wooded with pine, oak, dogwood and other timber. The natural slope is such that the drainage is excellent. This, together with the elevation, the good water supply, and the adequate space available, makes the land well adapted for institutional purposes.

The farm is in a part of Forsyth County in which there are both white and Negro families. There is a Negro district school within a few miles of the institution. In the rear of the administration building is a large grove which has been cleared and which the board of the institution has made available to

Negro Sunday Schools and other Negro groups wishing to have picnics.

Most of the tillable land lies on one side of the road and the buildings are on the other side. The superintendent is responsible for the area on one side and the farm superintendent for that on the other.

There is an administration building which contains four school rooms, an auditorium, living quarters for the superintendent, offices and several small wards with toilet facilities which are used for isolation at the time of admission.

There is one cottage for boys, one for girls, and one for children from two to ten years of age. The cottages are of one story construction and are complete units, each one containing a dining room and kitchen. The administration building has two stories. All of the buildings are fireproof. The laundry, which is equipped with an ordinary household size washer and tubs, is located in the basement of the boys' cottage.

The investment in the administration building, the cottages, the power plant, the septic tank, the farm building, etc., is estimated as follows: Administration building $50,195; cottage for small children $26,145; boys' cottage $26,671; girls' cottage $26,850; power plant $1,880; septic tank $2,750. The farm buildings, which include the barns and residence of the farm superintendent, are valued at $10,118.

In addition to the above facilities there is also a refrigeration plant and an adequate amount of ice is manufactured for the use of the institution. The general utilities have been so planned that they will be adequate if the time comes when additional cottage units are constructed. The water supply comes from a drilled well and all precautions have been taken to safeguard it against contamination. The County Health officer and the State Department of Health state that in the installation of the septic tank every sanitary requirement was complied with and that the facilities are sufficient to take care of considerable building expansion.

Each house has its own heating plant in addition to the fireplaces which add greatly to the attractiveness of the cottages.

Each cottage has a living room and a dining room which are

pleasant rooms having the minimum essentials in the way of equipment. These two rooms do a great deal toward making the cottages home-like and decreasing the formal institutional atmosphere. With competent cottage mothers who have some imagination in charge of each house the cottages, with practically no additional major expenditures, can be made much more attractive than most of the institutions in the state caring either for white or Negro children.

In each cottage there are toilet facilities; lockers in which the clothing of children and their personal belongings are kept; storage closets; and a bedroom and bath room for the cottage mother. Both showers and bath tubs are provided for the older children. The tub in the cottage for the young children is elevated. The number of toilets in the bath rooms of the cottage for small children was not adequate at the time of the study, but additional equipment was later installed. When the cottages were planned it was expected that each would have a capacity for 30 children. Figuring strictly on a basis of 500 cubic feet of air space per child the dormitories in the boys' and girls' cottages have a capacity for 26 children. The casement windows on three sides provide such a free sweep of air through each room that a few additional beds would not be particularly objectionable from the standpoint of air space. On the basis of 50 square feet of floor space per child each dormitory can accommodate 28 children. This figure is the one to be observed as otherwise the beds would be too close together.

In the cottage for the younger children there are two dormitories, each planned to care for fifteen children. On the basis of floor space the number in each of these rooms should also be somewhat under the planned maximum. All of the beds are single iron beds with springs and mattresses of a good grade. Each bed was equipped with the necessary bed linen, blankets and spreads which were clean and neat.

The school rooms in the administration building have standard desks secured from the Board of Education of Winston-Salem. These desks have been refinished and answer the purpose very well. The school rooms are well lighted and the arrangement is such that they meet the requirements of school room construction and equipment. Toilet facilities are provided for the school building.

The auditorium has a stage, is well lighted, and has a seating capacity in excess of the present population. Both the school rooms and the auditorium were planned on the basis of meeting future needs which was a wise procedure.

The institutional facilities for Negro children provided by the Memorial Industrial School are the best in North Carolina. They are probably superior to those for Negro children in any of the other southern states. The fact that the cottages were planned to care for not more than 30 children and that each was equipped as a complete unit indicates that the administration contemplated carrying out a modern program of institutional care. The institution provides a proper setting for such a program.

The chief difficulty which the institution presents in so far as physical features are concerned is its distance from Winston-Salem, as there are neither car lines nor bus lines to make it easily accessible. This is somewhat of a hardship for respectable parents who should be allowed to see their children and who cannot afford taxi-hire. The location may also make it somewhat more difficult to secure workers as people who do not enjoy an isolated rural setting might not appreciate the great natural beauty of the site. However, with the good roads and the almost universal use of machines, the distance from the city should not be a deterring factor in the development of the program when there are so many advantages to offset this one drawback.

LIFE OF THE CHILDREN

The older children assist with the routine household and yard tasks and a number of the older boys help with the various farm activities. At the time the study was made the farm chores consisted of caring for the animals, and of clearing up some of the fields. Later in the season the boys will help with the planting and cultivation of the crops.

There is, as yet, no definite schedule of work shifted at regular intervals. Children work on whatever assignments are given them and for such length of time as is required to finish the tasks.

The school includes the first seven grades. Classes run from 9 to 12 for the older children who are in the fifth, sixth and seventh grades. The younger children who are in the first four grades go to school in the afternoon from one to four. There was no formal vocational teaching at the time of the study.

The one teacher who is also in charge of the boys' cottage has been at the institution for four years. She has had a years' training at Bennett College and has spent several summers at the Winston-Salem Teachers Training College. She holds a "Grammar C" certificate.

The school runs for an eight months' term.

There is no nursery school or kindergarten training for the pre-school children and no special planning for their activities. The woman in charge of them, who is well along in years and has been on the staff for a long time, tries to take care of their physical needs as best she can and she lets them play among themselves. Three older girls assist in this cottage in which there are 27 children, nine of whom were under six.

When school is out the older children who have no duties play among themselves. The others go to their various tasks..

On Friday evenings a special program is usually given by the children or an evening of games is enjoyed. Saturday afternoon from 3 to 6 is devoted to athletics. On Wednesday evening there is prayer meeting and on Sunday evening a vesper service. Sunday School is held Sunday morning.

There is no provision as yet for any economic training for the older children so they have no experience in earning or in handling any money or in learning how to save.

COMMENTS AND RECOMMENDATIONS ON LIFE OF THE CHILDREN

Reference has been made earlier in this report to the important part which a capable cottage mother who understands her children and is interested in giving them a substitute for family life, plays in the work of an institution. The superintendent, teachers, recreation leaders, physicians, nurses and social worker may all contribute to a constructive program but if the cottage mothers are inferior, unintelligent women with no capacity for carrying out recommendations and plans made for the children and for creating a wholesome family atmosphere in their cottages, the work of the professional staff will be largely nullified. Thus, the first step in making the service side of the Memorial Industrial School consistent with the high quality of its plant and equipment is to get each cottage to functioning as it should with the material resources already provided. In other words, a highly satisfactory machine has been created and the logical next step is to employ cottage mothers equipped to run it in such a way that it will have a constructive effect upon the lives of the children accepted.

In checking over the daily schedule of the children it seemed that there were some readjustments needed. For example, the older boys who help with the milking are up for three hours before breakfast is served which seems like an unduly long interim between the rising and breakfast hours. These children also should have a minimum of eight hours sleep and they were getting but seven and a half hours on the basis of the schedule followed in February.

There is some question, too, as to the value of a study hour for older children from 7:30 to 9:00 p.m. after they have worked the best part of a half day. The chances are that quite as much real study would be done in a forty-five minute period as in an hour and a half at that time of night.

Work assignments should be made from the standpoint of what it is reasonable to expect from growing children, rather than from the standpoint of the multitudinous tasks always pressing to be done in an institution. Habits of industry should be established and all children should work a reasonable amount, but no child should be exploited because he happens to be dependent and must be cared for in an institution. With a better organized system of academic and vocational education and a more diversified recreational program, and with a frequent

8

check-up on health conditions any unwise planning of work assignments should be easily corrected.

During the time the children remain in the institution it is important that they be taught thrift and the value of saving some portion of what they earn. While it is not desirable for children to be paid for doing ordinary routine tasks such as the cottage mothers will ask them to do in the cottages, there should be some opportunity for the older children to earn small sums in order to teach them that upon their own industry will depend in large measure what they have in the way of material possessions. The older boys and girls should be taken into the city occasionally by twos and threes and given a chance to make purchases for themselves. A considerable number of institutions in the country have worked out satisfactory systems of economic training so that children learn to earn, to save and to spend while still under supervision.

The attitude of the children was friendly and spontaneous and the atmosphere was not that of a formalized, inflexible institutional regime. The superintendent was attempting to handle problems of discipline through mutual understanding between him and the children rather than through fear. Boys who had disobeyed the farm manager were being sent to the superintendent for reprimand. How well this plan will work out depends upon the reasonableness of the two men and the extent to which their attitudes toward the discipline of children differ.

The psychologists have taught us there is little of constructive value gained when the disciplinary system is motivated entirely by fear as fear provides only an outer control of conduct and does not touch the inner life of a child from which ethical conduct must spring. If moral training and discipline are to have lasting values they must become a part of the child himself. Extraneous conformity by which he gains a degree of peace and freedom from annoyance while he is in the institution does not mean a great deal in the development of a child's character. The finest ethical training which an institution can give is that which the children gain through observation and imitation of the adults with whom they live.

It is for this reason that only those who have something to contribute to the children by their example of wholesome daily living be employed to care for the children.

The development of the educational program and of the recreational and leisure time facilities will be considered in some detail at this point. A school operated under private auspices has certain advantages and certain disadvantages. If it is not interested in maintaining proper standards and in meeting the minimum requirements of the public schools, it is still possible in some states to avoid maintaining such minimums. On the other hand if an institution is so disposed it may equip itself to carry out an educational program unhampered by the limitations of public school standardization.

Many of the children accepted by the Memorial Industrial School will be those who have neither the mental capacity nor the inclination for a great amount of purely academic training. Nevertheless the facilities of the school ought to be such that each child will have his chance to develop to the maximum his native capacity.

As will be discussed later under social policies it does not seem desirable for the Memorial Industrial School to embark on a program of long time custodial care; or to utilize its resources chiefly to provide educational opportunities for a limited group of children. There are few communities in North Carolina where public school facilities for Negro children are better than in Winston-Salem and Forsyth County from which at present practically all the children come. Judging by what has taken place during the past ten years the educational facilities for Negro children will be greatly improved in the counties adjacent to Forsyth County and elsewhere in North Carolina during the next decade. The emphasis of the institution should be upon providing care for socially and perhaps physically handicapped children for such length of time as care may be needed. This does not change the need for adequate educational facilities but it does change the approach to the problem of education.

Institutions so located that they may send their children to public schools are doing so increasingly in order that pupils

may have the advantages of the public educational system
and of competing with children coming from all types of homes.
It has a bad psychological effect for children in an institution
to feel that they are too different from children living elsewhere.
When they come in daily contact with others and form friend-
ships among them, it counteracts the instinctive feeling of being
set apart which institutional children are prone to have. The
fact that the Memorial Industrial School had a number of unfortunate experiences while in its previous site through sending its children to public school does not prove that the plan
is impracticable but that the administration of the institution
at that time was unable to carry out such a plan successfully.

The nearest public school is now a one-room rural school.
It does not offer the advantages which the schools in Winston-
Salem afforded nor does it offer the possibilities for development which the institution itself possesses at this time. Therefore, the recommendation is made that the institution proceed
with the development of its own educational system. The time
might conceivably come when the school at the institution
might become the public school for the school district in which
the institution is located but this is not the time to consider
such a plan.

Increasingly institutions are becoming more discriminating
in the classification of the educational opportunities which they
offer. Instead of labeling all the tasks to which children are
assigned industrial training, they frankly face the fact that
many things have no vocational content after being repeated
a few times and should be classified merely as work. Children
need to learn that there are many routine tasks which must
be done in the world and that most people have to do their
proportionate share of them throughout their life time. Boys
and girls who are old enough should do a reasonable amount
of routine labor and should be taught to do it properly. There
is serious objection, however, to the assumption that an institution is providing technical training when it is merely having
its children do daily tasks on the farm and in the house. Because children are primitive they derive personal satisfaction
from the elementary processes required to provide food, cloth-

ing and shelter if the adults who supervise them have any conception of what a child's approach is and what it is reasonable to expect from him.

The Memorial Industrial School through its exceptionally beautiful site, its farm operation under the direction of a technically trained farm manager, and its modern buildings and equipment offers distinct advantages for developing a wide diversity of manual skills. In addition there should be facilities for exploratory courses in a variety of other vocational fields through which special aptitudes may be discovered and manual dexterity stimulated. This will not require the elaborate equipment such as is found in schools for delinquents where an effort is made to approximate the conditions found in industrial concerns but it will require some simple tools and other materials and a qualified teaching staff. With the changes which have taken place in the swing from the apprentice system to mass production an institution for dependent children stands a better chance to make a worth while contribution to the vocational adjustment of its children by giving them a wide range of opportunities for discovering special aptitudes, for self-expression and for developing manual dexterity through a variety of arts and crafts than it would by installing some shop machinery and assuming it could then turn out finished mechanics.

The time is past when an institution walled itself in and went its way oblivious of the community in which it was situated and the resources which that community possessed. Today the tendency is to use all available facilities to improve its own standards of service; and to contribute to the promotion of better standards of care for all children whether in or out of the institution. The Memorial Industrial School is well located to profit materially from community resources and to stimulate interest in safeguarding the well-being of all children.

As has been indicated the one teacher in charge of the School during the past year has also been responsible for the boys' cottage. She is not equipped to develop an educational program or to integrate the academic and vocational aspects of the school.

The superintendent of the institution has a background of training and experience which should enable him to make a distinct contribution to a well organized educational department. However, in developing the program he needs the stimulation and advice which would come through a tie-up with a broader educational system.

The following recommendations are presented for consideration:

1. The board of the Memorial Industrial School should determine to what extent the Winston-Salem Teachers' Training College for Negroes would coöperate with the institution in the development of its educational program; and upon what basis the College would be willing to take on the institution school as a demonstration school in which to experiment with various educational procedures in a controlled environment. Such a plan of coöperation would, we believe, be of mutual value to the institution and to the College. The fact that the superintendent was formerly on the staff of the College and respects and is respected by the president assures personal support of a coöperative plan.

2. It does not lie within the province of this report to make specific suggestions as to what the institution should be responsible for and what can reasonably be expected of the College as these are matters to be determined by the local representatives of both groups. As a basis for discussion, however, the following points are enumerated and certain questions raised:

(a) All of the details of institutional administration should be carried by the superintendent as at present. In making plans for the operation of the school he should participate as without his full coöperation nothing can be carried out successfully. Furthermore he is qualified to assume considerable responsibility in outlining such plans.

(b) Any service which the Teachers' Training College gives should be confined to the educational and recreational programs. Through staff meetings of teachers and cottage mothers the objectives to be attained would be thoroughly understood and each group would feel a sense of participation in the attainments of the children.

(c)   Teachers or play leaders should confine their authority to the school rooms, the work rooms and the playground, and not interfere in the administration of the cottages in details of administration which must lie wholly with the superintendent. If schedules are worked out jointly and there is ample opportunity for open discussion there should be no difficulty in carrying out the assignments of time for school, for work and for play.

(d)   The Teachers' Training College provides training for teachers of pre-school children and for teachers of physical education, vocational arts and crafts as well as academic subjects. Thus all of the phases of education which should be included in the program of the institution are being taught at the College. The extent to which students in these various fields might be used under clearly defined conditions in the work of the institution is a question to be determined locally.

(e)   It would seem that a prerequisite to the use of students at the institution would be the employment of an experienced teacher who would rank with the critic teachers at the College in professional standing and who would be acceptable to the president and faculty of the College.

(f)   The superintendent is well qualified to teach certain types of vocational subjects. On the basis of his experience during the first year he has been in charge of the institution he should be able to tell how many periods he can give to formal teaching and project supervision. To what extent the vocational teaching of the boys by the superintendent will have to be supplemented is a matter to determine after a decision has been reached as to what should be included in the training.

(g)   The cottage in which the older girls live is so planned and equipped that with a limited amount of additional equipment it can well serve as the laboratory for the practical teaching of home economics. The class room phases of the subject could be taught in the school building or in the living room of the cottage. To what extent the wife of the superintendent could carry responsibility for such teaching if capable cottage mothers were employed, would have to be determined.

(*h*)　One of the most serious gaps in the present program of the institution is the entire lack of proper training and recreational facilities of the pre-school children. With a competent cottage mother giving full time service, a helper and a student teacher who would direct the activities of these young children for definite periods each day and see that proper play equipment and material were available, the many serious difficulties which arise because there is no one in the cottage competent to give intelligent direction to young children would be overcome.

3.　Additional equipment for vocational training is needed. However, no investment should be made until the educational program has been carefully planned and the resources now available have been analyzed in order to determine how they may be integrated with the general educational scheme. Such planning requires leadership from the field of specialized education and the facilities which Winston-Salem and the state of North Carolina provide should be utilized to the fullest extent.

4.　The 1930 budget of the Memorial Industrial School includes an item of $1,080 for the salary of one person who would teach and also do the social work. This is not a practical combination of service since it will require the full time of one social worker if proper social standards are to be established. As both the social worker and the teacher are equally important it is difficult to see just how the institution can get a well organized program under way on its present budget. Even though the Teachers' Training College were willing to give service it would seem that in addition to the student teachers who would serve in various departments there ought to be two experienced persons employed as regular members of the staff. One of these would be the teacher previously referred to. The other ought to be a person with special training in physical education and recreation. One of the teachers ought to be particularly skillful in planning activities for little children and be able to direct the student and cottage mother in charge of the pre-school children. Since the largest age grouping is from six years through twelve and since the boys have the influence of the superintendent and the farm manager the teachers should probably be women although ability, training and interest in the job are more important than sex. A tentative estimate as to additional funds needed in order to develop the academic, vocational, recreational and pre-school program is as follows:

Salaries for two staff teachers for one year........................$2,500
Transportation for student teachers.............................. 250
  (Daily operation of bus which has been purchased but not paid for.)
Additional equipment for vocational and recreational purposes...... 1,000

    Total for first year..$3,750

This estimate would have to be revised after plans are formulated for the operation of the various school departments but it is presented as a concrete basis for discussion. As indicated earlier the advice of specialists in the field of education must determine the final decisions regarding the educational set-up. In this report only an attempt to sketch the broader outlines of the picture has been made.

At this time the Memorial Industrial School is without the necessary funds to put the suggested educational program into effect. It is carrying a large indebtedness incurred because the hazards to the life and safety of the children were so great in the old plant that new quarters were imperative. When one compares the total investment with the remaining indebtedness, however, what has been achieved in a period of five years has been a noteworthy accomplishment. Yet the interest on the indebtedness is a drain on the operating budget and thus slows up the development of the institution's program.

To sum up, there are three steps to be taken in organizing the educational program of the Memorial Industrial School:

1. The board of the institution should decide whether or not it wishes to consider the suggestion that the Teachers' Training College be asked to take on the school as a demon-

stration project. If this seems desirable the president of the board should appoint a committee of from three to five members to serve as a special educational committee and to carry on the necessary negotiations with the officials of the Teachers' Training College. There will be many details to be worked out and a small committee of persons interested in academic and vocational education will function more effectively than a larger group.

2.   Detailed planning with which the assistance of specialists should be sought should precede any investment in equipment for additional vocational training. The resources which the institution already possesses both in its plant and equipment and in the presence of two technically trained men on its staff should be taken into account in such planning.

3.   When final decisions as to policies are reached and it is known what is needed in the way of staff and equipment in order to provide a proper educational program it is suggested that the possibility of securing additional funds from private sources be considered.

MEDICAL SERVICE

Since August, 1929, when the institution was moved to the new plant, children have been admitted only upon the recommendation of the City and County Departments of Public Welfare or the Associated Charities. The majority of admissions have come through the City Department. In these cases the City Physician has examined the children prior to admission in order to determine the presence of contagious or infectious diseases. The admission blank prepared by the institution provides a space for the report of the physician. This blank is a record of medical inspection rather than a record of a thorough and complete physical examination.

On the second floor of the administration building there are several wards which are used for the isolation of new admissions. There are also the necessary toilet facilities adjacent to the wards. Early in the fall a number of children having whooping cough were admitted, but due to the fact that isolation was provided none of the other children contracted it.

This one experience proved the value of admission quarantine.

There are no diet kitchen facilities in connection with the isolation department and the food had to be brought from the boys' cottage in which the cooking is done. This is not a particularly convenient arrangement, but it has been possible, according to the wife of the superintendent, to carry out a fairly satisfactory isolation regime in spite of this handicap.

A physician, who is a member of the board of the institution, is on call and gives his services when necessary. His relationship to the institution is that of a family physician. There is no nurse on the staff but it was stated that the wife of the superintendent had had some nurse's training.

At the time the study of the institution was begun the medical program did not include a thorough physical examination after admission in order to supplement the medical inspection prior to admission. Neither was there any plan for routine correction of defects and for immunizing the children against contagious diseases.

In a modern institutional program the medical service is largely preventive and corrective rather than curative. Such a program includes intensive physical examination by a pediatrician at the time of admission; Wassermann, Neisser, Schick and Von Pirquet tests; immediate correction of defects and the carrying out of prescribed treatment; immunization against contagious diseases, such as smallpox, typhoid fever and malaria; keeping records of the initial examination and the corrections, laboratory tests, immunizations and illnesses which a child may have while in the institution; routine re-examination; records on weight and height taken at regular intervals; and a summary on physical conditions at the time of dismissal, together with recommendations which parents or foster parents should carry out after the child leaves the institution. Nursing service should be available either through having a nurse on the staff or through frequent visits of a public health nurse. The medical service of the Memorial Industrial School was checked against the above essentials when the study was begun and it was found that there were many gaps in procedure.

In the budget for 1930 the amount allocated for medical service is $50. With this small amount it is evident that if the children are to receive the service required physicians will have to give volunteer service; or else the public health units of service will have to be utilized.

As part of the study an effort was made to determine just what the resources of Winston-Salem and Forsyth County were in order to be able to make a recommendation about the medical service which would cover at least the minimum essentials and would also be consistent with the public health facilities provided. It was found that Forsyth County has a well organized county public health program and that Winston-Salem has a city department of health and a city hospital. Because the institution is located outside the city limits it seemed logical to confer with the county health officials rather than with city officials. It was found that the county unit was in a position to render the type of service through which a complete program could be set up at the Memorial Industrial School if requested to do so. There was a Negro public health nurse who visited the schools in the territory adjacent to the institution and her assignment could also include the Memorial Industrial School.

While the study in North Carolina was still in progress the county health department was asked by the president of the board to make complete examinations of all of the children in the Memorial Industrial School. Arrangements were also made to have the public health nurse make routine visits. The following summary prepared by the county health commissioner gives a graphic picture of what was done in a space of a few weeks toward laying the foundation for what he terms a "one hundred per cent" health program.

The nutrition of the children is above normal. The physical defects are not as numerous as in the average Negro child. The county nurse makes two visits a week to this institution. We have already started a program that will give each child a thorough and complete examination. This will include the general physical examination given to all school children in the county. All remediable physical defects will be corrected. We have already vaccinated the entire school for smallpox. They have been given the Schick test and our readings show a very small per cent of positives. These will be immunized. We did the Von Pirquet test for tuberculosis last week on the entire group. Fifteen of these children showed a positive reaction to this test. This positive group will be X-Rayed and those found to have activity either in the bronchial glands or lungs, will be isolated and treated under the supervision of the school nurse and the Superintendent of the tuberculosis hospital. We have taken blood Wassermanns on some twenty odd. The report shows only one of this twenty odd to have a positive Wassermann. This one is receiving treatment at the present time. Typhoid vaccine clinics will be held there during the summer. A baby clinic is being organized for the school and the surrounding community and will be held in the school building.

We are planning to have a complete health record for each child. This will be filed in the superintendent's office at the institution.

The nurse reports that she has found three or four children that were in need of visual corrections. They have been ordered to be examined by an eye, ear, nose and throat specialist and glasses fitted.

We are working out a program to dispose of all diseased tonsils in this institution, either at a clinic at the school or a series of small clinics in one of the local hospitals. There are some ten or twelve in need of correction.

I have asked the school nurse to arrange with the Negro dentists of the city to do all of the necessary dental work for this school. In event the Negro dentists do not respond to this opportunity to serve the institution, I will ask the president of the board to allow these children to be treated by the industrial dentist at the R. J. Reynolds office.

There could be no better illustration of the possibilities of integrating an institution with high standard community resources than that afforded by the Memorial Industrial School and the Forsyth County Department of Health. The time will undoubtedly come when the institution will be in a position to have a pediatrician and a nurse on its own staff. Until that time, however, the facilities provided by the county should be utilized to the fullest extent.

The following recommendations on medical service are presented for consideration:

1.   The present plan of having the City Department of Health make medical inspections of all children prior to admission should be continued and new children should be isolated until laboratory reports are received and any suspicious conditions cleared up.

2.   The County Department of Health should continue the intensive program already begun, following through on necessary treatments and corrections on the present population; and examining all new children before they are transferred from the isolation department to the cottages.

3.   The public health nurse should continue her routine visits to the institution and carry the responsibility for seeing that corrections and treatments are carried out; and that proper records are kept. If the health commissioner decides to use the type of record of which samples have already been sent to him, it is suggested that during the time a child remains in the institution these records be kept in a loose leaf notebook in the office of the superintendent so that they will be easily accessible and notations can be made without going through the folders; and that when a child leaves the record then be filed in his folder.

The size of the population of the Memorial Industrial School at the present time scarcely warrants the employment of a full time graduate nurse when public health nursing service is available and no infants are accepted for care.

4.   The majority of the children accepted for care are legal residents of Winston-Salem. Since the city owns and operates a general hospital it is recommended that the board of the Memorial Industrial School determine whether the city would make an agreement whereby children who need hospitalization subsequent to admission and who are legal residents may be cared for without charge. The distribution of service between city and county would then be—

(a) Medical inspections to determine the presence of contagious or infectious diseases or serious mental retardation prior to admission by the city department of health;

(b) Intensive examinations, laboratory tests, immunizations, nursing service and general health supervision by the county department of health;

(c) Hospitalization and corrective surgery by the city hospital. Since neither the city nor the county pays board for any of the children this would seem to be an equitable arrangement.

5. The staff physician should continue to serve as family physician and should be on call for all cases of acute illness. As such an arrangement has been satisfactorily carried out in other institutions over a long enough period to demonstrate its practicability this recommendation does not involve procedure which violates the ethics of the medical profession.

6. The many assets for the development of a program of child health and protection which the institution has should be utilized to the fullest extent both for children in the institution and for others in the neighborhood through clinics as has already been planned. Overcrowding should be avoided regardless of demands for additional service in order that the advantages of elevation and of spaciousness of site will not be sacrificed by unhygienic housing.

PSYCHOLOGICAL AND PSYCHIATRIC SERVICE

At present the institution has no facilities for the psychological study of its children or for any psychiatric treatment. From its own resources it will not be able to supply such service for some time to come and any suggestion at this time that the institution so equip itself would be unreasonable. This does not alter the fact that these services are desirable and that they enable any institution to do a much more discriminating piece of work. It is urged that the officials of the institution acquaint themselves with the mental hygiene resources of Winston-Salem and the state of North Carolina and that it utilize such professional services as are made available to it through other agencies and organizations.

PERSONAL HYGIENE

Modern plumbing facilities make it possible for the children to be bathed frequently and to be taught the fundamentals of personal hygiene. With a qualified cottage mother in each house it should not be too difficult to have every child use his own wash cloth and towel; and to keep tooth brushes, combs and brushes individually.

At the time of the study this was not being done in all the cottages. While it is difficult to teach children coming from poor homes the importance of using and taking proper care of their own toilet articles it is by no means an impossible task and should be regarded as an important part of a child's general training.

DIET

The wife of the superintendent who has had some training in dietetics plans the meals. At the time of the study she was doing the cooking for the entire population as previously stated. The home demonstration worker from the State Department of Agriculture had also given service to the institution.

A dairy herd of Guernsey and Jersey cattle furnishes the milk for the institution and it is intended to have the herd large enough to furnish an adequate supply at all times. Chickens and hogs are kept and a variety of vegetables will be raised this season which is the first summer the new buildings have been occupied. Thus, the products from the farm will furnish the major portion of the necessary food stuffs.

The chief criticism to be made of the menus which were checked is that except for the coffee, the food served to the matrons and not to the children consisted of eggs, butter and in one case, milk, all of which growing children need much more than adults do. Most institutions are getting away from the policy of serving one kind of food to the children and another to the staff except for such variations in beverages and desserts as are consistent with the proper feeding of children. As soon as the Memorial Industrial School equips itself to operate each cottage unit it is urged that the food prepared be practically the same for both children and adults. When the cooking is done on a family basis in each unit for a small group of the children the cottage mother should eat with her children and the variety and quality of the food should be such that both adults and children will be properly fed.

The plan of having the home demonstration agent come into the institution occasionally for consultation should be continued. The older children could take turns in keeping a record of foods served at each meal as it provides an opportunity for training the children in accurate observation and notation of their observation. Institutions occasionally have the experience of having someone on the outside criticise the feeding of the children. Keeping a careful record of each days' menus is a protection against unfair criticism as well as a means of furnishing data for checking on the food served over a given period, which should be done from time to time. If consultation service from the outside is available, it is particularly valuable to have a written record. It is also preferable to have this record based on the foods actually served the children than on the menus prepared by the executive and given the supervisors in the various cottages.

With an adequate supply of milk, fresh eggs, green vegetables, a moderate amount of meat or fish, and occasional simple desserts; and with intelligent planning of meals so that there are proper food combinations the record for proper nutrition of the children which the institution has already established should easily be maintained. The administration deserves credit for having a food per capita sufficiently high to insure proper feeding.

SOCIAL POLICIES

At the time of the study applications for admission were being referred to a committee of the board and children were being accepted almost entirely upon the recommendation of the Winston-Salem Department of Public Welfare, the Forsyth County Department of Public Welfare, or the Winston-Salem Associated Charities.

9

As shown by the data on population given earlier, approximately 36 per cent of the children were full orphans; 47 per cent were half orphans; and the remainder had both parents living but separated or divorced or otherwise unable to care for them. Fifty-three per cent were admitted during 1929. No board was being paid for any of the children under care in February, 1930. The lack of adequate social data makes it impossible to attempt any detailed case analysis of the entire population.

In a special section of this report will be found a discussion of the need for social service in connection with every institution. Thus, this report will be confined to a discussion of the development of the social program of the Memorial Industrial School.

The service provided by the departments of public welfare and the Associated Charities has been focused primarily on solving a social problem in a family by getting the children into the institution. Because of the pressure of work in these various agencies and the lack of certain resources a discriminating case work job has not been done.

While the institution has not done any amount of child-placing several of the older children who wished to continue their high school courses were placed in wage homes in the fall of 1930 as it seemed impracticable to transport them to and from school each day. The superintendent made an effort to determine the suitability of the families to which the children went but there has been no plan for subsequent supervision. The placements were made as a means of meeting a concrete situation and not because the policy of making placements in foster homes had been adopted by the board.

As indicated previously if the Memorial Industrial School were located in a community where there were few educational facilities for Negro children or where the Negro population was so sparse that it would be years before good schools could be established, it would seem logical to use the facilities of the institution for long time custodial care in order to give children educational advantages. Since Winston-Salem and Forsyth County have public school facilities for Negro children, we do not believe that emphasis should be placed upon keeping a limited number of children for a long time but rather upon meeting a variety of needs of a large number of children for varying periods. The investment in the Memorial Industrial School will probably yield the largest returns if it is used as a center through which diversified forms of social and health service for Negro children will be made available. Such a program would be built around adequate social and medical service rather than around academic and vocational education. While there should be proper educational facilities children should not be accepted primarily in order to give them an education.

North Carolina appears to be ready for a demonstration of what is involved in a modern program for the care of dependent and neglected Negro children. The Memorial Industrial School provides the best setting in the state for such a demonstration which should be so organized as to utilize the institutional facilties to the greatest advantage and the maximum extent; and to supplement the intra-mural service through careful intake study, family adjustment, a limited amount of placement and adequate follow-up. The following comments and recommendations are presented for consideration:

1. A full time social worker having technical training in the children's field should be employed. Cases referred by social agencies and individuals should be investigated by her and upon the basis of the facts secured by her the admissions committee should decide to accept cases or refer them elsewhere.

2. If the institution equips itself with social service, plans for the children will be individualized upon the basis of need. In some instances long time care may be desirable but the program of the institution should not be developed with the idea of providing long time care for all children accepted. Instead the service should be sufficiently flexible to meet a variety of situations which may involve both short time and long time care.

3. Infant care should not be undertaken by the Memorial Industrial School within the institution as it does not have

the physical facilities or an adequate staff for such specialized service.

Pediatricians and psychologists agree that young children develop more rapidly, both physically and mentally, in families than in groups. Group care which is even approximately satisfactory requires an investment beyond what most institutions can afford. For this reason foster home care for young children is being used to supplement institutional service, board being paid by the agency. Inquiry made in Winston-Salem during the study brought out the fact that there was a considerable number of thrifty middle class Negroes living in the community. It is upon this group that child-placing agencies largely depend for the development of foster home programs. Not more than one or two small children should be placed in one family, so that the foster mother can give them the amount of care and attention which a good mother gives her own children. Under the supervision of the social worker and of the nurse and physician who are responsible for the medical program of the organization such homes afford a valuable means of meeting the needs of young children without investment in special facilities and equipment. The investment is in direct service to the children and adequate supervision. The development of such a program must be slow. Otherwise there will be careless selection of homes and lax supervision. If a limited development of foster home care were undertaken by the Memorial Industrial School as a demonstration of the practicability of this form of care for Negro children in certain southern communities it would be a distinct contribution to the development of the social program of the entire state. If such a project were initiated, special funds would have to be allocated for boarding purposes in order that when proper homes were found there would be no question about securing the necessary board. Whenever possible, parents or relatives should contribute to the support of their children whether placed in foster homes or in the institution. On the other hand, proper placement should not depend upon a parent's financial ability to pay board, and for this reason there would have to be a special budget for boarding purposes. The amount for the first year would not be large as with one worker to do everything, only a few homes could be developed since the selection would have to be made with the utmost care.

4. The institution should use a few carefully selected Negro working homes for the placement of older children who have the ability to continue their high school work successfully. The number of children for whom such placement should be made will not be large. If the social worker uses care and good judgment in the selection of homes and supervises the children after placement, there is every reason to believe that this policy will prove to be satisfactory.

5. When applications for admission are under consideration one of the deciding factors as to whether or not a child should be accepted should be his physical condition. There may be cases in which, from the standpoint of safeguarding the child physically, it is highly desirable for him to have a period of residence in a controlled environment even though he does not need hospital or sanatorium care. At the present time the institution has no data as to how greatly this type of service is needed. The information which the social worker would gather during twelve months would furnish a basis for deciding whether cardiac cases, convalescents, children suffering from malnutrition, etc., should be cared for by the institution at a later period of its development. If the health aspects of the program were to be emphasized an additional cottage would be needed and a more complete isolation unit would have to be provided.

6. It is not possible to state with exactness how large a budget would be required to carry on a case work demonstration as part of the program of the Memorial Industrial School but a tentative budget would be as follows:

Salary for one worker and maintenance.....................$1,200 per year
A car and upkeep for a year............................... 800
Funds for a demonstration of boarding home care........ 1,000

                                                  $3,000

The board of the institution and the Winston-Salem Community Chest cannot, with resources now available, underwrite the cost of such a demonstration. As stated previously, the sum of $1,080 was allocated for the salary of one person who would do the socal work and also teach. If $540 of this amount goes into the salary of teachers and $540 toward the salary of the social worker, there would still be a balance of $2,460 needed for the case work service on the basis of the above tentative estimate.

Conclusion

Practically all of the recommendations made are confined to what should be done in the immediate future in order to get the Memorial Industrial School to functioning to the limit of its present potentialities. If by the end of a five year period it has accomplished this result it will have made satisfactory progress as the development of the more intangible aspects of the program will be much slower than the construction of the new plant and the clearing and improving of the farm.

In addition to caring for dependent children, the institution is in a position also to render important service in the field of social training for Negro workers. In various parts of the country institutions which for years have confined their service to long time custodial care are reshaping their programs in order to be of larger usefulness. Mothers' aid, workmen's compensation laws, public health service and increasing interest in psychological and psychiatric service and other factors have all had an influence upon institutional care. More and more, emphasis is being placed upon those aspects of economic and community life which will insure to every child his inherent right to be brought up as a member of his own family.

The Memorial Industrial School does not have to repeat the experience of institutions which have been in existence for nearly a century before it embarks on a course which will insure a flexible and individualized service for dependent and neglected children. Instead it can profit from the experience of these older institutions and initiate a program which will meet present day needs and conditions most effectively, and will utilize the new techniques which have been hammered out of the old trial and error methods. If this is done it should then make its resources available for the training of workers since as yet the number of trained Negro workers in the children's field is much more limited than in other phases of social work or in the nursing profession. This would come later in the development of the institution but it should be kept in mind as an additional contribution which the Memorial Industrial School might make to the care and protection of Negro children.

At this time it is not possible to make definite recommendations regarding the future. Whether eventually the institution should increase its facilities so that it may care for children from the western half of North Carolina is a question which the social development of the state during the next five years will help to answer. Whether a cottage for physically handicapped children is needed will be determined by the experience of the institution itself gained through its social service department during the next year or two.

Some indication has been given as to the amount of funds required to develop the educational and social service programs which have been outlined. Since there is no institution for dependent Negro children either in North or South Carolina which has as yet been able to put into effect accepted child-welfare standards or to provide a cottage plan plant and equipment it is hoped that private philanthrophy will make it possible for the Memorial Industrial School to focus its attention on doing a qualitative job which will serve as a demonstration of what child welfare service really includes and what it may accomplish.

SUMMARY

1. There should be some reorganization of the board for reasons set forth in the body of this report.

2. As soon as possible each cottage should be operated as a complete unit. This cannot be done until competent cottage mothers are employed.

3. If, after discussion among the members of the board and other interested local persons it seems at all practicable, it is urged that the Winston-Salem Teachers' Training College be asked to take over the school as a demonstration of what can

be accomplished in the fields of academic and vocational education of Negro children in an institutional environment.

4. The Memorial Industrial School should develop its program around the social needs of dependent children and their families rather than primarily around the idea of proving educational opportunities.

5. The medical service should be so organized that the physical and mental health of the children will be properly safeguarded.

6. Since no institution for Negro children in the south has as yet been able to put into practice modern standards of social case work, it is recommended that the Memorial Industrial School initiate such a program. The first step in the establishment of such service is the employment of a social worker who will bring to her field of endeavor the same technical skill and scientific approach that the farm manager brings to his field of service.

7. Future expansion and development of the institution should depend upon the experience gathered during the next five years. At this point the board should bend its energies to putting a regime into effect which is consistent with the high standards of the material equipment already available.

CHAPTER VI

THE NORTH CAROLINA ORTHOPEDIC HOSPITAL[1]

DUKE MEMORIAL WARD FOR NEGRO CHILDREN

IN 1921 THE North Carolina Orthopedic Hospital was opened. As the word orthopedic implies, the purpose of this institution has been to make the crooked or crippled child straight, and to prevent as far as possible, deformities and limitation of activity in children who have suffered some mishap, or who have become afflicted with some deforming disease. This institution was founded primarily for indigent cases of white children.

As a result of clinics held at this hospital, and subsequently, at various places in the state, such as Goldsboro, Bryson City, Greenville, Kinston, Lenoir, Murphy, Raleigh, etc., it became apparent that a ward for the care of Negro crippled children was needed.

In March, 1926, the first Negro ward was opened. The late Benjamin N. Duke donated the funds which were necessary for the erection of this building, which contained the living quarters for the Negro nurses and two small wards, each accommodating ten beds. The building is now used entirely for a nurses' home.

The beds were filled immediately. The need for a larger fireproof building was felt. In his will, Mr. Duke left the Negro crippled children of North Carolina a sum sufficient for the erection of the desired building.

The fifty bed unit, known as the Benjamin N. Duke Memorial Ward, was formally opened in November 1930. The one-story

---

[1] This section was written by Dr. O. L. Miller, Chief Surgeon, Orthopedic Hospital, Gastonia.

brick structure was planned so that there would be a maximum of light and air. An enclosed porch, well supplied with casement windows, extends across the front of the building. The porch opens on to a wide stretch of cement that is used daily in good weather for the sunning of all the children.

This building is equipped sufficiently for the adequate care of the children, though there is a need of such things as bedside tables, a food truck, etc.

The money for operating this unit is appropriated from state funds to the North Carolina Orthopedic Hospital. For the past six months the daily average of patients has been 35. Funds do not permit that greater numbers be cared for. The needs at present, however, for hospitalization are fairly well met.

The treatment and care of the children comes under the direction of the staff of the hospital. The head nurse in this division is Anna B. Crawford, a graduate of Conner Street Hospital, Charleston, South Carolina (1905). She became a registered nurse in Tennessee in 1915. She has been with this institution for the past six years. The children are cared for by a group of nursing aides or attendants. The six who are here at present (March, 1932) have received no training in nursing elsewhere. One of this number has had one year of college work at Bennett College, Greensboro, N. C.; three have completed high school; and two have finished grammar school. All of these except one have been employed over two years. The educational background and the continuity of services make this group quite valuable in insuring proper orthopedic care for these children. We feel that there is an excellent spirit of integrity and loyalty in the group.

In July, 1931, a study was made of the education of the children in this institution. From that study the following data were gathered:

Daily average of white children.................................... 110
Daily average of Negro children................................. 30
    Total average of patients...................................... 140

White children of school age....................................... 73
Negro children of school age....................................... 23
    Total children of school age.................................... 96

White children from 6-19 who have had no schooling.................. 7
Negro children from 6-19 who have had no schooling.................. 6
    Total 13

White children behind grade...................................... 43
Negro children behind grade...................................... 11
    Total 54

Average No. Years the 43 white are behind grade........2 years 2 months
Average No. Years the 11 Negroes are behind grade....2 years 3 months

Many of these children have had few of the educational advantages of normal children, due to their inability to go to and from school. Some, even after leaving, will be unable to attend school. Hence, it would seem doubly desirable to have the children adequately taught while they are here. There is no teacher for the Negro children.

Though there is no formal educational program carried out, emphasis is placed on teaching the children proper habits in eating, personal hygiene, speech, etc.

The teacher from the Occupational Therapy Department encourages sewing, basketry and various handicrafts. Were there another worker in this department, the children would be able to derive much more pleasure and profit from this phase of the work.

There is a small collection of books in the ward to which the children have easy access at all times.

The problems of discipline are negligible.

Since opening the ward, Sunday School has been held each Sunday. Six churches of Gastonia have faithfully carried on this work.

Crippled children as a group are surprisingly happy in spite of the fact that most of them are confined to bed. The ones who are able to be up and about are dismissed as soon as possible.

One activity which furnishes an endless amount of enjoyment to the children, and is surely a real source of pleasure to the rest of us, is the singing. As does the race as a whole, these children sing well. Even the tiny ones are endowed with melody and rhythm.

A simple well balanced diet is furnished. Each child drinks a quart of milk or buttermilk each day. It is a matter of honor that each child eats everything on his tray. A child soon learns to like foods which at one time he refused. Occasionally a problem arises, such as that of a rachitic child who refuses to eat carrots. But a touch of hunger and a bit of patience will solve such a problem.

Up to January 1932 there had been 233 children admitted to the Negro ward for treatment. The disease incidence in this number is as follows:

Tuberculous arthritis 52

Non-tuberculous arthritis 23

Osteomyelitis 32

Congenital deformities 26

Paralysis 46

Burns 10

Miscellaneous, including fracture, etc.............................. 44

Of these 233 cases, 25 are still in the hospital, 12 of them have been permanently dismissed, 13 have died, and the remainder are being followed in the clinics.

Of the thirteen deaths, 11 were caused by tuberculosis of the bone. Six of these had shown signs of the disease a year or more before they were examined at the clinic. The disease had had ample time to make devastating inroads. The other five had been ill for some months before they were seen. Mention is made of this because early diagnosis and early treatment increase so much the chance of recovery for a child who is afflicted with tuberculosis.

Clinics have been held over the state in some 28 towns. At these about 400 Negro children have been seen. At present only two clinics are held with regularity, the one at Gastonia on each Tuesday afternoon, and the one at Goldsboro on the third Thursday of each month. After a child has been dismissed from the hospital he is seen at intervals, varying according to the needs of the case, from once a month to once every two years, until the case is dismissed permanently. The hospital is dependent entirely upon correspondence and the invaluable aid of the welfare officers in getting these children to the clinics.

There follows a brief account of four cases who have been treated here:

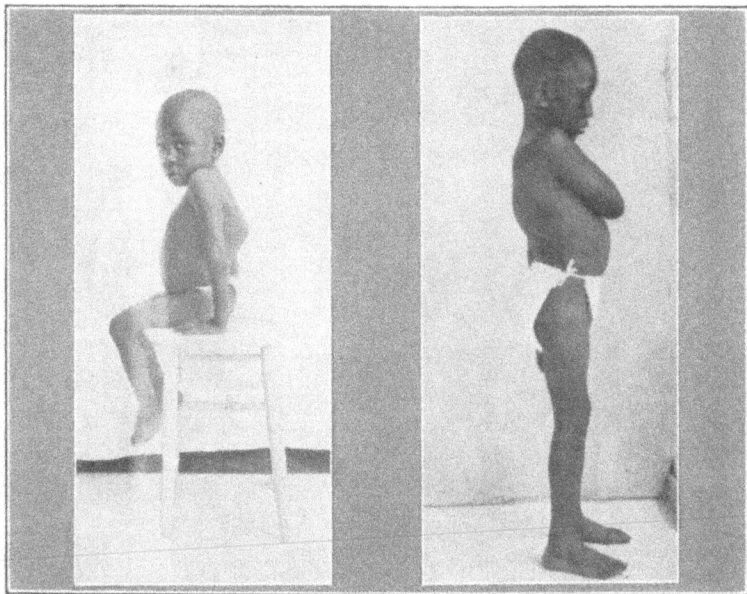

I.   Leroy, a boy of four years from Robeson County came to the hospital for examination in July 1927. A large hump was on his back. He had apparently been suffering with tuberculosis of the upper part of his spine for a long period of time. He was unable to walk. He held his legs in the position shown in the first picture. Apparently he had gotten around by walking on his hands and knees. During the first year of his hospital stay, his general health was built up. During the second year he had two operations on his spine. Two years after admission he was walking. Six months later he was dismissed. The last picture shows the child in March 1931.

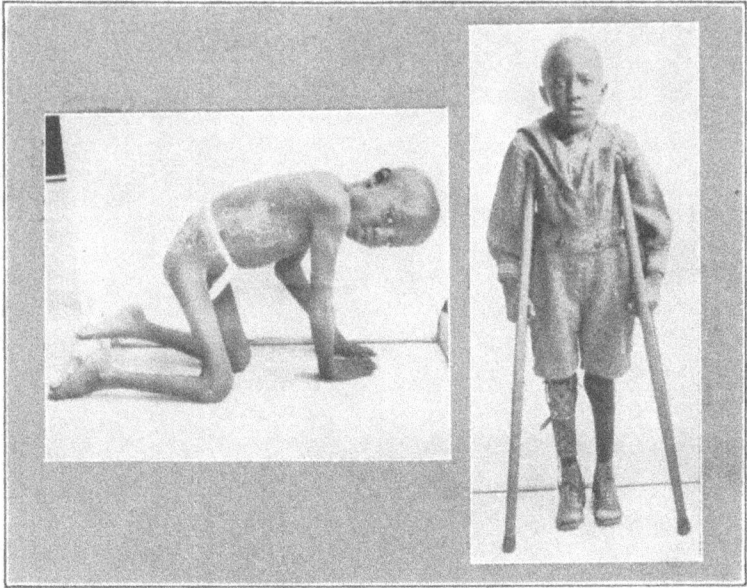

II.   Moses is from Cabarrus County. The mother and father are both dead. The child had infantile paralysis in June 1926. He was first brought to clinic in April 1927, at which time an application was filed for admission to the hospital for treatment at a later date. In March 1928 he was admitted. Two operations followed. In four months he was dismissed wearing a brace, as shown in the last picture. This boy came to the clinic in November 1931. He still wears a brace but walks quite well without the aid of a crutch or cane.

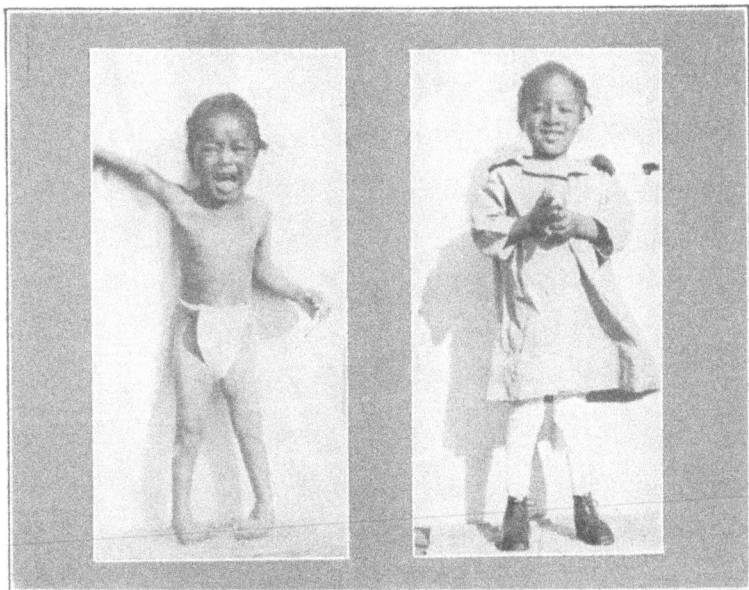

III. Larcina, a little girl from Richmond County, was born with club-feet. She was the sixth Negro child to be admitted for treatment. She came in February 1926. Ten months later, after treatment with casts, she was sent home in shoes as shown in the second picture. She is now being seen in clinic about every six months.

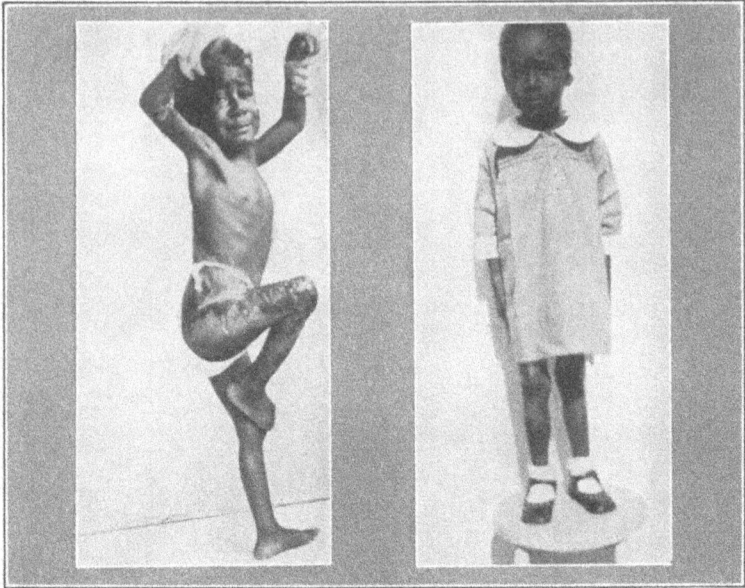

IV.   Pearlie, a little three year old girl from Craven County, fell into the fire one day in January 1930. When she was first examined, she appeared as in the first picture. The scar tissue had contracted until she had a sharp flexion deformity which made her unable to walk. She was brought to the clinic in Goldsboro and later to the Hospital for treatment by a Negro welfare worker. The second picture shows Pearlie ready to go home after a year's stay in the hospital, during which time a series of operations had been performed.

The state of North Carolina is rendering to its Negro crippled children a great service, eliminating for the individual years of unnecessary discomfort and unhappiness, and lifting an economic burden from the state while the burden is still light.

Some months ago there came to the hospital a girl sixteen years of age, who had had from birth club-feet as extreme as those of the little girl shown in Plate III. Yet she was being seen for the first time in an orthopedic clinic. Undoubtedly, there are many such cripples in the state who for years have been in need of aid.

So far as we know, no institution in the South offers in excellence such service to Negro crippled children. The Duke Memorial unit, a part of the North Carolina Orthopedic Hospital, stands as a useful monument to its benefactor, as an expression of sincere interest on the part of the white race and as a beacon modestly lighting the Negro race onward in its destiny.

CHAPTER VII

NORTH CAROLINA SANATORIUM

TREATMENT OF NEGRO CHILDREN[1]

ALTHOUGH THE North Carolina Sanatorium for the Treatment of Tuberculosis was established in 1907, it was not until the fall of 1923 that a division for Negroes was created. As far as treatment of children is concerned, there is at present at the Sanatorium a separate children's building for white children suffering from tuberculosis, but there is no separate unit or ward, and no special provision for taking care of Negro tuberculous children. There are rarely more than three or four Negro children at a time in the Sanatorium. From the fall of 1923 until March 1932, there were ninety-nine Negro children sixteen years of age and under cared for in the Sanatorium. The ages of these children upon admission were as follows: 1, four years old; 2, five years old; 1, seven years; 2, eight years; 4, nine years; 8, ten years; 6, eleven years; 14, twelve years; 8, thirteen years; 12, fourteen years; 20, fifteen years; 21, sixteen years. The number of orphan Negro children among those admitted to the Sanatorium is strikingly high. Fifty-five of these children had lost one or both parents, while forty-four had both parents living. Of the fathers of these children, sixty-seven were living, and thirty-two were dead. Of the mothers, fifty-nine were living and forty dead. Seven of the fathers and twenty-two of the mothers are known to have died of tuberculosis.

The number of Negro children admitted to the Sanatorium represents a very small fraction of the number throughout the state in need of hospital treatment, but unfortunately there is

---

[1] The data and descriptive material for this section were secured from Dr. P. P. McCain, Superintendent of the Sanatorium.

no provision for any patient with tuberculosis, either child or adult, white or Negro, to receive treatment at the Sanatorium at less than $1 per day. The present law permits county and city authorities to pay this amount for their indigent cases, but it does not require them to make provision for such cases, and very few of the counties send their indigent cases to the Sanatorium. For a number of years the Sanatorium officials have been trying to get the law changed so that counties will be required either to provide their own institutions to take care of indigent cases, or to pay for their care at the Sanatorium, but so far these efforts have failed. Practically all Negro patients who do not have insurance are indigent, and almost 100 per cent of the children come from indigent families. The source of support of the ninety-nine Negro children admitted to the institution, 1923-1932, was listed as follows: relatives, 55; public welfare department, 12; county, 10; friends, 8; city, 6; Red Cross, 4; health department, 2; self-supporting, 2.

Since most of the Negro children admitted to the Sanatorium were suffering from the adult type of disease, which involves the lung tissue itself, their chance for recovery was described as not at all probable. There were ten cases of the childhood type, where the disease was limited to the glands at the root of the lungs with a very small primary focus in the lungs. In such cases the chance of recovery is said to be excellent if proper treatment is secured. Of the ninety-nine cases, the prognosis is described as good in twenty-nine instances.

During the past six years the extension department of the Sanatorium, in coöperation with the health, school, and public welfare authorities of the various counties, has made a study of tuberculosis in the schools of North Carolina, both among the white and the Negro children. The method of study has been to give the tuberculosis test to all school children whose parents give their consent. If this test is positive, it shows that the child has tuberculous infection, but not necessarily tuberculous disease. All the positive reactors are given a careful physical examination and two X-ray pictures, one postero-anterior and one oblique, are made of their chests. During this six year period, 19,867 Negro children were studied. Of this number, 3,632, or 18.28 per cent, gave positive reactions. Of these positive reactors, 501, or 13.8 per cent, were found to have demonstrable tuberculosis. About 2.5 per cent, therefore, of all Negro school children examined were suffering from tuberculosis.

These studies of school children also show that, while the percentage of Negro children showing positive tuberculin reaction compares fairly well with white children, 18.28 per cent for the Negro, and 15.29 per cent for the white, the percentage of positive reactors among the Negroes showing demonstrable tuberculosis is 13.8 per cent, that of the white reactors showing demonstrable tuberculosis is only 8.2 per cent. This is probably to be explained by the fact that Negro children usually live in much more crowded quarters and when they are exposed to infection they are usually more closely exposed than are white children.

At present none of the public or private sanatoria in North Carolina have separate buildings for Negro children. Last year (1931) the Cabarrus County Tuberculosis Association ran a small preventorium for a few weeks for a few Negro children. Within the near future also Mrs. Percy Rockefeller of Overhills, N. C. is to establish a preventorium which is to operate the whole year round, and will provide for sixteen Negro children, and sixteen white. The admissions, however, will probably be limited to the residents of Harnett and Cumberland counties.

CHAPTER VIII

STATE HOSPITAL FOR NEGRO INSANE
GOLDSBORO[1]

TREATMENT OF FEEBLEMINDED AND EPILEPTIC
NEGRO CHILDREN

THE STATE HOSPITAL at Goldsboro was established in 1880 for the purpose of treating and caring for Negro mental patients, including inebriates.

Legally, children who are mentally sick are eligible for admission, but few have been received because no special provision has ever been made for them. The institution is crowded and, since suitable arrangements have not been made, the presence of children there serves to complicate matters for the administrative authorities.

The institution was never intended to care for the feebleminded, although several urgent cases have been received from time to time. A ward has been set aside for the feebleminded children who have been committed.

Epileptic children are housed in the regular epileptic wards and pellagra cases are cared for in the pellagra wards.

Under the circumstances the treatment and care of the children in the institution is as good as can be expected. The quarters used for the children are clean and comfortable. The officers of the institution do their best to provide adequate treatment and care.

The following table shows age, sex, and mental status of children in the institution at the end of the year 1931:

---

[1] This section was contributed by Dr. W. C. Linville, Superintendent of the State Hospital at Goldsboro.

TABLE II

NEGRO CHILDREN IN STATE HOSPITAL AT GOLDSBORO, DECEMBER 31, 1931
AGE OF CHILDREN WITH REFERENCE TO MENTAL STATUS AND SEX

Age Years	Boys				Girls				Total
	Total	Epileptic	Feeble-Minded	Pellagra	Total	Epileptic	Feeble-Minded	Pellagra	
8	2	..	2	..	2	..	..	..	..
9	2	1	1	..	2	..	..	..	..
11	3	..	2	..	2	1	..	..	1
12	5	2	..	..	2	1	2	..	3
13	5	..	3	..	3	1	1	..	2
14	8	1	1	..	2	3	1	2	6
15	6	1	2	..	3	2	..	1	3
Totals	31	5	11	..	16	8	4	3	15

RECOMMENDATIONS

1. Ample provisions should be made either at Caswell Training School or at the State Hospital at Goldsboro' for the care, treatment, and training of Negro feebleminded children.

2. Better facilities should be provided at Goldsboro State Hospital for the care and treatment of epileptic children, and those suffering with pellagra, who are committed to the institution. A suitable children's cottage would serve this purpose.

CHAPTER IX

SCHOOL FOR BLIND AND DEAF, RALEIGH, N. C.

THE SCHOOL FOR the Blind and Deaf was established in Raleigh in 1845 for the purpose of providing education and training of blind and deaf children who could not take advantage of educational opportunities provided in schools for normal children. The law also provided that the curable blind should be treated in the institution. In 1868 provisions were made for Negro blind and deaf children. White deaf were provided for in the School for the Deaf at Morganton in 1894.

School attendance was made compulsory for deaf children in 1907 and for blind children in 1908, while the general compulsory school attendance law was not enacted until 1919. In 1921 school attendance was made compulsory for the blind and deaf between the ages of seven and twenty-one years of age; but amended in 1923 to read seven to eighteen. It provides that such children must attend school for a term of nine months each year and it also provides that children who are not self-supporting at the age of eighteen may continue in school until they reach the age of twenty-one. The law should be amended to make attendance compulsory between the ages of seven and twenty-one unless excused by the Superintendent of the school.

In the cases of indigent children the county is required to provide clothing and traveling expenses in an amount not to exceed $45 a year.

The Negro Department of the School for the Blind and Deaf had been housed in inadequate quarters on East Lenoir Street until it was moved into a new plant on the Garner Road east of Raleigh, in September 1931. The new plant is located on a 233 acre farm with approximately 200 acres under cultivation. The capacity of the new plant is 240.

The population of the school on December 31, 1931 was as follows:

	Negro Department			White Department		
	Boys	Girls	Total	Boys	Girls	Total
Blind	46	31	77	85	71	156
Deaf	48	66	114	..	..	...
	94	97	191	85	71	156

During the ten year period ending December 31, 1931, the following number of students were admitted to the school for the Blind and Deaf at Raleigh:

	Negro			White		
	Boys	Girls	Total	Boys	Girls	Total
Blind	71	47	118	152	103	255
Deaf	62	64	126	...	...	...
	133	111	244	152	103	255

For the fiscal year 1930-31 the State appropriated $148,-800 for maintenance to this institution. Of this amount the School was permitted to use $112,460. (It is not possible to state just what part of this amount was used for the Negro Department.)

The School is under the control of a Board of eleven directors with overlapping terms. The Board elects a superintendent, who has charge of the administration and management of the school. The Board also elects the staff of employees for the institution.

The staff of the Negro Department of the School is composed of a principal, seven teachers for the deaf and six teachers for the blind. In addition to these, seven other teachers have charge of handicraft, domestic science, sewing and mending, broom and mattress and chair work, wood-work and carpentry and shoe repairing. There are also four matrons, one for each of four cottages; a girls' supervisor, a boys' supervisor, a housekeeper who has charge of the kitchen and dining room and an assistant housekeeper.

The School for the Blind and Deaf would probably be more efficiently administered if the superintendent were made entirely responsible for the employment of all teachers and staff members. It would also seem that the administration of the Negro Department could be made more effective if more responsibility were placed on the principal of that Department. The Principal and the Superintendent should select the teachers instead of leaving the selection to the Board.

There are now eleven grades for the blind. There should be a complete staff of teachers for the blind and another for the deaf.

PLANT AND EQUIPMENT

The administration building includes on the two main floors the school rooms for both the deaf and blind, and a kitchen and dining room on the basement floor. There are four dormitories with a capacity of 60 each. One of these is used for the deaf boys, one for deaf girls, one for blind boys, and one for blind girls. Each dormitory is equipped with adequate bathing and toilet facilities and running hot and cold water. There is also a small hospital ward for each dormitory. Equipment does not compare favorably with the building. Most of the furniture which was moved from the old buildings is entirely inadequate. More adequate provisions should be made for the kitchen and dining room.

In addition to these buildings there are three small frame buildings, one for a shoe shop, one for a wood shop, and one for broom, mattress and chair work.

There is also a central heating plant. Water is supplied from a deep well, equipped with an electrically driven pump.

When money is available the plan is to have a separate building for the kitchen and dining room. When this is done the present quarters will be used for teaching domestic science and certain crafts.

With present facilities the Principal must either live in one of the dormitories or off the grounds. It is important that the

Principal live on the grounds and a cottage should be constructed for this purpose when money is available.

The fact that all the regular teachers are graduates of a college or normal school and have in addition, in most cases, several years of experience in the institution indicates that good educational and cultural opportunities for the children are provided. As has been pointed out above, additional teachers are needed.

With reference to ages, the distribution of the population of the Negro Department is as follows:

TABLE III

| Age | Blind | | Deaf | | Total |
	Boys	Girls	Boys	Girls	
Under 10	7	0	1	2	10
10	1	0	4	6	11
11	1	1	4	5	11
12	3	1	1	2	7
13	3	3	9	4	19
14	3	2	5	11	21
15	5	2	4	6	17
16	2	2	4	4	12
17	3	4	1	5	13
18	4	2	2	8	16
19	1	4	3	4	12
20	4	3	5	2	14
Over 20	10	6	5	7	28
Total	47	30	48	66	191

EDUCATION

Both the elementary school and the high school for the blind are on the state list of standard schools. The course of study for the deaf had not been accredited at the time this information was secured.

The following distribution shows the blind and deaf boys and girls by grades. Twenty deaf boys and twenty-nine deaf girls are being taught to communicate orally. Thirty-one deaf boys and 33 girls are being taught to communicate manually.

TABLE IV

	Boys	Girls	Total
BLIND			
First grade and Kindergarten.....................	14	5	19
Elementary grades	25	17	42
High School	8	9	17
	—	—	—
Total	47	31	78
DEAF			
Beginners and lower first grade..................	8	8	16
First grade	11	12	23
Second grade	7	13	20
Third grade ....,....................	11	10	21
Fourth grade	4	6	10
Fifth grade	4	4	8
Sixth and Seventh grades........................	4	9	13
Tenth grade	2	0	2
	—	—	—
Total	51	62	113
Total Blind and Deaf...........................	98	93	191

Staff conferences are held by the Principal of the Negro Department twice a month for the purpose of studying the individual pupil. Teachers are requested to obtain social histories of their pupils to present at the conferences. They are now making a special study of the bright pupil.

Quite a number of the deaf are able to learn to talk. For the others, the method of teaching and reciting is manual. It is not possible to go into detail about the various methods of teaching the blind and deaf, but it should be noted that results are obtained. Many boys and girls have been able to provide for themselves after they have received training in the school. Following graduation from the school, several students have done creditable college work.

For the purpose of enabling blind students to pursue any course of study, profession, art, or science in any university, college or conservatory of music located in North Carolina, the General Assembly has appropriated $2,000 annually to the

School for the Blind and Deaf. No student can receive more than $200 in one year.

HANDICRAFTS AND INDUSTRIES

Students, in addition to the regular work, are taught to do handwork, rug weaving, basketry, chair caning, and to make stools. Deaf boys are taught to repair shoes, to do wood work, make brooms and mattresses. They also do farm work under supervision.

MUSIC

Although there is only one music teacher, music has a large place in the lives of the blind students. Seven pianos are provided. Two quartettes of boys and a glee club made up of fifteen boys and girls have been developed. Public school music is taught each class of blind students and chorus classes are conducted every afternoon.

Two blind boys, formerly students, are now living from their work as piano tuners.

RELIGIOUS SERVICES

The teachers conduct Sunday School for both the blind and deaf every Sunday. Preaching services are conducted twice a month and chapel services are conducted every morning at eight o'clock.

MEDICAL SERVICE

Medical service includes three eye specialists, one general physician, a dentist provided by the State Board of Health but paid by the School, and a full-time registered nurse.

As a general rule, the Superintendent says, the blind and deaf are more delicate than other people. A variety of wholesome food with a large quantity of milk is necessary.

FOLLOWING UP FORMER STUDENTS

The School has never been able to put into effect any sort of a follow-up program. However, many of the students keep in touch with the School, return to the School for brief visits and in this way the School is able to assist a number of students in making satisfactory adjustments.

The following cases show what some of the former students are doing. The Principal states that most of them are following the trades which they learned while in the institution:

Roger (deaf) entered the school in 1892, remained for some time doing work required of him. He later entered Shaw University and, having done his work so well, they recommended him to Yale, where he graduated in law. He is now the only deaf and dumb lawyer in the state, so far as the School knows. He was a teacher in the School in 1918-1919.

Herman (deaf) entered school in 1896. He took the carpenter's trade. He did his work well and is now a contractor, making a good living and doing creditable work in a North Carolina city.

Jack (deaf) entered school in 1896 and took the trade of shoe making. He is married and has a family supported by his trade. He is running a creditable shoe shop in a North Carolina city.

Lizzie (deaf) entered school at an early age. She has completed her work and is now employed as assistant housekeeper in the school.

Daniel (blind) entered the School for the Blind in 1897 and is now doing Evangelistic work in New York state. He was at one time a teacher in the mattress making department of the school.

Macie (blind) entered school in 1907. She was able to secure work at a School for the Blind in another state.

Robert (blind) is making a good living as a soloist. He was in the School from 1911 until 1920.

Edgar, totally blind, entered school in 1915. He received his certificate in broom making, etc. In 1922 he returned to his home where he set up a shop. He helped his mother pay off the mortgage on the home and at the same time cared for them both. Edgar is now doing business in a North Carolina city as a mattress maker and chair bottomer.

Emma entered school in September, 1926. She was graduated in 1931 and is making a living selling baskets and other fancy articles. She also does chair bottoming and gives concerts in churches in her spare time.

Esther entered the Blind School in 1916. She remained until she graduated and is now an honor student at Shaw University, having won the prize in scholarship each year for the past two years.

SUMMARY

When work on the Negro Department's grounds has been completed, the place will present an attractive appearance. The plans for the grounds include playgrounds for both the boys and girls.

Additional building facilities and additional equipment already indicated can be provided only when more money is available. Plans for better organization and more efficient administration of the Negro Department can be worked out by the Board of Directors and the Superintendent of the School.

CHAPTER X

DISCUSSION OF SOCIAL POLICIES AND THE NEED FOR CASE WORK IN INSTITUTIONS

INTRODUCTION

IN ORDER TO avoid repetition it seemed desirable to discuss the need for social case work in a general report rather than in the individual reports on the four institutions caring exclusively for Negro children.

None of these four institutions have case workers on their own staffs. The Memorial Industrial School at Winston-Salem and the Negro Orphanage at Oxford have adopted the plan of accepting cases only upon the recommendation of the superintendents of public welfare in the communities from which the children come. The Morrison Training School for Boys and the Industrial School for Negro Girls at Efland receive children upon commitment by the courts. The information being sent to the respective institutions at the time of admission was chiefly identifying data. In none of the institutions were there complete social histories on the entire population.

It is only during the past quarter of a century that there has been anything like a professional approach to the problems of social welfare. Even now, although a philosophy of procedure has been evolved, performance based upon that philosophy still lags behind. Throughout the United States we find that service for both dependent and delinquent children is still in many ways unsatisfactory because there are not the necessary social resources for making a careful social diagnosis and planning intelligent treatment. This implies a gathering together of available information about a child's family, about the reasons for his dependency or delinquency, the probabilities of remedying conditions so that ultimately his own parents or other relatives may care for him, about his personality, his school record, his medical history, his mental capacity and his social attitudes as a basis for deciding what plan of treatment will be most effective for the child himself and for his family.

Social case work is predicated upon the assumption that both biologically and socially children are integral parts of their families and cannot nor should not be considered as isolated units. The Negro family in the south has been a self determining unit only since the Civil War. Standards of family life among Negroes are too often measured by the accepted norm among the white race. An assumption that family integrity is something which cannot be achieved to any large extent among the class of Negroes coming to the attention of social agencies is hardly fair when we consider that only 65 years have elapsed since the close of the Civil War. Social evolution is a slow process and too much cannot be expected from the Negro or any other racial group in a short space of time.

If family life is desirable for one group of people it must be considered desirable for all groups regardless of race and color. Furthermore, there are many evidences that among Negroes there is a strong recognition of kinship ties which tends to foster the development of self-help in times of stress. This social trait is something which should be conserved rather than broken down. It also should make it easier to put into effect fundamental case work principles than is often possible with those groups less accustomed to sharing both their joys and their sorrows with their kinsfolk and neighbors.

Any social program which concerns itself merely with the care of a child away from his own home and which disregards his family relationships is limiting itself to a minor phase of the problems of dependency and delinquency. The following discussion of the need for social service as an integral part of the work of the four institutions caring exclusively for Negro children in North Carolina is based upon the premise that family life should be made possible and desirable for "all children everywhere."

INSTITUTIONS FOR DEPENDENTS

On the basis of such figures as are available it has been stated that between 80 and 90 per cent of the children coming to the attention of children's institutions eventually go back to their own people. Sometimes the re-uniting is delayed for years but finally most children find their way back which goes to prove that at least in most cases "blood is thicker than water."

What separation from his own group means to a child in terms of emotional stress and a feeling of insecurity because he doubts his own status, cannot as yet be measured. Through child guidance clinics and the application of better case work methods, however, we are gradually accumulating data which show that serious mental conflicts and unwholesome social attitudes may grow out of such separation.

The figures given in the individual reports on the Colored Orphanage at Oxford and the Memorial Industrial School at Winston-Salem on parental status indicate that (1) at the Colored Orphanage approximately 46 per cent of the children cared for in one year were orphans; 28 per cent were the children of widows; 20 per cent were the children of widowers; 76 per cent were twelve years of age or younger; 16 per cent were admitted during a period of 12 months; and (2) at the Memorial Industrial School 36 per cent of the population on a given date were orphans; 15 per cent were the children of widows; 32 per cent were the children of widowers; 75 per cent were twelve years of age or younger and 50 per cent were admitted during a period of 12 months.

While the Colored Orphanage was caring for children from 46 counties and the Memorial Industrial School was confining its intake largely to one county, the case work service being provided by the counties did not vary greatly as to quality in so far as the records available revealed case work standards. In some instances probably much more service had been given by the workers in the counties than the records at the institutions revealed.

The figures given above show that both of these institutions

are caring for children whose social problems will never be
solved by a few years' care in an orphanage. The number of
orphans which is larger than that found in most institutions
in North Carolina or elsewhere, makes the problems of adjustment when the children can no longer remain in the institution
unusually difficult. To care for orphans over a long period of
years and then dismiss them without definite plans for the
future is a short sighted and expensive policy to say nothing
of the obvious suffering and moral risk which many children
will undoubtedly experience during their reabsorption into
community life. If, at the time of admission, it were possible
to determine the social resources which exist among the relatives of children and to make some plan whereby the natural
inclination of the Negro to share what he has with his kinsfolk
might be utilized, institutional care of orphans would not in
all cases be necessary. Even if some assistance had to be given
in order to provide care in a family setting it would cost less
than institutional care.

In other cases involving orphan children, they might be accepted but during their stay in the institution such remnants
of families as they had would not be lost sight of and whenever possible, would be utilized in making plans for the future.

The children of widows reveal the need in North Carolina
for more adequate provision for mothers' aid. Since the first
White House Conference in 1909 we have been saying that a
child should not be removed from his mother solely because
she is economically unable to support him. No phase of social
welfare is so clearly the responsibility of public agencies as
that which has for its objective the preservation of family life.
It is not possible to say what per cent of the children of widowed
mothers might be returned to them if there was a comprehensive mothers' aid program in North Carolina but if proper
standards of administration prevailed generally and enough
funds were available, the chances are that the majority of the
children in this group now receiving institutional care could

be better cared for by their own mothers at less expense.

The following tables* giving the position which North Carolina occupies in its provision for mothers' aid and that of a group of other states and the District of Columbia from which data were secured, may be of interest:

TABLE V

State	Number of Children Receiving Aid per 10,000 Total Population
Minnesota	38
South Dakota	34
Michigan	33
Wisconsin	33
New York	30
Idaho	28
New Jersey	27
Montana	27
Delaware	26
Maine	24
Oregon	19
Colorado	18
Massachusetts	18
Rhode Island	17
Connecticut	14
Pennsylvania	13
New Hampshire	11
Oklahoma	8
Arizona	7
District of Columbia	7
Indiana	6
North Carolina	5
Vermont	4
Louisiana	2
Virginia	1

* Emma O. Lundberg, "Progress of Mothers' Aid Administration," *Social Service Review*, Vol. II, No. 3, September, 1928.

TABLE VI

State	Per capita Expenditure for Grants
Arizona	$ 0.07
Colorado	0.17
Connecticut	0.25
Delaware	0.26
Idaho	0.24
Louisiana	0.07
Maine	0.20
Massachusetts	0.48
Michigan	0.43
Minnesota	0.36
Montana	0.32
New Hampshire	0.08
New Jersey	0.31
New York	0.56
North Carolina	0.15
Ohio	0.21
Pennsylvania	0.16
Rhode Island	0.27
South Dakota	0.48
Vermont	0.04
Virginia	0.01
Wisconsin	0.43

TABLE VII

State	Average monthly Grant per Family
Massachusetts	$60.00
Rhode Island	52.00
Connecticut	47.70
New York	42.50
Pennsylvania	36.35
Colorado	28.36
Maine	27.12
Michigan	27.12
Montana	26.30

State	Average monthly Grant per Family
New Jersey	26.30
Minnesota	25.90
Vermont	25.70
Wisconsin	23.89
South Dakota	23.60
Arizona	22.80
Delaware	21.60
New Hampshire	20.50
Ohio	19.20
North Carolina	18.35
Virginia	15.60
Louisiana	15.35
Idaho	14.12

In cases where the mother has died and a father is left with a family of children, institutional care is not always the only method of solving the problem. The number of children of widowers in the Colored Orphanage and the Memorial Industrial School would undoubtedly be materially reduced if proper intake service were available so that applications might be more carefully investigated and more help given in making other plans. The fathers of children who need the type of care which the institution can give, should be made to feel a sense of responsibility for their children and encouraged to look forward to the day when they can again care for them. This is a part of good case work procedure which should continue throughout the time a child remains in the institution. For the child who has no family ties or whose parents and other relatives are so irresponsible and degraded that there can be no hope of family rehabilitation, a new family should be found into which he can grow and for which he will develop a strong sense of attachment. Neither of the institutions under discussion is at present in a position to undertake any family home placing. Unless families are selected with discrimination and there is proper supervision after placement, child-placing becomes a dangerous experiment. On the other hand, if child-

11

placing is carefully done by persons having special training
for the task; and if it is not confined to free home placements
but also includes those homes in which some remuneration is
paid in order to secure a particular type of service, it is one
of the best social instruments known for meeting the peculiar
needs of individual children.

The most dominant note in children's work today is the
emphasis upon first determining what a child's needs are and
then supplying the type of treatment which seems best adapted
to meet those needs. This may be long or short time institutional care, placement for adoption, temporary placement in a
boarding home or, for an older child, placement in a wage
home.

In any child caring program it is important that parents
pay toward the support of their children to the limit of their
ability as otherwise they gradually lose all sense of responsibility for them. How much a parent should pay can only be
determined after the facts regarding his earning capacity,
his financial obligations and his own needs are known. To
gather such information is an essential part of the case work
process.

Practically no board was being paid by parents for the
care of any of the children in either of the two institutions
for dependent children. While the earning capacity of the
parents and other relatives is undoubtedly low, the failure to
secure payment for any child is more significant of the lack
of case work service than of the inability of all parents or
relatives to pay even small sums for board.

When counties can send children to institutions supported
by the state or by private philanthropy without paying any
share of the cost, there is a temptation to dispose of cases
through utilizing institutional care rather than by trying to
work out a plan for the entire family which may cost the
county something. Without any initiative being taken by the
institutions themselves to stimulate the local communities in
making plans by which children may be returned as soon as
possible to their own families, there is undoubtedly a tendency

to forget about the children in the institution until a crisis arises and the superintendent insists that some action be taken.

It would be interesting to see what would happen if in one of the counties from which the largest number of children have been sent to the Colored Orphanage over a five year period, a demonstration were set up which would make it possible to give adequate mothers' aid and family relief; and which would be so staffed that high administrative standards could be observed. Such a project would clearly show the relation between the prevention of child dependency and high-grade family welfare service, mothers' aid, public health measures and economic opportunities.

The figures previously given show that the turnover in population was greater at the Memorial Industrial School where 50 per cent of the children under care were admitted during a twelve months period than at the Colored Orphanage where only 16 per cent of the total population came in during the same period. The fact that the Memorial Industrial School moved into a new plant during 1929 is largely responsible for the difference in these figures.

A well organized social work program will tend to increase the rate of turn-over as children will not remain beyond the period for which institutional care is actually needed. Thus more children can be aided each year by means of the facilities already provided. Investment in service which stimulates a more rapid turn-over in the long run pays for itself. It is analogous to investment in salesmanship by means of which the stock in a manufacturing plant or in a store is kept moving. Without this type of service an institution runs the risk of crippling its effectiveness by caring for a static group of children for an indefinite period.

CASE STUDIES

As part of the study of Negro child welfare in North Carolina some cases of families whose children have been or are now in institutions were investigated. The data gathered through these case studies illustrate what happens when institutions are not equipped to render case work service. They bring out, too, the family integrity which can be found in Negro families.

Case 1.—A woman was left with three young children at the death of her husband. She was able to maintain her family by doing washing except when the weather was bad and the clothes would not dry. At such times of the year she could not do enough work in a week to get along and would have to ask for assistance from the local family agency. It appears that she was helped willingly for some time. Finally, however, when she had to ask for help it was suggested that she put her children in an institution. This she refused to do and no aid was given her. The case worker in the report of her investigation of this case writes: "The next day (after the family agency refused aid) the superintendent of public welfare came to tell the mother what a wonderful idea it would be if she allowed the children to go to the Home. But she thought her own home comfortable and wanting her children with her she refused. Later the same day, he returned with a worker to say that they were desirous of having the three oldest children examined. She allowed the children to go with them, thinking that they would soon return. That night the children had not returned and the next day their clothing was sent for and she was told they were in the institution. She at once went to a woman for whom she works and who has known her for a number of years. This woman and her husband interested themselves in the case and after several days they were able to get the children back.

"The mother, who is said to be entirely reliable, is a pleasant, clean and matronly sort of a person. She shows signs of having done hard work. She abhors the fact of her children having been taken from her.

"Smeed Alley, where this family lives, is really not what the name implies. It is a small stretch of land which extends to the railroad track. Small houses are built close together on opposite sides of the lot. The houses are dilapidated and show years of standing. Many are vacant. There are no fences but the entire place is fairly clean and orderly.

"The family lives in two rooms of a four room double tenement one-story frame house. The front room, which has two double beds, is used for both sleeping and living purposes. The kitchen is used for cooking and eating purposes. Both rooms are neat, clean and fully furnished.

"Since the children were returned from the institution they have not gone to school, although they went regularly previous to this experience. It is evident that the mother is afraid to let them go for fear they may again be taken from her."

This case, which appears to be a mothers' aid case, illustrates (1) the way in which the social assets in this family situation were ignored; (2) the economic shortsightedness of attempting to meet a situation which demanded only a small amount of relief by putting three children in an institution having a per capita of over $200 per year; and (3) the way in which a poor social plan has interfered with the education of the children.

Fortunately, in this case, the mother had a friend at court so that her children's residence in the institution was brief. That such an incident occurred, however, is in itself a commentary on the social practice of the community which requires no further elaboration.

Case 2.—This case involves a mother, a deserting father and five children. The case worker's summary is as follows:

"Things went well until the father deserted the mother and five children in September, 1929. Previous to that time he had spent one or two nights away from home but always paid the rent, bought plenty of food and good clothes for all. But this time he left them in need and it became necessary to apply for aid. In the meantime the mother became ill with influenza. For two or three weeks the family agency gave food and the father brought money to her with the promise of more. It was after a request for help that one of the workers from the agency came to ask the mother how she would like to let the children go to the institution. This she was unwilling to do. The next day the superintendent of public welfare came to tell her if she allowed the children to go to the institution she could get them back as soon as she was well and able to work, so she consented.

"As soon as she was better she moved to a smaller place where the rent was cheaper. In the meantime she had gotten a job at the tobacco factory and the father had promised to do for the children as soon as they were returned home.

"The mother states she went to the agency office and was told she could not have the children. She feels that she is being mistreated. And as much as she would like to see her children she cannot visit them often as the orphanage is outside the city and she does not have money for taxi fare.

"She states that her plan for caring for them when she gets them back is to pay someone to care for the youngest ones. The oldest ones will be in school.

"For about a week the mother has lived on the second floor in one rear room of a two-story eight-room house. The house is rented by one and two rooms. The room is clean but a bit crowded with two double beds, dining table, chairs, trunks and stove. She informed us that she disposed of some of her furniture after the children were refused her.

"The neighborhood for the most part is fairly quiet. Near-by there are a few land owners who have very attractive homes. There are, however, a few cottages and apartment houses which are built for rent.

"The mother appears to be good natured, pleasant, congenial and still very much in love with her husband and devoted to her children. She gives one the impression of being reliable and truthful.

"The social worker of the Congregational Church informs us that the woman is a hard working, reliable, good woman who is interested in her children."

In this case temporary placement of the children during the mother's illness was no doubt advisable. But the lack of any effort to straighten out the trouble between the father and mother, to make the father continue to contribute to the support of the children and to help the mother plan for geting her children home again reveals the assumption on the part of the referring agency that all the problems of this family were solved by placing the children in the institution. The satisfactory vocational history of the father, his former willingness to provide for his family, the mother's good character and her love for her husband and her children are social assets which should have been recognized by the agency to which the mother turned for aid when ill. Instead, the father's sense of responsibility has undoubtedly been lessened, the mother is suffering because of her isolation from both her children and her husband, and the cost of caring for the children in the institution for an extended period will be greater than the cost of constructive family service would have been. While the children may be getting certain physical advantages, the institution cannot provide a substitute for the care and affection of a devoted mother.

Institutions throughout the country are recognizing that they need to do more than merely provide care within their own four walls if they are to do their full duty by the children whom they accept. For this reason a modern institution is not content to serve merely as a repository for children referred to it by other agencies. It also equips itself with the service necessary to look into the cases referred and to make sure that what is done will be in the direction of conserving family life rather than of contributing to its disintegration.

There is sometimes a tendency to regard investment in case work service as a luxury which can be dispensed with. As a matter of fact, it is the one investment which more than any other safeguards expenditures for institutional care. It insures an institution against caring for children whose families should bear their own responsibilities. It conserves the resources of an organization for those whose needs are greatest. It attempts to use such social and economic assets as exist in a family in a process of rehabilitation in order that the period of care in the institution will not be unnecessarily prolonged. It sees to it that parents who are able, share the burden of support even though the children must be separated from them. It plans continually for the return of children to family and community life and aids them during this difficult period of readjustment. And, it forever searches for the truth by means of which children may be understood by those who, for a time at least, serve as parent-substitutes.

Neither the Colored Orphanage nor the Memorial Industrial School is able at present to undertake any of the services above indicated. Definite recommendations regarding the development of case work service are included in the report on the Memorial Industrial School since that institution has certain advantages which make it seem desirable for it to undertake a demonstration case work program.

The need for social service in connection with the Colored Orphanage is just as great. The fact that it cares for a larger number of children from a wider area adds to the social problems inherent in the task of caring for children away from their own homes.

The following recapitulation and recommendations are presented for consideration:

1. An institution cannot function properly without high-grade case work service. At present, the county units of public welfare in North Carolina are for the most part unable to give an adequate amount of service to the institutions caring for dependent and neglected Negro children. For this reason the institutions themselves should supplement the service which the county units can give by having case workers on their own staffs.

2. Practically no children are being placed either in free homes or boarding homes by the institutions. This is a wise policy since neither institution has the necessary staff to undertake such a program. As the case work service is developed, however, a limited amount of placement work should be done since family home care is more desirable for infants and very young children than group care; and also for certain types of older children who have special problems. This supplementary placement service should be a gradual development and not a wholesale attempt to dispose of a large number of children in a hit or miss fashion.

3. The populations of both institutions need to be carefully analyzed to determine what plans should be formulated

for the subsequent care of the children. This task could not be undertaken as part of the special study of Negro child welfare but it needs to be done as the starting point of a well-organized case work program.

4. The institutions should participate in every effort to secure more adequate mothers' aid, better family welfare service, better public health facilities, etc., as these are all important factors in the prevention of child dependency.

5. The Memorial Industrial School has certain assets which make it particularly well adapted for carrying on a demonstration in children's case work. Its modern plant and equipment, limited population, private support and community resources, provide a medium in which a complete child-caring service can be developed in a way that will prove the value of integrating modern case work procedure with institutional care. If such a demonstration is undertaken by the Memorial Industrial School, the lessons which grow out of it should be made available to the Colored Orphanage.

INSTITUTIONS FOR DELINQUENTS

In the past there was a tendency to draw a sharp line of demarcation between the care and treatment of delinquent children and of dependent and neglected children. We have learned, however, that delinquency frequently has its roots in dependency and neglect and thus social treatment of the two groups of children should not vary greatly in its fundamentals. For this reason, practically every point raised in the foregoing discussion of the need for social service in the institutions caring for dependents is equally applicable to the Morrison Training School for Boys and the Industrial School for Girls at Efland. In addition there are special problems because the children committed to these correctional institutions have presumably violated laws against property, have been habitual truants or have disregarded accepted moral codes. As a matter of fact, there were evidences that had there been better case work in some of the counties from which the children came, it would not have been necessary to send so many young boys to the Morrison Training School for what appeared to be minor offenses resulting from poor environment or failure to adjust in school.

At the present time the boys and girls sent to these two institutions remain until they have earned a parole by good conduct or until they reach the age limit of jurisdiction. Then they return to their own homes or else seek employment. Many of them go back to the same environmental conditions which were largely responsible for their delinquency in the first place. As neither institution has a parole officer, the superintendents of public welfare in the counties from which the children come must be depended upon for any work done with families and for supervision after parole. While the superintendent of Morrison Training School makes an effort to keep in touch with the boys who have left, it is an informal type of service.

CASE STUDIES

The following case summaries based on investigations made during the study of Negro child welfare illustrate the weaknesses of the present plan of procedure.

Case 1.—William was ten years old when admitted to the Morrison Training School on a charge of truancy and he remained for two and a half years.

His father and mother are both living but the father deserted his family five years ago. It then became necessary for the mother to go to work. The oldest boy in the family also worked, the baby was cared for by a neighbor and William was supposed to go to school. However, he was out of school more than he was in. The record in the Juvenile Court is as follows:

"On 3/13/26 William was brought into juvenile court for truancy. The disposition was that he was put on probation and told to attend school regularly. If he violated this order he was to be brought to court and whipped. 3/20/26 he was again brought into court for truancy and his probation was continued after he was again warned of being whipped. 4/23/26 he was again brought into court for truancy but no action was taken. 5/1/26 another truancy charge was filed and the judge ordered that he be sent to the county reformatory. There is no record indicating that this order was carried out. 11/12/26 he was again brought into court for truancy and the judge ordered that he be committed to Morrison Training School at Hoffman, North Carolina."

When William was paroled he was told by the executive of the institution that upon his arrival at home he should report at the office of the superintendent of public welfare. This he did. The report of the case worker states, "He was cautioned and told that it was not necessary to come back."

William had been at home for six months at the time of the study. The mother made the following comments when interviewed: "William is an entirely different boy. He attends school regularly now. He cleans the house before going to school and he has the fire made and preparations for supper under way when I get home from work at night."

In this instance the training which William received at the school is apparently enabling him to stay on the right track. But the failure on the part of the superintendent of public welfare to assume any responsibility for seeing that the good work which the institution did was carried on following parole, indicates the lack of systematic planning for supervision.

This case also illustrates the failure of the Juvenile Court to do anything about the repeated truancy of this boy except to bring him into court, threaten him with whipping and confinement in the county reformatory and release him. The record shows no evidences of any effort to determine why he disliked school, which should be the starting point in the treatment of truancy in a ten-year-old child.

Case 2.—In May, 1928, an eleven-year-old boy was committed to the Morrison Training School for house-breaking, larceny and truancy. In July, 1929, he was paroled. In February, 1930, the records at the institution showed that no word had been received from this boy and nothing was known about what he was doing.

The report of the case worker who visited the home of this boy's mother is as follows:

"The superintendent of public welfare did not know of Harold's return until he got into trouble four months after he came back from the Training School. At this time he committed larceny and was reported as a truant. An order was made committing him to the county reformatory. Later he was paroled from the reformatory and in January, 1930, he took a bicycle and a child's automobile. He was again committed to the county reformatory but for only a few days.

"The mother also stated that for nearly three months Harold has been sleeping away from home. She has been trying to locate his whereabouts. The neighbors tell her that he comes to the house very often in the afternoon for clean clothing and food but leaves when it is time for her to return from work. She has seen him running from the house as she neared it.

"She has been near enough to talk to him about twice in the three months that he has been away. During their conversation he cries and tells her how anxious he is to stay at home and do what is right but he cannot. As soon as her back is turned he is gone again. She states that he was told at Morrison to go to the welfare office upon his return home but she does not think that he went."

If there were proper facilities for the supervision of children paroled from the Morrison Training School, this boy would have been returned to the School when he violated his parole instead of being sent to a county reformatory ill-suited to the care of juvenile delinquents. Furthermore, there would have been some effort made during the first few months of parole to prevent him from getting into trouble and to improve the family situation if possible. Instead, it appears that nothing at all was done to safeguard the investment which the Morrison Training School put into the retraining of this lad.

Case 3.—Frank, an 8-year-old boy, was committed to the Morrison Training School in December, 1928, and was still in the institution in February, 1930. The superintendent of public schools serves as the superintendent of public welfare in the county from which this child came. The reason for commitment as given in the records was "boy continually on the streets and cannot be controlled."

A visit to this community and an interview with the mother revealed the fact that Frank is the younger of two illegitimate children. The mother stated that the fathers of the children were both Negroes and that she had never been married.

The Juvenile Court records showed that Frank was brought into court for larceny and that there was no record of any charge previous to the one for which he was committed to the Training School.

On the basis of interviews with employers of the mother, the minister, the superintendent of schools and the mother herself, the case worker writes the following summary:

"We went to see the lady where the mother had worked so long. She was out but we talked to her daughter who is about thirty years old. She spoke highly of the mother and expressed regret at her leaving their employ. She felt as if the woman was one of the family and there was nothing they would not do for her.

"The daughter referred to Frank as the 'dearest colored boy' in town who was loved by white people both young and old. She told how white women would pick him up in their cars and take him shopping with them or to their homes. She states further that white boys carried him around with them at all times. She thinks that he was learning how to drink and smoke by going for motor rides into the country with them.

"The mother's minister states that she is a member of his church but attends only occasionally. He states further that because of being seen frequently with white women and girls he and the mother thought it advisable to take steps to send Frank away. He also states that white boys older than Frank were teaching him many bad habits.

"The mother also gave us information similar to the above. She added that on one or two occasions when Frank spent the night away from home she learned that he had been at some white residence at bed time and they insisted on his remaining. He did so, sleeping with some member of the family.

"The mother also told us of the daughter of a prominent white citizen who came home with her little son about Frank's age. The two became 'pals' and learned how to steal fruit at fruit stands along the street. Nothing, however, was ever done as the grandfather of the white child and Frank's mother paid each dealer the bill presented by him.

"On one occasion Frank, seeing a horse tied at a gate, took the horse and rode where he was going and brought the horse back after doing his errand. Upon his return the owner was waiting for the horse. When asked why he took the horse, the boy replied that he saw the horse standing and having to do the errand decided to use it to save time and, too, he was tired. The white man did nothing about it and referred to it as being 'cute'."

It would appear that in this instance the community had contributed to the delinquency of Frank during his eight years of life in a thorough-going manner. If the Training School is able to establish new behavior patterns and to substitute new social attitudes for those which have grown out of being regarded by the white residents as the "cutest boy in town" it will have accomplished a stupendous task. However, still greater difficulties will be faced when the time comes to parole Frank. If he goes back to the same environment there is grave doubt that his institutional experience will bear fruit.

This is the type of case which illustrates the need for work with the family while the child is in the institution. If Frank is to go back to his mother, it should be only upon condition that she change her environment and her mode of living. She will need help and encouragement if she is to do either. Neither the community in which she lives nor the institution is now equipped to render such service.

In addition to the purely social problems which institutions caring for delinquent children must face there is also the problem of vocational adjustment of boys and girls. Very often the success or failure of a child after parole depends largely upon his ability to get work which he can do satisfactorily. The time is past when it can be assumed that every boy who has been delinquent should get a job on a farm and every girl should be placed at domestic service.

Schools having modern educational systems seek to diversify the training given so that special aptitudes and bents may be discovered. When the time comes for parole, every effort is made to guide children into vocational pursuits for which they are best fitted. This adjustment service upon which a child's future so largely hinges demands skill and training of high order and is an important part of a well-organized social service program.

The social service program of an institution for delinquent minors may be developed in two ways, namely, through the creation of a central parole bureau serving all the institutions as is done, for example, in New Jersey and Massachusetts; or by providing a case work staff for each institution as is done at Sleighton Farms, a school for delinquent girls at Darlington, Pennsylvania, and at Long Lane Farm, Middletown, Connecticut.

It does not lie within the scope of this report to recommend the adoption of a particular administrative method but it is urged that North Carolina inquire into the advantages and disadvantages of each as a preliminary to rounding out its own program for the prevention and treatment of juvenile delinquency. Until both intra-mural and extra-mural care are provided, the program cannot be regarded as complete.

The following suggestions and recommendations are presented for consideration:

1. The Morrison Training School and the Industrial School for Negro Girls at Efland, pending the development of more adequate social service, should take the initiative in securing better coöperation from superintendents of public welfare by:

a. Asking them to furnish more complete social information at the time of commitment;

b. Making frequent inquiries regarding the families from which children come in order to know whether the institution can look forward to the return of children to their own homes and to secure the aid of the county workers in making plans for children who cannot go home;

c. Notifying the superintendent of public welfare formally when a child has been paroled and requesting that some supervision be given and reports on progress made to the school.

2. The State of North Carolina should, during the next

five years, supplement its institutional program for the care of delinquent children by the development of a modern social service program. The experience of other states and the special needs of North Carolina should determine the selection of administrative methods.

Conclusion

In attempting to point out the need for social service resources as an integral part of the institutional service provided for Negro children in North Carolina, the practical difficulties in the path of achievement have not been lost sight of. Changes will not be effected next week nor next month nor even next year. But the idea that no program for children is complete without such facilities can be nurtured by its acceptance on the part of the state and the private groups and individuals interested in the care and protection of socially handicapped children. If the study of Negro child welfare in North Carolina promotes a more general acceptance of this idea it will have achieved one of its major purposes.

PART III

NEGRO CHILDREN AND THE LAW

CHAPTER XI

CHILDREN IN THE COUNTY JUVENILE COURTS IN NORTH CAROLINA, 1919-1929, WITH SPECIAL EMPHASIS UPON NEGRO CHILDREN

ALTHOUGH THE General Assembly of North Carolina in 1915 passed an act (Public Laws, 1915, Ch. 222, pp. 294-296) embodying the essential provisions of a juvenile court, namely, separate hearings for children's cases, probation service, and the keeping of social case records on the children appearing before the court, the act was so loosely drawn, and was so indefinite in its provisions, that outside of a few of the cities, such as Asheville, Winston-Salem, Wilmington, and Raleigh, it had little effect.[1] In 1919, however, when the public welfare system was strengthened by making it mandatory for each of the 100 counties, with a population of as much as 32,000, in the State to employ a welfare officer, the county superintendent of schools serving ex-officio in this capacity in the remaining counties, a state-wide system of juvenile courts, with the county as the unit, was established. Under this reorganization the clerk of the Superior Court in each county was made ex-officio judge of the county juvenile court, while the county welfare officer was made chief probation officer. It is required of both the judge of the juvenile court and the chief probation officer that they keep full and complete records of all children appearing before the juvenile court, but unfortunately no provision was made in the juvenile court act for any periodical reporting of cases to any State authority, so that no one knows the number or type of cases appearing before the county juvenile courts throughout the State for a

---

[1] National Child Labor Committee, *Child Welfare in North Carolina* (1918), pp. 22-35.

given year. The only way such information could be secured would be by writing to each of the one hundred counties for such information, and the investigator would think himself fortunate if he received replies from ninety per cent of the counties.

At the beginning of the Negro child welfare study, therefore, it was felt that the most satisfactory method of securing data on the Negro children appearing before the one hundred county juvenile courts[2] in North Carolina would be to have the field representatives and other members of the staff of the State Board of Charities and Public Welfare to visit each of the one hundred counties, and to transcribe on cards the important social data contained in the county juvenile court records. For purposes of comparison it was decided that such social data should be secured on the white children as well as on the Negro children, and that the period to be covered should be ten years, from July 1, 1919, until the summer of 1929.[3]

---

[2] The juvenile court act further provides (C. S. 5062) that cities with a population of ten thousand or more by the census of 1920 shall maintain a city juvenile court, or make provision therefor, while towns of five thousand population under certain conditions may establish such courts. The cities with ten thousand population in 1920 are Asheville, Charlotte, Durham, Gastonia, Goldsboro, Greensboro, High Point, New Bern, Raleigh, Rocky Mount, Salisbury, Wilmington, and Winston-Salem. Of these cities, seven maintain separate juvenile courts, namely, Winston-Salem, Raleigh, High Point, Greensboro, Wilmington, Gastonia, and Rocky Mount. Hickory is the only town of less than ten thousand to maintain a separate juvenile court. Those having combined city and county juvenile courts are Asheville, Charlotte, Durham, Goldsboro, New Bern, and Salisbury. This study does not include the records of the separate juvenile courts of Greensboro, High Point, Rocky Mount, Hickory, nor of Asheville previous to the consolidation, March 24, 1924.

[3] Since the field workers spent several months in securing this information, it was not possible to cover exactly ten years. For example, in some counties the cards were filled out in May, 1929, two months before the expiration of the ten year period, while in other counties the cards were filled out through August and September, 1929, but on the average the period covered was approximately ten years.

NATURE AND LIMITATIONS OF JUVENILE COURT RECORDS

Everyone acquainted with public affairs knows that in the final analysis state laws depend for their effectiveness, not upon the legislators who write them, but upon the county courthouse officers who interpret and enforce them. One may readily understand, therefore, that the passage of a law creating a juvenile court in every county did not immediately result in the establishment of an actively functioning juvenile court in each of the one hundred counties. Many of the county juvenile court judges were unfamiliar with the principles and the procedure of juvenile courts, and in some instances the judges were actually hostile to the juvenile court movement, thinking it was merely a method of "letting the youthful criminal go free." Another difficulty in the way of establishing effective juvenile courts was the indifference of the counties in the matter of paying a salary to the clerk of court for his juvenile court work. Although the juvenile court act specifies that the judge "shall be paid a reasonable compensation for his services," as late as 1929 approximately one-third of the counties paid no salary to the county juvenile court judge, and almost a third of the counties paid no juvenile court costs. Then, too, in about two-fifths of the counties there are no separate welfare officers, but the county superintendent of schools is ex-officio welfare officer, and consequently chief probation officer for the county. In such case the superintendent of schools receives no salary for his welfare and probation work. It is but natural to expect a public official, already holding a full-time position to which he is appointed or elected and for which he is paid, to have little interest, even if he had the time, in carrying out supplementary duties for which he receives no compensation. As a result the juvenile court work has been neglected in many of the counties of the state. For example, in five counties of the state (Beaufort, Bladen, Burke, Dare, and Lincoln) there are no juvenile court records covering the first ten years after the establishment of the juvenile

court system, 1919-1929, although in the first four of these
counties during this period delinquent children have been committed to state training schools for juvenile delinquents, and
in the last named county several cases of white children were
handled unofficially.[4] In at least twenty-eight other counties
there was an average of less than four juvenile court cases
per year during the ten year period, or less than one case
every three months. In twenty-nine additional counties there
was an average of less than one juvenile court case per month.
In one county, Edgecombe, the clerk of the court refused to
allow the staff members of the State Board of Charities and
Public Welfare to consult his juvenile court records.

Perhaps there is no better indication of the carelessness in
juvenile court procedure and the lack of uniform standards
than the method of record keeping in the various county
juvenile courts. In a considerable number of the counties the
clerk of the Superior Court (as judge of the juvenile court)
keeps a *Juvenile Court Docket Book*, published by Edwards &
Broughton, in Raleigh, N. C. Only the barest facts about each
child's case are requested for the record, namely, county, date,
name, address, race, sex, age, name of parents, others responsible, charges, witnesses, and disposition. In many counties there
is no docket book, but some record (such as court papers)
is kept on the children appearing before the juvenile court. In
some of the larger counties the juvenile court docket book,
containing hundreds of cases, had been "lost." As a general
rule, even where there is a record on each child, many of the
items are lacking, such as age, date, disposition, and in numerous instances, even race, and sex. Almost six per cent of the
cards tabulated for this study from the juvenile court records
had to be thrown out because of inadequate information—as
failure to indicate race, sex, or charge. Because of such widespread carelessness in filling out the individual record blanks
in the juvenile court docket book, it has been impossible to
secure adequate information about a number of the most im-

---

[4] It should be noted also that the only juvenile court records in New Han-
over County are those of the Wilmington city juvenile court.

portant phases of the study. For example, due to the carelessness in listing the date of the juvenile court hearing in many of
the counties, it has not been possible to tabulate juvenile court
cases by years, to determine whether delinquency, or dependency, was increasing or decreasing. The same carelessness applies to the listing of the age of the child, especially the Negro
child, so that it is impossible to show the relationship between
age of the child and the type of charge, or between age and
type of disposition. Another important phase of the study
about which it was impossible to get satisfactory information
according to the present method of record keeping, is the
number of times a child appears before the juvenile court.
Under the present system each time a child appears before
the juvenile court he is counted as a new case, and there is no
way of telling, except possibly by classifying all cases by name
and date of appearance, whether a particular record card
represents a child's first appearance or his sixth. Finally, there
is no way to evaluate the success or failure of the juvenile
court method of procedure under present methods of record
keeping. The final entry on the child's record card is what
disposition was made at the time of the juvenile court hearing.
Whether the disposition were placing on probation or commitment to a training school, it is impossible to tell from the
records to what extent the disposition succeeded or failed. The
record closes before it is fairly begun. It is. vitally important
to know what proportion of delinquent children succeed when
placed on probation, or what per cent of delinquents sent to
training schools fail to make good, or whether dependent children placed in foster homes make a satisfactory adjustment.
Unless some provision is made for following-up and recording
in the juvenile court records the outcome of children handled
by the juvenile court, at least a year after the original hearing, who can tell whether the juvenile court is succeeding in its
rôle of guardian and protector of delinquent and neglected
youth? In contrast to the attitude of indifference in keeping
juvenile court records, is the attitude occasionally found that
it is unfair to the child to preserve any record against him.
In one county, for instance, where the public welfare work is

highly developed, the clerk of court says, "I don't like court records for juveniles. Cases should be settled unofficially. A court record is the same downstairs (in juvenile court) as it is upstairs (in the criminal court)." In another county, the attitude of the clerk, as described by a field representative, is as follows:

"The clerk states that when a child is brought before him for a minor offense, he puts him on probation. He shows him the Superior Court docket book and tells him there is a record that will always stand against the persons entered in it. He then explains to the child the seriousness of having a record of this kind against his name. He then tells him that he will give him a six months' trial. If he behaves himself and lives up to the rules of probation, he will not make any record of his ever having come before the juvenile court. At the end of the six months, if the child has behaved, the clerk, then, destroys before him any papers regarding the trouble that he has been in."

It might be said, therefore, that no two counties keep their juvenile court records alike, and that whether they keep records at all, or not, or whether they lose, or purposely destroy their juvenile court records, is, apparently, of little concern to the state. One can hope for little improvement in the methods of record keeping, or in standards of procedure, in the county juvenile courts in North Carolina, until some more adequate method of state supervision and regulation of county juvenile courts is provided, as, for example, the establishment of a special bureau of juvenile courts and probation, in the State Board of Charities and Public Welfare, with sufficient traveling expenses to make it possible for a juvenile court expert to visit and instruct the county juvenile court judges throughout the state in the practice and procedure of juvenile court work.[5] As additional checks the state authority should have some control over the salary of the juvenile court judge—as refusing to allow the payment of the juvenile court judge's

[5] *Biennial Report of the North Carolina State Board of Charities and Public Welfare, July 1, 1928-June 30, 1930*, p. 50.

salary unless the minimum standards were met—and also, annual reports should be required of all county juvenile courts to the state authority.

While it is apparent from the above considerations that there is no fair basis for making comparisons between counties with regard to number and types of cases, types of charge and disposition, still the large number of cases included in the study—more than twenty-three thousand—would tend to even up the differences between the various counties, so that the final tabulations, as presented in the following tables, may be accepted at their face value, as an accurate picture of the cases officially handled by the county juvenile courts in North Carolina. It may be added that the number of cases handled unofficially by the probation officer, without a juvenile court hearing, equals or exceeds the number of cases actually brought before the juvenile court.[6]

NUMBER AND TYPE OF CHILDREN HANDLED BY THE COUNTY JUVENILE COURTS

Since five counties reported no juvenile court records, and one county refused access to its records, the tables presented here represent the returns from ninety-four counties, for the ten year period, July, 1919-July, 1929. A total of 24,897 children were recorded as having been handled by these ninety-four county juvenile courts during this period. Of this number, 1,441 cases had to be excluded because the juvenile court records as kept by the county officials were so incompletely filled out as to be unintelligible. Furthermore, because their numbers were so small, twelve Indian children (5 delinquent boys, 2 delinquent girls, 4 dependent boys, and 1 dependent girl) and one dependent and neglected Chinese boy, were excluded. The tables presented here are based, therefore, upon 23,443 cases of white and of Negro children handled by the county juvenile courts, and whose records were complete enough to identify them by race, sex, and type of jurisdiction. According to Table VIII, there were 18,059 delinquent chil-

---

[6] *Ibid.*

dren handled by the juvenile courts, or 77 per cent of the total cases tabulated, while the dependent and neglected children numbered only 4,998, or 21.3 per cent of the total. By way of explanation, it may be pointed out that when the record card listed a child as being delinquent, dependent and neglected, the child is listed only once as a delinquent child. There were only 129 children, or 6 per cent of the total, who appeared before the juvenile court solely because their custody was subject to dispute, and who were not delinquent, dependent or neglected. The miscellaneous group, made up of 257 cases, or 1.1 per cent of the total, represent chiefly the mentally and physically defective child, the abandoned child, the illegitimate child, those unable to attend school because of poverty (without suitable clothing or school books), and a scattering of other cases.

RACE AND SEX OF CHILDREN HANDLED BY COUNTY JUVENILE COURTS

From Table IX it may be seen that 61 per cent of the cases represent white children, and 39 per cent represent Negro children. The question at once arises as to how this distribution according to race of children appearing before the county juvenile courts of North Carolina compares with the distribution of children of juvenile court age according to race in the general population. Some light may be thrown upon this question by taking the total number of children in North Carolina, 7-15 years inclusive, according to the census of 1920, (579,112) and adding it to the number of children of same age group under the census of 1930 (706,709) and dividing the total (1,285,821) by 2 to get an average for the ten years of 642,911 children of juvenile court age. By following the same method for white children and for Negro children, it is found that the ten year average for white children is 439,431, and for Negro children, 199,875. Reduced to a percentage basis, it is found that white children compose approximately 69 per cent of all children in North Carolina of juvenile court age, and the Negro children compose approximately 31 per cent. By comparing these figures with Table IX, it is apparent that Negro children are over-represented in the juvenile court cases (39 per cent as compared with 31 per cent) and the white children are under-represented (61 per cent as compared with 69 per cent).

With regard to sex distribution, a little over one-fifth were girls (21.2 per cent) and a little less than four-fifths (78.8 per cent) were boys. For purposes of comparison it may be pointed out that a recent report of the Federal Children's Bureau on juvenile court statistics, covering 96 juvenile courts during the year 1929, showed that girls represented 26.2 per cent of the cases, while boys represented 73.8 per cent of the cases.[7]

In Table X the outstanding fact is the great variation in distribution according to type of jurisdiction for the two races and sexes. Of all the white boys appearing before the juvenile courts, 80.9 per cent are delinquent, while only 35.9 per cent of all the white girls are so classified. On the other hand, 91 per cent of the Negro boys are delinquent, and 69.6 per cent of the Negro girls. Attention also should be called to the small number, and proportion, of dependent and neglected Negro children before the juvenile courts: 8.4 per cent of the Negro boys and 28.2 per cent of the Negro girls, as contrasted with 17.6 per cent for the white boys and 59.9 per cent for the white girls. In Table XI the arrangement of the figures is reversed. While it was shown in a preceding section that the white children represent 69 per cent of all children of juvenile court age in North Carolina, it is seen by referring to Table XI that the white children represent only 55.9 per cent of all delinquency cases, and 77.6 per cent of all the cases of dependency and neglect. On the other hand, the Negro children comprising 31 per cent of the children of juvenile court age in North Carolina make up 44.1 per cent of all the delinquency cases, and only 22.4 per cent of dependency and neglect cases. Apparently, therefore, the Negro children have considerably more than their share of delinquency cases, and far less than their share of dependency cases. If

---

[7] *Juvenile Court Statistics* (1929), p. 3.

however, the rate of delinquency and of dependency is worked out according to the method employed in the discussion of Table IX, it is found that the white delinquency rate is 2.29 per cent, and the Negro delinquency rate is 3.98 per cent. The rate of dependency and neglect, by the same method of calculation, is for the white children .88 per cent and for the Negro children .56 per cent.

If one considers the defective and dangerous environmental conditions under which so many Negro children are brought up—presented so vividly in the case studies of delinquent Negro children—one is not surprised that the proportion of delinquency of Negro children is greater than that for the white. The surprising fact is that the proportion is so low, or that all Negro children do not become delinquent.

On the other hand if one considers the fact that the Negroes have a higher illegitimacy rate, a higher death rate, a less stable form of family life, more desertion, etc., than the whites, it appears that there should be a considerably higher proportion of dependency and neglect among Negro children than among the white children, and yet the juvenile court statistics show less dependency among Negroes. The same condition exists if a comparison is made of the white and the Negro dependent children cared for in institutions in North Carolina. There are two colored orphans' homes in North Carolina, caring for 355 children, while there are twenty-eight institutions to care for 4,528 dependent white children.[8] The lack of institutional facilities for dependent Negro children is one reason they do not appear so frequently before the juvenile court, the judge preferring not to have a juvenile court hearing unless he feels that there is an institution available to which he can commit the child. A more plausible explanation, however, is that the Negroes, since they are a minority group, have developed a persecuted-race-complex and stand by one another in time of trouble to a far greater degree than the white people. When Negro children are left orphans through the death of their

---

[8] Duke Endowment, *Sixth Annual Report of the Orphan Section* (1930), pp. 51-52.

parents, their relatives, or even their neighbors gladly take the orphans into their own home, but when white children are left orphans, the first impulse of the white community, including the white relatives, is to send the children to an orphan asylum. If some supervision were provided, and some financial relief to ease the burden of the family taking the orphan children, who would say that the Negroes' method of caring for their dependent children was not superior to that of the whites?

DELINQUENCY CASES BEFORE THE COUNTY JUVENILE COURTS

Charges.—Before making a detailed comparison of the charges on which white and Negro boys and girls were brought before the county juvenile courts in North Carolina, it must be pointed out that the juvenile courts are *white* courts—that is to say, the judge of the juvenile court and the chief probation officer in every case is a white official, and in only a few instances are there subordinate Negro probation officers for handling the cases of Negro children. Then, too, the judges of the juvenile court are all *men*, which might color the attitude of the judges in handling boys' cases as compared with girls. Again, the fact that the judge of the juvenile court is the clerk of the Superior Court where adult criminals are handled, might influence his attitude in making out the charge—using the same terminology in describing the offense of the child as is used in the case of the adult, as, for example, "assault with deadly weapon," "carrying concealed weapon," "fornication and adultery," etc., and it might also influence him in making his disposition of the child, as committing him to an institution.

By referring to Tables XII and XIII, it may be seen that by far the most common charge on which children are brought before the county juvenile courts is larceny, making up 31.7 per cent of all delinquency charges. Approximately 10 per cent more Negro children are brought before the juvenile courts for larceny than white children. By comparing the sexes, we find that about 9 per cent more Negro boys are up for larceny than white boys, but about three and one-half times as many Negro girls as white girls for the same offense. The next most common offense in order of frequency is *delinquency*—a blanket term which may mean anything in the category of juvenile offenses—comprising 10.1 per cent of all charges. Breaking and entering comes next with 9 per cent, and it is almost altogether a boys' offense—the white boys exceeding the Negro boys in this respect. Fighting is fourth, with 8.7 per cent, but here there is considerable variation in race and sex distribution. Nearly twice as high a proportion of Negro children are charged with fighting as white children, 11.5 per cent as compared with 6.4 per cent. The Negro girls, strange to say, lead them all in fighting, having over twice as high a proportion as Negro boys, over three times as high as white boys, and six times as high as white girls. One-fifth of all Negro girls were before the county juvenile courts on the charge of fighting. The Negro children again lead in assault with deadly weapon, exceeding the white children by two to one. On the other hand, the white children lead in injury to property, having about two and one-half times as high a proportion as the Negro children. From three to five times as high a proportion of girls are beyond parental control as boys.

Immorality, or sex offenses, comprise only 2.2 per cent of the total charges, but there is the widest variation in distribution according to race and sex.[9] As for race differences, white children are up for sex offenses in 3.1 per cent of their cases, while only 1 per cent of Negro children are charged with immorality. Of all the white girls appearing before the county juvenile courts, 23.7 per cent were charged with immorality, while only 5.8 per cent of the Negro girls were up for sex offenses. These figures, however, are so much at variance with the experience of both white and Negro social workers in North Carolina, and so contrary to the figures on illegitimacy among the whites and the Negroes in the state, that they deserve some detailed consideration. In the first place, just as there is a dual standard of morality for boys and girls, there is a dual standard of morality for the whites and the Negroes. The juvenile court judges are *white* officials, and consequently regard a

---

[9] Sex offenses of boys are practically never brought to the attention of the juvenile court—only one-half of one per cent of white boys, and one-tenth of one per cent of Negro boys appearing on this charge.

sex offense by a white girl far more seriously than a similar offense by a Negro girl. Many white people, among them court-house officials, hold the view that practically all Negro girls are sexually delinquent, and if a judge of a juvenile court began hearing cases of this sort he would be swamped with work. The writer recalls a number of years ago visiting a certain county in North Carolina for the purpose of interview-ing, on behalf of the State Board of Charities and Public Welfare, a man who had applied for the position of county superintendent of public welfare. This man was asked among other things whether there was much juvenile delinquency in his county. He replied that there was practically none among the white girls. Of course, there were some white boys, he said, who had sex relations with the Negro girls, but "it was a good thing, because it protected the white girls." Then, too, it must be considered that there is a well-equipped institution to which white delinquent girl sex offenders can be committed, while the institution for the same type of Negro girl is so small and poorly equipped as to be entirely inadequate.

A third possible explanation why so few sexually delinquent Negro girls come to the attention of the juvenile court is that Negroes have had such a hard time getting justice in the white man's adult criminal court, that they refuse to report their delinquent children to the white man's juvenile court. It is perhaps true, therefore, that the great majority of immoral Negro girls never get to the juvenile court, while most of the sexually delinquent white girls, known to the community as such, are promptly haled before this tribunal.

Summarizing the social differences in types of charge, we see that the Negro children exceed the white children in larceny, fighting, and assault with deadly weapon, while the white chil-dren exceed the Negro children in such charges as delinquency, breaking and entering, nuisance and disorderly, truancy, injury to property, beyond parental control, trespass, immorality, violation of the liquor law, and drunkenness. Table XII shows the race and sex distribution for each charge, although in in-terpreting this table it should be kept in mind that the white children have a higher representation among the delinquents,

55.9 per cent, as compared with 44.1 per cent among the Negroes.

DISPOSITION OF DELINQUENCY CASES

With regard to the disposition of the delinquency cases handled by the county juvenile courts in North Carolina, as presented in Tables XV, XVI, and XVII, it is seen that more than two-fifths of the cases, 42.9 per cent were placed on probation, and that the proportion of Negro children so handled slightly exceeded that of the white children. Next in order of frequency comes commitment to institutions for delinquents, comprising a little over one-seventh of all dispositions, or 14.7 per cent. Here, however, the proportion of white children so disposed of is more than twice as high as that of the Negro children, or 19.9 per cent, as compared with 8.1 per cent. There is a simple explanation for this—namely, the great difference in institutional facilities for white and for Negro juvenile delinquents. This would not explain, however, why 43.1 per cent of white girls were sent to institutions, as compared with only 16.8 per cent of the white boys. The answer to this probably lies in the fact that such a high percentage of the white delinquent girls are sex offenders, which is usually regarded as of such serious consequence as to require institutional care, while boys who have been brought before the juvenile courts for larceny—especially first offenders—are regarded as fit subjects for probation. About one-seventh of the cases are dismissed, with the Negro children slightly in the majority for this type of disposition. Each of the remaining types of disposition represent a comparatively small proportion of the total, but there are some important differences according to race and sex distribution. For instance, 5.5 per cent of the Negro children were placed in foster homes, while only 1.9 per cent of white children were disposed of in this way—perhaps, again a reflection of the difference in institutional facilities for the two races.

There are several types of disposition of cases of delinquent children by the county juvenile courts of North Carolina, which are altogether foreign to the spirit of the juvenile court, and contrary to the recognized standards of juvenile court procedure, namely, such dispositions as, fine and cost, placing in jail, county home, or workhouse, or having the child whipped by its parents or by a public officer. Such methods of handling children should be abandoned. Where a child has stolen or damaged property, he should, if possible, be required to earn through his own efforts enough money to pay the owner for the stolen or damaged article. Such treatment has character building qualities. But where a fine and cost order is made, the fine is usually paid by the child's father and the money goes to the county school fund. In such case the delinquent child is not benefitted and all too frequently the money paid as a fine is badly needed by the other members of the delinquent's family for food and clothing. Twenty-one counties of North Carolina sent white children to jail, and twenty-five counties sent Negro children to jail. This is legal, provided the child is kept apart from adult criminals, but it is wholly unnecessary, except in rare instances, and has a most demoralizing effect upon the child's personality, for it brands him with the inevitable stigma of jail confinement. Eighty-eight white children and one hundred forty Negro children were sent to jail by the county juvenile courts from 1919-1929. Twenty-two of these children were girls, four white and eighteen Negro. Ten counties sent delinquent white children as well as delinquent Negro children to the county home, where the dangers of moral contamination are almost as great as in the county jail. It should be possible to keep any of these children, except those suffering from venereal diseases, in private homes at the expense of the county, if they must be removed from their own homes.

The most unnecessary, and brutalizing, type of disposition of delinquent children is to order them whipped. During the ten year period, white children were whipped in seven counties, while in twenty-two counties Negro children were whipped. In all, one hundred and fifty-nine children were whipped, twenty-five white and one hundred and thirty-four Negro children. One was a white girl and fourteen were Negro girls. There is a widespread feeling among the county juvenile court judges that

13

whipping is the most effective way of handling delinquent Negro boys. One county welfare officer coming from one of the larger cities of North Carolina told the writer (July, 1932) that he sends his delinquent Negro boys downstairs with a big police officer and has them flogged. On July 22, 1932, there appeared also in the *News and Observer* an account from one of the eastern counties of North Carolina of three Negro boys, all under age, who "were found guilty of breaking into the residence of ————— and stealing over a hundred dollars worth of family silver, jewelry, clothing and money. Due to the boys' age, they were ordered publicly whipped, rather than sentenced to a reformatory. A Negro girl . . . connected with the robbery, was sent to the county farm."

Under the Constitution of North Carolina, 1868 (Art. II, Sec. 1) corporal punishment was removed from the statute books of the state. If it is unconstitutional, therefore, to punish an adult in a criminal court by whipping, it would appear that it would be equally unlawful to administer such discipline to a child in the juvenile court, which is a branch of the Superior Court. In fact, two rulings have been secured from the State Attorney General relative to the whipping of children under authority of the juvenile court. On April 13, 1923, the Attorney General was asked by the Commissioner of Public Welfare—"Does the judge of a juvenile court have authority to order a child to be flogged by the police, and if so, under what conditions?" The Attorney General replied as follows: "To this we answer emphatically *No*. . . . The Juvenile Court Act is based upon the fundamental idea that the proceedings allowed therein are not for the punishment of the delinquent child, but for his protection and training. It is the State acting as a parent when dealing with them. We are very clear, then, that these courts should never in any instance require these delinquents to be punished by flogging, administered by a police officer." To the other question put to the Attorney General, May 27, 1921, whether the juvenile court could order a parent to flog a delinquent child in the presence of the court, the reply was that if the juvenile court had this authority it would be more honored in the breach than in the observance, for the parent "would accomplish more by administering the punishment privately than he would by outraging the sense of justice of this little irresponsible Arab by a thrashing in public." To whip girls of either race is a relic of our barbaric past when we branded felons with a red hot iron, and nailed their ears to a pillory. To whip delinquent Negro boys, but not the white, is racial discrimination of the grossest kind. Whipping of delinquents has no place in our civilization.

DISPOSITION OF DEPENDENT AND NEGLECTED CHILDREN

Since there are only two Negro orphan homes in North Carolina—a state institution (Oxford Colored Orphanage) and a county institution (Memorial Industrial School near Winston-Salem)—it may readily be understood why such a small proportion of the dependent and neglected Negro children, 9.4 per cent, are cared for in institutions (see Tables XVII, XVIII, XIX, XX, and why more than half of them, 52.6 per cent, are placed in foster homes, and 9 per cent more in homes of relatives.[10] A little over a fourth of the white dependent and neglected children (27.3 per cent) were placed in foster homes, an additional 7.8 per cent were placed with relatives, and 23.6 per cent were sent to institutions. About one-tenth of the white children (10.1 per cent) were committed to the Greensboro Children's Home Society for placement in free foster homes for adoption. There is no comparable state home placing society for the Negro children.

In the final table, Table XXI, is presented the number of cases of delinquent, dependent and neglected children before the county juvenile courts of North Carolina, 1919-1929, by county, race and sex, together with the number of cases dis-

---

[10] It was quite difficult in many cases to determine whether the child placed in a foster home was placed with relatives. If the record stated the relationship, or if the foster parents had the same name as the child, the child was listed as being placed with relatives. It is quite probable, however, that many cases listed as placed in foster homes should be listed as placed with relatives—but there was no way to check the relationship.

carded for each county because of incomplete records. Among the more significant facts set forth here might be listed the concentration of Negro children's cases in the counties of Mecklenburg, Forsyth, Wayne, and Pitt. It is also of interest to note that thirteen counties listed no cases of delinquent Negro children, and forty-six counties listed no dependent and neglected Negro children, during the entire ten year period.

TABLE VIII

CASES BEFORE THE COUNTY JUVENILE COURTS OF NORTH CAROLINA, 1919-1929, BY TYPE OF JURISDICTION

Classes	Number	Per Cent Distribution
Delinquent	18,059	77.0
Dependent and Neglected	4,998	21.3
Disputed Custody	129	.6
Miscellaneous	257	1.1
Total	23,443	100.0

TABLE IX

CASES BEFORE THE COUNTY JUVENILE COURTS OF NORTH CAROLINA, 1919-1929, BY RACE AND SEX

Race and Sex	Number	Per Cent Distribution
White	14,285	61.0
Boys	11,058	47.2
Girls	3,227	13.8
Negro	9,158	39.0
Boys	7,412	31.6
Girls	1,746	7.4
Total	23,443	100.0

TABLE X

Cases Before the County Juvenile Courts of North Carolina, 1919-1929, By Race, Sex, and Type of Jurisdiction

Classes of Children	Number				Per Cent			
	White Boys	Negro Boys	White Girls	Negro Girls	White Boys	Negro Boys	White Girls	Negro Girls
Delinquent	8,942	6,742	1,159	1,216	80.9	91.0	35.9	69.6
Dependent and Neglected	1,945	626	1,934	493	17.6	8.4	59.9	28.2
Disputed Custody	54	20	33	22	.5	.3	1.1	1.3
Miscellaneous ..	117	24	101	15	1.0	.3	3.1	.9
Total	11,058	7,412	3,227	1,746	100.0	100.0	100.0	100.0

TABLE XI

Per Cent Distribution of Cases Before the County Juvenile Courts of North Carolina 1919-1929, by Type of Jurisdiction, Race and Sex

	Delinquent	Dependent and Neglected	Custody Disputed	Miscellaneous
White	55.9	77.6	67.4	84.8
Boys	49.5	38.9	41.8	45.5
Girls	6.4	38.7	25.6	39.3
Negro	44.1	22.4	32.6	15.2
Boys	37.3	12.5	15.5	9.3
Girls	6.8	9.9	17.1	5.9

TABLE XII

DELINQUENCY CASES BEFORE THE COUNTY JUVENILE COURTS OF NORTH
CAROLINA, 1919-1929, BY RACE, SEX, AND CHARGE

Charge	Total Cases	Total	White Male	Female	Negro Total	Male	Female
Larceny	5,722	2,770	2,684	86	2,952	2,647	305
Delinquency	1,818	1,266	924	342	552	413	139
Breaking and Entering	1,619	1,035	1,025	10	584	563	21
Fighting	1,563	644	603	41	919	669	250
Nuisance & Disorderly	1,154	703	639	64	451	384	67
Truancy	1,078	614	510	104	464	395	69
Injury to Property	719	540	527	13	179	165	14
Beyond P't'l Control	566	362	261	101	204	105	99
Assault Deadly W'p'n	522	200	195	5	322	266	56
Trespass	405	256	252	4	149	139	10
Immorality	400	318	43	275	82	12	70
Violation Probation	355	153	144	9	202	174	28
Larceny of Auto	340	177	177	0	163	157	6
Runaway	297	168	122	46	129	85	44
Viol. Liquor Law	192	130	125	5	62	55	7
Viol. Traffic Ord	184	132	128	4	52	52	0
Forgery	163	104	93	11	59	52	7
Car. Concealed W'p'n	154	85	83	2	69	68	1
Viol. City Ord	154	67	66	1	87	86	1
Gambling	126	75	75	0	51	50	1
Drunkenness	104	86	79	7	18	14	4
Other Burning	41	24	21	3	17	17	0
Attempted Rape	37	16	16	0	21	21	0
Robbery	29	16	16	0	13	12	1
Burglary	17	6	6	0	11	11	0
Murder	12	4	4	0	8	7	1
Manslaughter	12	7	7	0	5	4	1
Rape	12	4	4	0	8	8	0
Crime vs. Nature	10	7	7	0	3	3	0
Arson	9	2	2	0	7	6	1
Incest	6	6	0	6	0	0	0
Miscellaneous	239	124	104	20	115	102	13
Total	18,059	10,101	8,942	1,159	7,958	6,742	1,216

TABLE XIII

PER CENT DISTRIBUTION OF DELINQUENCY CASES BEFORE THE COUNTY JUVE-
NILE COURTS OF NORTH CAROLINA, 1919-1929, BY CHARGE, FOR EACH
RACE AND SEX

Charge	Total Cases	Total	White Male	Female	Negro Total	Male	Female
Larceny	31.7	27.4	30.0	7.4	37.1	39.2	25.1
Delinquency	10.1	12.5	10.3	29.6	6.9	6.1	11.4
Breaking and Entering	9.0	10.2	11.4	.9	7.3	8.4	1.7
Fighting	8.7	6.4	6.7	3.5	11.5	9.9	20.6
Nuisance & Disorderly	6.4	7.0	7.1	5.6	5.7	5.7	5.5
Truancy	6.0	6.1	5.7	9.0	5.8	5.9	5.7
Injury to Property..	4.0	5.3	5.9	1.1	2.2	2.4	1.2
Beyond P't'l Control.	3.1	3.6	2.9	8.7	2.6	1.6	8.1
Assault Deadly W'p'n	2.9	2.0	2.2	.4	4.0	3.9	4.6
Trespass	2.2	2.5	2.8	.3	1.9	2.1	.8
Immorality	2.2	3.1	.5	23.7	1.0	.2	5.8
Violation Probation..	2.0	1.5	1.6	.8	2.5	2.6	2.3
Larceny of Auto....	1.9	1.8	2.0	..	2.0	2.3	.5
Runaway	1.6	1.7	1.4	4.0	1.6	1.3	3.6
Viol. Liquor Law....	1.1	1.3	1.4	.4	.8	.8	.6
Viol. Traffic Ord.....	1.0	1.3	1.4	.3	.7	.8	..
Forgery	.9	1.0	1.0	.9	.7	.8	.6
Car. Concealed W'p'n	.9	.9	.9	.2	.9	1.0	*
Viol. City Ord.	.9	.7	.7	.1	1.1	1.3	*
Gambling	.7	.7	.8	..	.6	.7	*
Drunkenness	.6	.9	.9	.6	.2	.2	.3
Other Burning	.2	.2	.2	.3	.2	.3	..
Attempted Rape	.2	.2	.2	..	.3	.3	..
Robbery	.2	.2	.2	..	.2	.2	*
Burglary	.1	*	*	..	.1	.2	..
Murder	*	*	*	..	.1	.1	*
Manslaughter	*	*	*	..	*	*	*
Rape	*	*	*	..	.1	.1	..
Crime vs. Nature....	*	*	*	..	*	*	..
Arson	*	*	*	..	.1	.1	*
Incest	*	*	..	.5	..	..	..
Miscellaneous	1.3	1.2	1.2	1.7	1.4	1.5	1.1

* Less than one-tenth of one per cent.

TABLE XIV

Per Cent Distribution of Delinquency Cases Before the County Juvenile Courts of North Carolina, 1919-1929, by Race and Sex,
for Each Charge

Charge	Total	White Male	Female	Negro Total	Male	Female
Larceny 100.0	48.4	46.9	1.5	51.6	46.3	5.3
Delinquency 100.0	69.6	50.8	18.8	30.4	22.7	7.7
Breaking and Entering 100.0	63.9	63.3	.6	36.1	34.8	1.3
Fighting 100.0	41.2	38.6	2.6	58.8	42.8	16.0
Nuisance & Disorderly 100.0	60.9	55.4	5.5	39.1	33.3	5.8
Truancy 100.0	57.0	43.3	13.7	43.0	36.6	6.4
Injury to Property.. 100.0	75.1	73.3	1.8	24.9	22.9	2.0
Beyond P't'l Control. 100.0	64.0	46.1	17.9	36.0	18.6	17.4
Assault Deadly W'p'n 100.0	38.3	37.4	.9	61.7	51.0	10.7
Trespass 100.0	63.2	62.2	1.0	36.8	34.3	2.5
Immorality 100.0	79.5	10.7	68.8	20.5	3.0	17.5
Violation Probation.. 100.0	43.1	40.6	2.5	56.9	49.0	7.9
Larceny of Auto..... 100.0	52.1	52.1	...	47.9	46.2	1.7
Runaway 100.0	56.6	41.1	15.5	43.4	28.6	14.8
Viol. Liquor Law.... 100.0	67.7	65.1	2.6	32.3	28.6	3.7
Viol. Traffic Ord..... 100.0	71.7	69.6	2.1	28.3	28.3	...
Forgery 100.0	63.8	57.1	6.7	36.2	31.9	4.3
Car. Concealed W'p'n 100.0	55.2	53.9	1.3	44.8	44.2	.6
Viol. City Ord....... 100.0	43.5	42.9	.6	56.5	55.9	.6
Gambling 100.0	59.5	59.5	...	40.5	39.7	.8
Drunkenness 100.0	82.7	76.3	6.4	17.3	13.5	3.8
Other Burning 100.0	58.5	51.2	7.3	41.5	41.5	...
Attempted Rape 100.0	43.2	43.2	...	56.8	56.8	...
Robbery 100.0	55.2	55.2	...	44.8	41.4	3.4
Burglary 100.0	35.3	35.3	...	64.7	64.7	...
Murder 100.0	33.3	33.3	...	66.7	58.3	8.4
Manslaughter 100.0	58.3	58.3	...	41.7	33.3	8.4
Rape 100.0	33.3	33.3	...	66.7	66.7	...
Crime vs. Nature.... 100.0	70.0	70.0	...	30.0	30.0	...
Arson 100.0	22.2	22.2	...	77.8	66.7	11.1
Incest 100.0	100.0	...	100.0	...	...	...
Miscellaneous 100.0	51.9	43.5	8.4	48.1	42.7	5.4
Total 100.0	55.9	49.5	6.4	44.1	37.3	6.8

TABLE XV

DISPOSITION OF DELINQUENCY CASES BEFORE THE COUNTY JUVENILE COURTS OF NORTH CAROLINA, 1919-1929, BY RACE AND SEX

Disposition	Total	Total	White Male	Female	Negro Total	Male	Female
Probation	7,753	4,301	4,051	250	3,452	2,941	511
Placed in Institution.	2,649	2,006	1,506	500	643	579	64
Dismissed	2,525	1,295	1,203	92	1,230	1,002	228
Restitution or Dam'g's	765	388	382	6	377	323	54
No Disposition	677	482	415	67	195	165	30
Placed in Foster Home	634	195	153	42	439	374	65
Pending	615	327	280	47	288	226	62
Returned Home	559	355	293	62	204	166	38
Fine and Cost	515	320	277	43	195	173	22
Placed in Detention..	278	121	102	19	157	116	41
Placed in Jail	228	88	84	4	140	122	18
Placed with Relatives	183	63	57	6	120	95	25
Sent to County Home	173	30	22	8	143	132	11
Whipped	159	25	24	1	134	120	14
Sent to Higher Court	129	54	53	1	75	68	7
Punished by Parents.	126	20	11	9	106	101	5
Sent to Work House.	34	10	10	0	24	22	2
Sent to Another County	21	11	11	0	10	9	1
Hired Out	10	2	0	2	8	7	1
Other Disposition	26	8	8	0	18	1	17
Total	18,059	10,101	8,942	1,159	7,958	6,742	1,216

TABLE XVI

PER CENT DISTRIBUTION, ACCORDING TO DISPOSITION, OF DELINQUENCY CASES
BEFORE THE COUNTY JUVENILE COURTS OF NORTH CAROLINA 1919-1929,
FOR EACH RACE AND SEX

Disposition	Total	Total	White Male	Female	Negro Total	Male	Female
Probation	42.9	42.6	45.3	21.6	43.4	43.6	42.0
Placed in Institution.	14.7	19.9	16.8	43.1	8.1	8.6	5.3
Dismissed	14.0	12.8	13.5	7.9	15.5	14.9	18.8
Restitution or Dam'g's	4.2	3.8	4.3	.5	4.7	4.8	4.4
No Disposition	3.7	4.8	4.6	5.8	2.5	2.4	2.5
Placed in Foster Homes	3.5	1.9	1.7	3.6	5.5	5.5	5.3
Pending	3.4	3.2	3.1	4.1	3.6	3.4	5.1
Returned Home	3.1	3.5	3.3	5.3	2.6	2.5	3.1
Fine and Cost	2.9	3.2	3.1	3.7	2.5	2.6	1.8
Placed in Detention..	1.5	1.2	1.1	1.6	2.0	1.7	3.4
Placed in Jail.......	1.3	.9	.9	.3	1.8	1.8	1.5
Placed with Relatives	1.0	.6	.6	.5	1.5	1.4	2.1
Sent to County Home	1.0	.3	.2	.7	1.8	2.0	.8
Whipped	.9	.2	.3	.1	1.7	1.8	1.2
Sent to Higher Court	.7	.5	.6	.1	.9	1.0	.6
Punished by Parents.	.7	.2	.1	.8	1.3	1.5	.4
Sent to Work House.	.2	.1	.1	..	.3	.3	.2
Sent to Another County	.1	.1	.1	..	.1	.1	.1
Hired Out	*	*	..	.2	.1	.1	.1
Other Disposition....	.1	*	.1	..	.2	*	1.4

* Less than one-tenth of one per cent.

TABLE XVII

PER CENT DISTRIBUTION OF DELINQUENCY CASES BEFORE THE COUNTY JUVE-
NILE COURTS OF NORTH CAROLINA 1919-1929, BY RACE AND SEX,
FOR EACH TYPE OF DISPOSITION

Disposition	Total	White			Negro		
		Total	Male	Female	Total	Male	Female
Probation	100.0	55.5	52.2	3.3	44.5	37.9	6.6
Placed in Institution.	100.0	75.7	56.9	18.8	24.3	21.9	2.4
Dismissed	100.0	51.3	47.6	3.7	48.7	39.7	9.0
Restitution or Dam'g's	100.0	50.7	49.9	.8	49.3	42.2	7.1
No Disposition	100.0	71.2	61.3	9.9	28.8	24.4	4.4
Placed in Foster Home	100.0	30.8	24.1	6.7	69.2	59.0	10.2
Pending	100.0	53.2	45.5	7.7	46.8	36.7	10.1
Returned Home	100.0	63.5	52.4	11.1	36.5	29.7	6.8
Fine and Cost.......	100.0	62.1	53.8	8.3	37.9	33.6	4.3
Placed in Detention..	100.0	43.5	36.7	6.8	56.5	41.7	14.8
Placed in Jail.......	100.0	38.6	36.8	1.8	61.4	53.5	7.9
Placed with Relatives	100.0	34.4	31.1	3.3	65.6	51.9	13.7
Sent to County Home	100.0	17.3	12.7	4.6	82.7	76.3	6.4
Whipped	100.0	15.7	15.1	.6	84.3	75.5	8.8
Sent to Higher Court	100.0	41.9	41.1	.8	58.1	52.7	5.4
Punished by Parents.	100.0	15.9	8.7	7.2	84.1	80.2	3.9
Sent to Work House.	100.0	29.4	29.4	...	70.6	64.8	5.8
Sent to Another County	100.0	52.4	52.4	...	47.6	42.9	4.7
Hired Out	100.0	20.0	...	20.0	80.0	70.0	10.0
Other Disposition ...	100.0	30.8	30.8	...	69.2	65.4	3.8
	100.0	55.9	49.5	6.4	44.1	37.3	6.8

TABLE XVIII

DISPOSITION OF DEPENDENCY AND NEGLECT CASES BEFORE THE COUNTY JUVE-
NILE COURTS OF NORTH CAROLINA, 1919-1929, BY RACE AND SEX

Disposition	Total	Total	White Male	Female	Total	Negro Male	Female
Placed in Foster Home	1,769	1,137	587	550	632	344	288
Placed in Institution	1,102	989	490	499	113	65	48
Returned Home	763	573	277	296	190	106	84
No Disposition	607	502	266	236	105	57	48
Placed with Relatives	435	327	162	165	108	68	40
Greensboro Children's Home Society	426	423	226	197	3	3	0
Continued	95	69	27	42	26	10	16
County Home (Temporary)	49	41	23	18	8	5	3
Sent to Another County	45	40	21	19	5	5	0
Sent to Detent'n Home	39	35	21	14	4	4	0
Other Disposition....	54	48	16	32	6	3	3
Total	5,384	4,184	2,116	2,068	1,200	670	530

TABLE XIX

Per Cent Distribution, According to Disposition of Dependency and Neglect Cases Before the County Juvenile Courts of North Carolina, 1919-1929, for Each Race and Sex

Disposition	Total	White			Negro		
		Total	Male	Female	Total	Male	Female
Placed in Foster Home	32.8	27.3	27.7	26.6	52.6	51.4	54.3
Placed in Institution.	20.5	23.6	23.2	24.1	9.4	9.7	9.1
Returned Home	14.2	13.7	13.1	14.3	15.8	15.9	15.8
No Disposition	11.3	12.0	12.5	11.4	8.8	8.5	9.1
Placed with Relatives	8.1	7.8	7.7	8.0	9.0	10.2	7.5
Greensboro Children's Home Society	7.9	10.1	10.6	9.5	.3	.4	...
Continued	1.8	1.6	1.3	2.1	2.2	1.5	3.0
County Home (Temporary)	.9	1.0	1.1	.9	.7	.7	.6
Sent to Another County	.8	1.0	1.0	.9	.4	.7	...
Sent to Detention Home	.7	.8	1.0	.7	.3	.6	...
Other Disposition	1.0	1.1	.8	1.5	.5	.4	.6
Total	100.0	100.0	100.0	100.0	100.0	100.0	100.0

TABLE XX

Per Cent Distribution of Dependency and Neglect Cases Before the County Juvenile Courts of North Carolina, 1919-1929, by Race and Sex, for Each Type of Disposition

Disposition	Total	White			Negro		
		Total	Male	Female	Total	Male	Female
Placed in Foster Home	100.0	64.3	33.2	31.1	35.7	19.4	16.3
Placed in Institution.	100.0	89.7	44.5	45.2	10.3	5.9	4.4
Returned Home	100.0	75.1	36.3	38.8	24.9	13.9	11.0
No Disposition	100.0	82.7	43.8	38.9	17.3	9.4	7.9
Placed with Relatives	100.0	75.2	37.2	38.0	24.8	15.6	9.2
Greensboro Children's Home Society	100.0	99.3	53.1	46.2	.7	.7	...
Continued	100.0	72.6	28.4	44.2	27.4	10.5	16.9
County Home (Temporary)	100.0	83.7	46.9	36.8	16.3	10.2	6.1
Sent to Another County	100.0	88.9	46.7	42.2	11.1	11.1	...
Sent to Detent'n Home	100.0	89.7	53.8	35.9	10.3	10.3	...
Other Disposition....	100.0	88.9	29.6	59.3	11.1	5.55	5.55
Total	100.0	77.7	39.3	38.4	22.3	12.5	9.8

TABLE XXI

Cases of Delinquency, Dependency and Neglect Before the County Juvenile Courts of North Carolina, 1919-1929, by County, Race and Sex

County	Delinquent							Dependent and Neglected							Incomplete	
	White Boys	White Girls	Negro Boys	Negro Girls	Indian Boys	Indian Girls	Total	White Boys	White Girls	Negro Boys	Negro Girls	Indian Boys	Indian Girls	Total	Total	Cards Not Counted
Alamance	145	18	52	6	0	0	221	29	43	5	4	0	0	81	14
Alexander	36	9	3	1	0	0	49	3	3	1	3	0	0	10	7
Alleghany	3	1	0	0	0	0	4	0	1	0	0	0	0	1	1
Anson	33	5	83	9	0	0	130	0	0	2	4	0	0	6	8
Ashe	12	3	0	0	0	0	15	4	0	0	0	0	0	4	1
Avery	29	11	0	0	0	0	40	0	2	0	0	0	0	2	10
Beaufort	0	0	0	0	0	0	0	0	0	0	0	0	0	0	0
Bertie	5	3	28	3	0	0	39	0	0	0	1	0	0	1	0
Bladen	0	0	0	0	0	0	0	0	0	0	0	0	0	0	0
Brunswick	73	4	42	3	0	0	122	13	16	2	0	0	0	31	11
Buncombe	944	114	540	104	0	0	1,702	390	380	39	27	0	0	836	102
Burke	0	0	0	0	0	0	0	0	0	0	0	0	0	0	0
Cabarrus	94	15	38	2	0	0	149	5	11	3	0	0	0	19	89
Caldwell......	103	6	21	0	0	0	130	6	8	1	0	0	0	15	19
Camden........	4	0	4	1	0	0	9	0	0	0	0	0	0	0	1
Carteret	42	0	27	1	0	0	70	0	1	0	0	0	0	1	8

County															
Caswell	3	2	7	0	0	0	12	0	2	1	2	0	0	5	1
Catawba	64	13	9	3	0	0	89	29	32	3	0	0	0	64	52
Chatham	6	0	2	0	0	0	8	0	1	0	0	0	0	1	2
Cherokee	16	8	0	0	0	0	24	4	3	0	0	0	0	7	3
Chowan	11	5	30	1	0	0	47	0	0	0	0	0	0	0	1
Clay	16	5	3	0	0	0	24	7	4	0	0	0	0	11	10
Cleveland	41	2	21	7	0	0	71	3	6	0	0	0	0	9	3
Columbus	95	9	29	0	0	0	133	16	15	9	3	0	0	43	4
Craven	42	16	48	7	0	0	113	29	40	12	0	0	0	81	0
Cumberland	173	35	234	15	0	0	457	65	79	25	28	0	0	197	0
Currituck	3	4	6	0	0	0	13	0	0	0	0	0	0	0	0
Dare	0	0	0	0	0	0	0	0	0	0	0	0	0	0	0
Davidson	44	13	4	0	0	0	61	9	6	0	0	0	0	15	5
Davie	29	9	23	5	0	0	66	10	11	4	7	0	0	32	6
Duplin	37	3	16	2	0	0	58	23	27	2	1	0	0	53	16
Durham	90	18	120	26	0	0	254	20	33	32	18	0	0	103	16
Edgecombe															
Forsyth	499	92	1,162	298	0	0	2,051	109	91	50	35	0	0	285	68
Franklin	35	3	37	7	0	0	82	21	9	21	10	0	0	61	13
Gaston	334	60	58	11	0	0	463	133	80	16	8	0	0	237	58
Gates	5	0	12	0	0	0	17	1	0	0	0	0	0	1	0
Graham	20	0	0	0	0	0	20	3	2	0	0	0	0	5	3
Granville	8	0	15	2	0	0	25	2	0	1	0	0	0	3	3
Green	2	2	3	0	0	0	7	0	0	2	2	0	0	4	0
Guilford	543	67	346	69	0	0	1,025	112	106	23	20	0	0	261	44
Halifax	11	3	8	2	0	0	24	3	3	2	0	0	0	8	7

County	Delinquent White Boys	White Girls	Negro Boys	Negro Girls	Indian Boys	Indian Girls	Total	Dependent and Neglected White Boys	White Girls	Negro Boys	Negro Girls	Indian Boys	Indian Girls	Incomplete Total	Cards Not Counted
Harnett	193	68	46	15	1	2	320	42	34	5	5	0	0	86	64
Haywood	122	7	30	2	0	0	161	13	13	0	0	0	0	26	13
Henderson	37	3	1	1	0	0	42	2	0	0	0	0	0	2	1
Hertford	11	1	26	3	0	0	41	1	1	1	0	0	0	3	22
Hoke	18	2	7	1	0	0	28	5	6	15	4	0	0	30	3
Hyde	2	1	7	0	0	0	10	1	0	0	0	0	0	1	0
Iredell	39	7	21	0	0	0	67	29	31	6	4	0	0	70	14
Jackson	52	5	6	0	0	0	63	3	3	0	0	0	0	6	32
Johnston	63	17	64	7	0	0	151	54	56	9	11	0	0	130	3
Jones	11	0	7	0	0	0	18	11	10	1	7	0	0	29	2
Lee	25	2	2	0	0	0	29	3	0	0	0	0	0	3	5
Lenoir	78	17	99	14	0	0	208	36	42	29	20	0	0	127	3
Lincoln	0	0	0	0	0	0	0	0	0	0	0	0	0	0	0
McDowell	62	4	5	0	0	0	71	9	4	0	0	0	0	13	6
Macon	44	1	0	0	0	0	45	15	14	0	0	0	0	29	1
Madison	31	1	0	0	0	0	32	1	1	0	0	0	0	2	5
Martin	0	0	2	0	0	0	2	0	1	0	0	0	0	1	4
Mecklenburg	1,448	111	1,226	322	0	0	3,107	243	262	78	97	0	0	680	145

County															
Mitchell	9	2	0	0	0	0	11	0	0	0	0	0	0	0	0
Montgomery	26	0	5	0	0	0	31	4	7	1	0	0	0	12	0
Moore	6	0	9	0	0	0	15	0	0	0	0	0	0	0	0
Nash	59	6	67	11	0	0	143	9	15	10	4	0	0	38	10
New Hanover	395	34	428	62	0	0	919	24	22	10	8	0	0	64	25
Northampton	3	1	4	1	0	0	9	4	3	0	0	0	0	7	1
Onslow	18	3	15	0	0	0	36	0	0	1	0	0	0	1	1
Orange	49	6	38	9	0	0	97	4	7	2	2	0	0	15	10
Pamlico	5	2	5	0	0	0	12	6	1	0	0	0	0	7	0
Pasquotank	99	6	77	11	0	0	193	2	2	0	0	0	0	4	6
Pender	19	4	16	3	0	0	42	1	7	0	0	0	0	8	1
Perquimans	2	0	46	3	0	0	51	0	0	0	0	0	0	0	1
Person	17	5	22	4	0	0	48	3	3	1	0	0	0	7	4
Pitt	108	33	184	24	0	0	294	55	64	78	65	0	0	262	14
Polk	16	1	3	0	0	0	20	3	8	2	2	0	0	15	2
Randolph	39	7	14	1	1	0	61	22	7	0	0	0	0	29	13
Richmond	51	12	71	1	2	0	136	1	7	0	4	0	0	12	7
Robeson	66	21	17	3	0	0	109	13	19	0	1	0	0	33	53
Rockingham	196	21	45	4	0	0	266	60	44	6	3	0	0	113	25
Rowan	240	24	138	20	0	0	417	19	17	9	7	0	0	52	70
Rutherford	184	7	57	1	1	0	249	11	13	1	1	0	1	26	15
Sampson	50	13	32	1	1	0	97	37	27	14	11	4	0	94	5
Scotland	32	2	22	2	0	0	58	1	3	0	0	0	0	4	5
Stanly	47	3	4	0	0	0	54	20	10	0	1	0	0	31	7
Stokes	11	1	8	0	0	0	20	9	9	0	0	0	0	18	0
Surry	107	6	7	0	0	0	120	29	30	0	0	0	0	59	18

14

County	Delinquent							Dependent and Neglected							Incomplete	
	White Boys	White Girls	Negro Boys	Negro Girls	Indian Boys	Indian Girls	Total	White Boys	White Girls	Negro Boys	Negro Girls	Indian Boys	Indian Girls	Total	Total	Cards Not Counted
Swain	44	6	1	0	0	0	51	3	3	0	0	0	0	6	6	8
Transylvania	77	20	10	1	0	0	108	3	4	0	0	0	0	7	7	14
Tyrrell	69	0	30	1	0	0	100	0	0	1	1	0	0	2	2	1
Union	67	5	50	9	0	0	131	20	39	3	1	0	0	63	63	11
Vance	11	3	8	1	0	0	23	2	2	0	0	0	0	4	4	6
Wake	460	59	423	54	0	0	996	78	51	28	22	0	0	179	179	88
Warren	5	1	25	2	0	0	33	0	1	2	3	0	0	6	6	27
Washington	11	2	36	4	0	0	53	0	0	0	0	0	0	0	0	9
Watauga	48	0	1	0	0	0	49	10	5	0	0	0	0	15	15	0
Wayne	195	20	223	31	0	0	469	123	126	90	58	0	0	397	397	36
Wilkes	140	14	9	1	0	0	164	8	6	1	3	0	0	18	18	8
Wilson	61	7	70	1	0	0	139	14	13	10	12	0	0	49	49	44
Yadkin	8	1	1	0	0	0	10	0	0	0	0	0	0	0	0	0
Yancey	11	1	1	0	0	0	13	1	0	0	0	0	0	1	1	3
Totals	8,942	1,159	6,742	1,216	5	2	18,066	2,116	2,068	670	530	4	1	5,389	5,389	1,441

CHAPTER XII

CASE STUDIES OF DELINQUENT NEGRO CHILDREN

CASE STUDY OF A DELINQUENT NEGRO BOY IN RALEIGH, N. C.
WALDO HARPER

Juvenile Court Record.—The Juvenile Court record of this delinquent Negro boy opens with a letter from the County Superintendent of Public Welfare to a white farmer living near Wendell, in the same county. The letter, dated Feb. 16, 1923, is as follows:

"Dear Sir,

I have a colored boy about 10, or 11 years old now, if you can use him. I will have him here in my office tomorrow by 12, or 1 o'clock.

Yours truly,
C. H. A————,
Supt. of Public Welfare."

There is no further record showing the circumstances why the boy came to the attention of the welfare officer, nor what disposition was made of the boy at this time.

July 31, 1923. Waldo was brought into court for stealing bathing caps, for which he was placed on probation in custody of his mother.

May 1, 1924. Waldo was arrested for stealing automobile parts, valued at $15. He was committed to Oxford Orphanage. (The boy ran away from the orphanage a few days after his commitment.)

June 4, 1924. Boy was arrested again for stealing, and was ordered recommitted to Oxford Orphanage, but the order was not carried out.

September 12, 1924. Waldo in court again for stealing money amounting to twenty dollars. He was placed in the country with a relative where he was to work and attend school, but he returned to town about same time as welfare officer.

November 21, 1924. Boy charged with taking a blow pipe through the window of a garage, and he was ordered placed with a private family in the country, but he promptly ran away again.

December 16, 1924. Charged with stealing merchandise from an automobile. He was ordered to remain in county jail until January 1st, pending further orders and disposition. He was finally placed with an uncle in a rural community near Raleigh. After a very short stay he returned home.

January 8, 1925. Waldo arrested for attempting to steal a bicycle. Was committed to Morrison Training School. During the months which followed, Waldo showed a marked improvement, became a grade "A" man, and did splendid work in school. About two years after his commitment, Waldo's mother died, and he was allowed to return home for the funeral. Upon his return to the institution he continued to show an improvement, then suffered a relapse, but was finally paroled August 21, 1929.

Waldo's institutional record at Morrison Training School is presented by the superintendent of that institution in the following report:

"His age was given as 12 years. While his delinquent character was in the making he made his home with his mother, who was looked upon by her community as an indecent woman. Her home it seemed was the hang-out for whiskey drinkers. This boy was the victim of much bad example from some source. He had no faith in the virtue of men or women. He had acquired several very bad habits. The most stubborn were the practice of sodomy and vulgarity. After about six or eight months special work with these stubborn factors he took a turn for the better. He finally broke the habits and learned to despise the very thought of them.

"He liked to do special duties. If his duties gave him the rating of a leader he worked untiringly and without complaint. Most of his associates were boys who delegated their wills to him. He learned, however, to respect their rights through our appeal to the finer manhood of all student officers and group leaders. At first his attitude towards his associates was ruthless and savage. In the end he developed a spirit of genuine sympathy and helpfulness.

"His earlier contacts here with teachers was marked by distrust. He felt that every command was a personal thrust at him personally. Fortunately for all concerned his first teacher here was one who understood his background and needs. She won him thoroughly within 60 days. He expressed in those early days that he had seen but three good teachers in his life. Through this opening he developed a most sane attitude towards all teachers; as for the school, he felt that it was the best home he had ever seen.

"He was dull in books, but learned to respect his obligations to his mother and sisters. His chief interest finally centered around his education. He longed to "get educated" so that he could buy a home for his sisters and mother. His teacher used this point as the motivating lever. The day of his parole was unannounced. One-half hour before he was sent away he was notified that the hour had come. He expressed a keen desire to remain."

1. FAMILY

(a) *Father.*—Lynn Harper, Waldo's father, was born and reared in Fayetteville, North Carolina. He had very little schooling. When quite a young man he came to Raleigh to work and make his home. After a short courtship, which followed the acquaintance in Raleigh, he married Amanda Jones. For a number of years he worked as fireman on the Seaboard railroad, but a few years previous to his death he was a train porter for the same railroad company. It is believed that he changed his work from fireman to the lighter job of porter because of high blood pressure, from which he died about May,

1922. According to all information available he was an honest, hard working man well liked by his fellowmen, a devoted husband and a good father. He was a member of the Fayetteville Street Baptist Church, where he attended regularly. He also belonged to several fraternal orders.

(b) *Father's Family.*—Little is known of Lynn's family except that they were good, hard working country people. His father was a tenant farmer.

(c) *Mother.*—Amanda Jones, Waldo's mother, was one of nineteen children. She was born in Wake County about sixteen miles from Raleigh. The family moved to town when she was quite a young girl. She attended school for several years, after which she secured work as a nurse and housemaid. Later she married Lynn and had several children. After her husband's death it became necessary to place all of the children except two with her relatives. She did laundry work at home and with the help of her brothers and sisters was able to maintain the family. She suffered with asthma and very often it was impossible for her to work. It became necessary for the oldest boy to go to work in order to help the little family. It was also learned from a reliable source that Amanda was loose morally, was a drug addict and drank intoxicating liquor. On September 10, 1926, Amanda died and the children were divided between her two sisters and one brother.

(d) *Mother's Family.*—Little is known of Amanda's family except that her father was at one time a farmer. He moved to Raleigh to work when his children were young. He died about twenty years ago. It is believed by his children that his death was the result of "high blood pressure." He is reported to have been a member of the Baptist Church and a good man. Amanda's mother died about ten years ago from "asthma." She gave birth to nineteen children of whom only seven are living. Cause of the deaths are unknown except in the case of Amanda. It is thought that some of the babies died after living only a few days.

(e) *Children.*—Albert: nine years, attends school regularly and is in the 2nd grade. He looks healthy and is full of life. Is devoted to his twin sister, Alberta, and always wants to be near her.

Alberta: nine years, also goes to school and is in 2nd grade. She looks well, but does not appear as strong as Albert.

Lynn: eleven years, is in 3rd grade. Lives with uncle, John Dover, 613 W. Bragg Street.

Rebecca: thirteen years, is in 3rd grade. Lives with her aunt, Rena Powers, who states that girl does not give a great deal of trouble.

Cleve: nearly sixteen years old, is not in school. He sometimes works as helper to a brick mason. Is not at all tidy. He states that he has no clothes, and has no way of getting any. He, too, has a juvenile court record, which began 12-5-25, when he was found out of school and working on a delivery wagon with the driver. He was continually reprimanded by the court for keeping late hours. Later on, he began staying out all night, and played truant from school.

Waldo (Subject): seventeen years old.

Charlie: about twenty years old. Is sick and unable to work. Charlie's delinquencies began at the age of eleven years when he was charged with giving a seven-year-old boy ammonia and turpentine. He was ordered to report weekly to the probation officer. In less than ten days he was again arrested for stealing tickets from a market but the case was dismissed. Until 2-28-29 he was continually giving trouble. He was an accomplice in the theft of a horse valued at from two to three hundred dollars, for which he was placed on probation and ordered to make restitution. Week after week he failed to report at the office as ordered. If met on the street he gave an excuse which was never plausible. If given a job in a store he would take cake and candy. Wasted lots of time when sent on errands. The Juvenile Court Record shows that Charlie did not report over once or twice while on probation and ran away from every home where he was placed. Seven months passed without the probation officer seeing him or knowing his whereabouts. He came to the funeral of his mother and decided to remain for the Christmas holidays. In an interview with him it was brought out that he had been working in the country for a man who had been feeding him, clothing him and giving him spending money with a promise of fifty dollars when the crop was sold. After the Christmas holidays Charlie did not return to the country, stating that he decided to remain in town and work. Last heard of him by the worker from the Juvenile Court, he was working as helper to a brick mason. During this time he was attending Wake County Clinic for treatment of syphilis.

2. Developmental History

Waldo's aunt, Mary Dover, with whom he is now living, states there was a normal pregnancy and birth and that his mother was attended by a mid-wife. Waldo was healthy but had the common diseases of children such a whooping cough, measles, etc. She stated that at about the age of nine years Waldo fell down on the railroad track injuring his neck. This accident "brought on meningitis from which he almost died." His mother before her death, is reported to have told the welfare officer that Waldo's mind had never been right since his attack of meningitis.

3. Home Influences and Neighborhood Conditions (Present)

For the last three years the five children have lived with their aunt, Mrs. Mary Dover, at 613 West North Street. The house in which they live is a two story, two family frame structure. The paved street in front of the house, on which there is a car line, is one of the main thoroughfares leading to a white residential section. The community in which the family lives is composed mostly of one story frame cottages and a few places of business such as a filling station, two or three cafes (including Mary Dover's), two grocery stores, a pool room, two barber shops and a pressing club. Most of the houses have little if any front yard as they are built near the sidewalk. The backyards are fairly large and a few, including Mary Dover's, appear to be used to catch cast-away clothing, cans and other rubbish. There is an old unoccupied school house on the corner nearest to the Dover residence where the neighborhood children play. It has been reported from a very reliable source that this place at night is used as a headquarters for all kinds of vice, for sale of liquor and for immoral purposes.

There are at present living in the seven rooms twelve people, eight making up the family and four being roomers. Waldo and his two youngest brothers sleep in the room which was formerly the kitchen. The only furniture beside the bed is an old safe. Charlie sleeps with one of the roomers upstairs. Two of Mary Dover's nephews have a room together. A woman and her five-year-old child, and a transient, occupying a room alone, make up the other roomers.

The Dover's cafe, which is three doors from the house, is where all the meals are cooked and eaten. And when not out playing the children spend their time there. On winter nights the children gather in the cafe until bed time.

4. Habits, Interests, Companions

Mary Dover says Waldo usually comes directly home from school. He goes to the cafe for dinner and after doing, willingly and cheerfully, any jobs he is told to do by Mary Dover he goes out to play in the back yard or on the grounds of the old school house. On Saturday he usually goes on his own school campus, which is about six blocks away, to play football with the boys who gather there for the game. These boys generally are school boys living near by. His main interest is football. If not playing the game he is often seen in his own back yard practicing kicking, calling signals or running.

Mary Dover states that she never sees Waldo with the boys who were his companions before he entered the training school.

5. School History

Waldo is in grade six A. But his teacher thinks he should be a grade or two below as he is not able to keep up in his classes. She states that he is mischievous in school and thinks about football more than anything else. She does not believe that he is very bright mentally as he laughs in school at things which are not at all funny. (The teacher who gave this information is quite old, almost feeble.) Waldo does not attend school regularly. It has been necessary for the teacher to go to the home to investigate the cause for his frequent absences.

Another teacher who taught Waldo about a month states that he is not very smart but thinks that he does "fairly well" due to the fact that he gets little if any help at home. Is not at all impudent or mean. Must be kept busy in school in order to keep out of mischief. Likes to lead in games. Most of the younger boys look up to him because he is a good football player which is Waldo's main interest on the play ground. He is often seen teaching the game to a group of small boys.

The principal who has known the family for a number of years states that he has been in touch with Waldo since he was a small boy, and knew the mother and father quite well. He has found Waldo to be good natured and obedient. States that he likes outdoor sports, especially football. Likes to lead and have under his direction a group of boys for work or play. For the most part he is seen playing with boys younger than himself. Gives little, if any, trouble at school. Though the training school has helped him in many respects he does not feel that Waldo has ever been a bad boy.

6. WORK

Little is known of Waldo's work record. It seems that he has never had a regular job. Before going to Morrison Training School he used to help out stores or run errands for neighbors. Mary Dover states that he has worked little since his return from school, probably two or three days at a time in order to get money to buy socks, a shirt or something he needed.

7. PHYSICAL EXAMINATION

Waldo's health certificate, filled out by the county health officer, on Jan. 29, 1925, when the boy was 13 years old, showed no symptoms of tuberculosis or venereal disease, that the boy was in good physical condition except that he was five pounds under weight. His lungs, kidneys, tonsils, ears, and throat were normal—no adenoids—two teeth decayed—eyes, eight-tenths; no pellagra or malaria; hookworm suspect; general nervous condition good.

8. MENTAL EXAMINATION

An examination made by the State Psychologist, March 3, 1930, showed Waldo to have an I. Q. of 71, and he was diagnosed as feebleminded. The report showed that "the reactions on the form board show lack of ability to meet concrete situations, with a tendency to become confused and emotionally disturbed when confronted by difficulties."

9. BOY'S OWN STORY

Waldo remembers his father and mother. Both were very good to all of the children. But they were never allowed to go out of the yard to play. There were enough of them to have a good time in the yard. The father made good money and the children used to have "nearly everything" they wanted.

Waldo believes that his delinquencies began about the time his father was sick or right after his death. Waldo happened to be at a store one day and saw a boy pick up some things and quickly put them in his pocket. When they got outside, the boy divided with Waldo. In the meantime he told Waldo that was the method to use in stealing—when the saleslady had her back turned snatch quickly whatever object you wanted, put it in your pocket and when she turned around smile and say, "I wish I could buy that," pointing to some object. At first Waldo said he did not see how he could steal as he knew that it was wrong to take what did not belong to you. But after one or two more experiences like the first, and after seeing the boys sell what they had stolen, he thought he would try it. He can't remember if he was successful the first time. But on one occasion he was successful and sold the article and had the money to spend. It was the custom with the boys to steal, sell and divide the money with the bunch.

It was a "terrible" bunch but he seemed to like them and couldn't break away. They used to teach him to pick pockets but he never did attempt this because he didn't have the nerve and was afraid he would be killed. He said that in order to pick pockets one must walk along close to the man or woman whose pocket you are going to pick, then put your arm around their back, slipping your hand into the pocket.

Each time he was arrested for stealing he would "swear" he was going to do better but he knew the "value of money" and had no other way of getting spending change after his father's death. Whenever he would take home any object his mother suspected was stolen, she would send him back with it, but since he was afraid of getting arrested he would tear or break up the stolen article, throw it away and upon his return home would tell his mother he had returned it.

Once when placed by the Juvenile Court, with his uncle, he ran away because he asked him to let him come to town with him one Saturday just for the trip and his uncle refused him. But he "came just the same and with him" but hiding underneath the wagon. When his legs would get tired he would get off and run or walk a bit, keeping to the rear, out of sight.

When sent to Oxford Orphanage he thought he would stay but a boy who had planned to run away told him how easy it would be and insisted on his leaving with him. Knowing of a football game he wanted to see in Raleigh he decided to leave also.

When sent to Morrison Training School he did not like it. But after a few days he learned to like it very much. Several boys were placed under him for the supervision of their work and play. He used to play football and teach the boys to play. The boys used to look up to him because the folks at the school used to call on him to do many things. He was taught laundering while there and can do it now fairly well, he thinks. Since his return home he washes his own clothes and sometimes assists with the family washing.

He likes school but does not like to go when he does not know his lesson. His cousin's wife helps him sometimes but often when she comes by the cafe from work she is tired. Another reason for cutting school is all the boys his age have nice clothes to wear and he does not. When he works he is able to buy only one thing at a time. And "if you don't look just right you feel funny." If he could get a regular job in the evening after school and on Saturday he knows he could buy some clothes.

Story of His Life Written by Boy Himself.—"I am sixteen years of age and my name is Waldo Harper. When I was a little boy about five years of age and I fell out of the door stepps and I cried so much that my mother put me to bed and I liked to see the trains and I all ways like to tak about a train and when I started to getting larger my father bought a cross cut saw and me and my brothers sawed wood and one day me and some more boys went to play and we got up on a bank and was sliding down and I was sliding down and I fell and hurt my neck and after that I became sick and I stayed sick for about a month and the doctor said that I had the menegious and I was sent to the hospital right away and was opporated on and stayed at the hospital for two months and after that I came back and stayed around home and my father nenver did fuss with my mother neather my mother fuss with my father but one treated me just as good as the other but I loved my mother the best and after while my father died and I went to staying with my aunt and she was good to me also and my mother went to working out and I went to school for about two weeks and one day a boy told me to go with him up town and he to— me to lest steal something and he stole a little car and handed it to me and I took it and after that I thought I could do it to so I started to steal and stole for a long time and after while the———— they sent me out to the school and when I went out there I change my min about stealing and that is why I am here today and after whili my mother died and I was out to the school at the present time and I came home and stayed for one day and went back and I had a good time out there and I had lots of friends and I wonted to become a foot-ball player and I stayed out

there four years and eight months and I was honored on jobs
and the had a way of digging aroung trees and pulling them
up by a tractor and so I studied a way that we could digg
them up by the roots so I had a good time out there and so
after while they paroll me."

10. SUBSEQUENT HISTORY OF SOCIAL TREATMENT

"We have seen Waldo constantly since the collection of the
above data. We have supplied him with clothing so that he may
go to school looking as neat as any of the boys. We have
caused the organist of the junior choir to become interested in
him. Consequently he is to take part in the Christmas programs
and become a member of the junior choir.

When Waldo visits our office he is neater and shows signs
of having giving his appearance some care. We have allowed
him to run errands which involve the spending of money, for
which we pay him. He is very quick and eager to do something."

(Signed)   Z. M.

CASE STUDY OF A DELINQUENT NEGRO GIRL IN RALEIGH, N. C.
ELSIE LOUISE HOLMES

Juvenile Court Record.—June 19, 1928. Case referred by
Mrs. Holmes that Elsie is uncontrollable, she previously had
promised to do better. Visited and warned Elsie that she would
have to be brought up before Juvenile Court if she continued
to give trouble.

July 23, 1928. Visited the home of Ellen Holmes, guardian
of Elsie, 642 Jackson Street. The house is a neat five room
cottage—guardian neat and clean—also girl. Woman calls
girl ugly names which girl resents—girl said she was sorry,
was going to do better. Woman's husband is deaf and aged—
does odd jobs which pay well sometimes. Woman takes in washing, Elsie goes for the clothes, which gives her an opportunity
to be in street more than she should where various inducements
are offered.

July 24, 1928. Plans made for a group of children to call
for Elsie to take her to Sunday school—at St. Ambrose
Episcopal Church.

May 5, 1929. Mrs. E. Holmes in office stating that Elsie was in City Jail, said she was under a $25 bond. She did not feel as if she wanted to get her out as she had been warned a number of times to do the right thing. Woman understands that she is in jail for fighting over Cassie Clawson, a boy with whom she has been keeping company for some time. She also states that she has been staying out late at night and is very impudent. Visitor advised woman that she would go to jail to see Elsie and if she were turned over to Juvenile Court we would notify her.

Later. Visited Elsie in City Jail. Stated that girl was following her and she fought her. Upon making a suggestion about having her turned over to Welfare Department she stated that she would rather serve time in jail than to go to the reformatory.

May 8, 1929. Case in City Court. Turned over to Juvenile Court for disposition. Taken to Detention Home pending Juvenile Court hearing.

NOTE. The following extract from a letter written by Elsie while in the detention home to her lover, Cassie, delivery boy for a local drug store, throws more light upon this "triangular" affair:

Dearest One:

"While sitting feeling so blue longing for you and thinking of no one but you I will write to let you hear from me and I trust when these few lines reach your loving hands they will find you well.

"Dear I am just worry to death, I can't do anything but think of you and what you told me Monday, but don't worry because if you are telling the truth it will come out allright. Listen Dear she love you and she want you to marry her and that is the only way she think she can get to it but if you was under the influence of whisky there is no danger because a man cannot do when he is like there, furthermore if it was done in Dec. it should come in August and not Sept. like you said she said. I don't believe it is yours I just can't believe, I will not believe, I will stick by you until the end I love you and you know I love you. I will do anything to help you."

May 5, 1929. Case before Juvenile Court. Cassie admitted that he had been going with Martha and he had promised to marry her, also that girl was pregnant by him. Stated to Judge that he would be ready to marry girl on 5-14-29 as he received his pay the day before. Elsie was advised to leave boy alone and that she would have to be placed in an institution if there was any further trouble. Judge ordered that she be placed back in Detention Home pending marriage of Cassie and Martha. Girl almost went into a panic after Cassie left and was returned to the Detention Home.

NOTE. Cassie was duly married to Martha Prince in Welfare Department, 5-14-29 at order of Judge B———. Martha's baby was born 9-29-29.

May 15, 1929. Girl returned to her home.

June 10, 1929. Home visit. Foster mother stated that Elsie is working and doing fairly well.

July 20, 1929. Phone message from Mrs. Holmes stating Elsie had left home, and she did not know where she was.

July 24, 1929. Met Elsie on street with Cassie. Stated that she had just met him up the street but that she was not going with him any more. Would not tell visitor where she was living, but stated that foster mother told her to get out and she left. Promised to go back home same afternoon.

September 14, 1929. Visited Elsie at home in regard to having application filled out for Efland School. Foster mother stated that Elsie is infected with a venereal disease. Her report was four plus. Girl has not changed in her disposition and is very impudent. Foster mother does not think it worth while to put her in Efland. She is attending the clinic for treatments.

1. FAMILY

(The information relating to Elsie's family background was secured first from Elsie's foster mother, Mrs. Ellen Holmes, of Raleigh, and later from an interview with Elsie's own mother in Philadelphia. It was impossible to locate Elsie's father.)

(a) *Father.*—A white man of foreign birth, variously described as an Italian, an Assyrian, or a Jew, by the name of George Goldstein. At the time he ran away with Elsie's mother, leaving a wife and four children, Goldstein was traveling for an insurance company in North Carolina.

(b) *Mother.*—Minnie Barnes, born in Elizabeth City, N. C., about 1898. Her father, who was supposed to be married to her mother, died when she was small. She stopped school about the 4th or 5th grade and went to work as cook and house girl. While working out she met Goldstein, became intimate with him, and gave birth to Elsie, Dec. 15, 1913. Goldstein left town previous to her confinement, leaving her some money. When the baby was a few months old Minnie's mother died, after which Goldstein wrote Minnie to come with Elsie to live with him in Raleigh. He furnished a place and took good care of both mother and baby until he found Minnie unfaithful, whereupon he left town, and later Minnie heard that he was dead. Minnie got a job as cook or helper in some Greek restaurant or eating house on Wilmington Street, Raleigh. During this time she became very intimate with another white man, and on one occasion was caught in immoral relations with him. Both were arrested but he "paid his way out" while she was kept in jail.

During her confinement in jail, Minnie heard of Ellen Holmes' charitable nature and interest in children and sent for her. Because Minnie was so young and was without relations in the city, Mrs. Holmes became quite interested in her and the baby, and finally persuaded the jailer to let Minnie and the baby come to live at her home, promising to be responsible for her good behavior. It was understood that if Minnie gave any trouble whatever she was to be returned to the jail. At the expiration of three or four months Minnie went back to work and her old room, leaving the baby with Mrs. Holmes. Soon Minnie was arrested again for immorality, this time with a Negro man. The judge ordered that she marry the man or go to jail. They were married and shortly afterward went to Philadelphia to live. They had two children and got along well for a while, but about three years ago they separated because

15

of her husband's jealousy. Her husband married again shortly
after their separation. Minnie had a hard time after this owing
to difficulty in finding work, but she finally met another Negro
man who became quite friendly, so they began living together.
She has had one child by this man. He lives in the house most
of the time but has a room with a cousin where he can go. He
is very mean to her when "full of liquor." On one of his recent
liquor sprees he knocked her out of a second story window
to the ground, breaking her ankle. She wants to leave the man
but seems afraid.

(c) *Mother's Family*.—The last report of Minnie's mother
was that she had left Elizabeth City, N. C., with a white man.
She had always lived with one and was well taken care of by
him. She had several children, besides Minnie, all of whom had
a white father. It is not certain that Minnie's mother was ever
married.

(d) *Foster Father*.—Is sickly and feeble due to old age, and
not able to work regularly. He does odd jobs about the house
for a white family for whom he has been working for a number
of years. He has always been kind to Elsie, treating her as his
own child. Many times has he kept his wife from scolding Elsie.

(e) *Foster Mother*.—Ellen Holmes: born during slavery in
———— County, not far from Raleigh—married at the age
of fifteen and shortly afterward came to Raleigh to live. She
was a hard worker and possessed a "missionary heart to help
others," particularly young girls. Has taken in young babies
for care and rearing for a number of years. Some of these
babies have been illegitimate, and others of working mothers.
Of the eighteen babies she has reared, only two have proven
worthy—both are married, one living in New York and the
other in Raleigh.

While rearing Elsie there were no other small children in
the house and she did not take any until Elsie was in high
school. Since then she has done laundry work at home and
cared for a few children. In this way she has been able to
complete payments for her home with the help of the "old
man." At present she has one washing. She is also caring for a

twenty-two months old child born in the St. Agnes hospital in Raleigh, whose mother is a young girl living in New Jersey in a boarding school as if nothing had happened. The girl's family knows nothing of this illegitimate child. Mrs. Holmes receives $25 per month for the care of this child. Mrs. Holmes is a member of the Congregational Church, and is regarded as a good, Christian woman. She also belongs to a religious order called "Sisters and Brothers of Mercy and Hope." She appeared pleasant and coöperative, and wanted help·in dealing with Elsie's behavior problems.

2. DEVELOPMENTAL HISTORY

Elsie was a full term baby and breast fed. Was taken by Mrs. Holmes when thirteen months old. Never had any serious ailments, was bright, smart, good natured and full of life. Began menstruating at twelve or thirteen years.

3. HOME AND NEIGHBORHOOD CONDITIONS

The Holmes live in their own home, a six room one story frame house, located in a quiet and respectable Negro neighborhood near the city limits of Raleigh. The house is fairly well furnished, including a player piano and a wall telephone. The beds were very clean looking. Mrs. Holmes sleeps in a large double bed with the baby, and Elsie sleeps in the same room on a cot. Mr. Holmes sleeps in another room alone.

The house is located on the corner in the center of a large lot. There are a few pecan trees, a grape arbor and a garden at the rear. Mrs. Holmes rents the lot at the right of the house where she also has a kitchen garden. There are a few chickens and a cow. There are no sidewalks and the streets are in bad condition.

4. SCHOOL AND WORK HISTORY

Elsie started to school at age of five years, was smart and interested in her work, and passed each year until she reached second year high school when she had to repeat this grade. It was during the year that she repeated this grade that she left school at the age of fourteen. Elsie was never a behavior problem in school. The school record from the high school shows that during her first year in high school she was not absent a single day, and was tardy only a few times. The first half of her second year also showed an excellent attendance record, but toward the end of the year she began to be absent frequently. During the year she had to repeat second year high she had a poor attendance record, and she began to show lower grade marks, which before had been good.

Elsie has worked a few weeks at a time in various white families as a nursing maid at $3.00 to $3.50 per week.

5. PHYSICAL EXAMINATION

Elsie's physical examination showed active case of syphilis, with a 4 plus Wasserman reaction. She received numerous treatments for syphilis at the Wake County Free Clinic during August and September, 1929.

6. MENTAL EXAMINATION

A psychological examination by the State Psychologist showed Elsie to have an Intelligence Quotient of 69, and she was diagnosed as feebleminded. It was recommended that "the greatest possibility for adequate handling of the case would be along manual lines, especially with those types dealing with very concrete situations where the subject would be under supervision in her work."

7. CHILD'S OWN STORY

Remembers her mother very little. Her mother came from Philadelphia on a visit about seven years ago to take Elsie back with her, but Mrs. Holmes would not let her go. Elsie thought her mother very attractive and kind, but Mrs. Holmes has talked about her mother as a "bad woman" ever since she can remember.

Elsie's childhood was a happy one. Her foster parents were always kind until the last two or three years. Her foster mother has been quite strict with her and would not permit her to go to movies and parties, but this Elsie feels is due to the fact that Mrs. Holmes has "old ideas."

Elsie's sex life began quite early, about the age of seven years. Her foster mother was very often away from home on business or out for her laundry which she did at home. The neighborhood children would come over to play "mama and papa" and Elsie was taught what the mothers and fathers were supposed to do. Her sex experiences were regular until she began menstruating. The girls began telling her that if she had sex relations with a boy she would "get a baby." It eventually happened, however, one late afternoon while coming from the store. She met a boy and he suggested "loving" her. Refusing him several times he finally pulled her into a high thicket which they were passing. She went home crying but was afraid to tell her foster mother. After this her sex relations continued with little if any fear. Elsie tries to have the will power to resist the advances of boys but finds that staying out of their company is the only remedy.

Elsie liked to go to school and feels that she is good in English as she likes it best and gave more time to it. She attended school regularly until her foster mother saw her walking from school with a fellow one day and kept her home two or three days as punishment. When she went back she was behind the class. Knowing how it hurt her to miss school her foster mother always kept her home from school for a few days as punishment. It was during these times that Mrs. Holmes would tell her that she was "no good" like her mother, calling her "ugly names." So she finally decided that perhaps she was "just born to be bad." When asked if she would like to return to school, she said that she would like it very much, but not in Raleigh. So many boys and girls knew of her sex experiences and teased her about them.

Tired of being "fussed with," called "nobody," not being allowed to go to the movies without a fuss, and not being allowed to entertain her friends at home, is the reason Elsie gives for staying away from home several days at a time. Elsie told of a day she went to pay the insurance for Mrs. Holmes. Elsie came back by the home of some girls who live together. They called her in and she went in thinking it would be for only a few minutes. She does not care for whiskey but one or two men who had come in insisted and before she realized it she had drunk enough to cause her to become "realy dizzy." When asked if she had any sex relation that day she said she did not know. When she realized it several hours had passed and she had been asleep. Thinks probably she did as there were three men and three girls there including herself when she awoke. All appeared to be "lying around."

She also told us of a man who continues to bother her. He offers her money and clothing. On one occasion when he passed the house, he threw a package containing a pair of hose over the fence and told her to come up to the house and he would give her a hat to wear to church the next day. Though she kept the hose and wore them she never did go to the man's house nor has she had relationship with him.

She states that at times she feels very unhappy because she does not have sufficient clothing and her foster mother is not able to give her all she needs. Lately Mrs. Holmes has tried to whip her and put her out but she has no other home. If she goes it is usually for just a few nights. She usually stays with some girls who live together or a woman who is "sorter fast."

Elsie wants to go live with her mother in Philadelphia. She wants to work and make money enough to buy clothes and pay her fare to Philadelphia. She also expressed a desire to see her father. She heard that he used to buy her pretty clothes and care for her mother until he found out that her mother was crooked. She does not know her father's name but has heard that he worked for some Insurance Company while in Raleigh and was later transferred to Greensboro.

8. SUBSEQUENT HISTORY OF SOCIAL TREATMENT

"We have attempted to keep in touch with Elsie since our first contact with her family. She has been either to the office, called us up by phone or we have called her. Lately Mrs. Holmes called us to say that Elsie went to the movies one evening and did not come home until 9:30 o'clock. When she did so Mr. Holmes requested that she would not let Elsie come in. Since then she has not been able to locate Elsie's whereabouts. Mrs. Holmes states further that Mr. Holmes has become worried, realizing that Elsie is not grown, and is trying to find her."

(Signed) Z. M.

A letter from the Boy's Probation Officer of the Wake County Juvenile Court, under date August 19, 1931, summarizes Elsie's present social condition as follows: "Elsie has no further record either in Juvenile or Police Court. She still has the reputation of associating with a 'gang' of questionable boys and girls. She has worked irregularly as nurse and girl of general work, but has not been employed in some time. Elsie is still living with her foster mother, the foster father having died recently. The mother reports that the girl leaves home and is away for several days at the time. It seems the old trouble of stubbornness is still a factor to be dealt with in managing the girl."

Case Studies of Two Delinquent Negro Boys From Asheville, N. C.

Explanatory Note.—During the January, 1929, term of the Henderson County Superior Court, two Negro boys from Asheville, Edward Thompson, 12, and Daniel Dawson, 13, were convicted of larceny of an automobile, and were sentenced each to a term of two years in the State's Prison in Raleigh. Since both boys were under fourteen years of age they were legally subject to the exclusive jurisdiction of the juvenile court, hence their commitment to the State's Prison was contrary to law. When the matter came to the attention of the State Commissioner of Public Welfare, she wrote to the clerk of court of Henderson County asking for certain information about these boys, in the attempt to find out why their cases had not been handled by the juvenile court. The clerk's reply was as follows:

"These boys were sent to the State Prison from this county charged with larceny. I understand that they lived in Buncombe County at the time. No one took any interest in them."

The Commissioner thereupon reported both cases to the Governor, with the result that both boys were transferred to Morrison Training School by Executive Order, February 25, 1929, and were admitted to the institution, March 12, 1929.

Since nothing was known about the social background of these boys, Miss Marshall, the case investigator for the Negro Child Welfare Study, went to Asheville and through interviews with the boys' relatives and others secured the social data presented in the following case studies.

I. DANIEL DAWSON

1. FAMILY

(a) *Father.*—James Dawson, 55 years old, born in Laurens, South Carolina. Attended school for only a few months. Worked as helper on farms and as common laborer. Immediately after marriage he worked as laborer in Laurens; later he farmed on halves with his mother-in-law. As a result of poor crops one year he moved his family to Columbia, South Carolina, where he worked as a common laborer. Later he moved to Atlanta, Ga., in search of work, but in less than a year he went on to Palmetto, Georgia, to farm on halves with a white man. For a while he did well, but the boll weevil soon began giving the farmers trouble. Then in response to a letter from his sister-in-law in Asheville who wrote them to say he could get work there, Dawson moved to Asheville. For nearly four years they have moved from one place to another, Dawson working as a common laborer. Mrs. Dawson states that it has been all she could do to keep her husband from taking the boys out of school to go to work.

Mrs. Dawson says that her husband has a "weakness for large automobiles which keeps them forever in debt paying for a second-hand car which gives trouble from the start." Often if he is out of a job she has to keep up the payments, but neither she nor the children often get a chance to enjoy a ride.

Some years ago Mr. Dawson gave her a great deal of trouble with women, gambling and liquor. But now "his only bad habits" are liquor and cursing. He has a very high temper, and resents advice from any woman. For instance, Mrs. Dawson says she was cooking for a very rich white woman until a short time before Christmas, when because of illness she had to give up the work. This woman, seeing the poor condition of the Dawson home, offered to pay for the moving and first month's rent and even promised to give them a ton of coal if they moved into a better house which both Mrs. Dawson and the lady had seen. When Mrs. Dawson joyfully told her husband about it he refused to move, stating that he was not "going to let any woman rule him."

Several reliable people, former teachers of the children, and neighbors expressed the feeling that while Mrs. Dawson is very smart and greatly interested in her children the man is "no account" and listless. He is the cause of a great deal of trouble the family has had. One man, who knows the family well, declares that Mr. Dawson is a gambler and has no sense of pride. As long as there is a "mouthful to eat and chips to burn" he is satisfied. Dawson thinks the children do not need to go to school—stating that he had no education and makes a living, and his children can do likewise. He is not a member of any church but he sometimes goes to the Methodist Church and with his wife to the Holiness Church, which he likes a great deal.

(b) *Father's Family.*—Mr. Dawson's mother and father separated when he was a small boy. His mother remained in Laurens, South Carolina, and worked, while his father went to Nebraska, where he died a few years ago, leaving, according to rumor, both property and money.

(c) *Mother.*—Florence Jones Dawson, 45 years old, born in Laurens, South Carolina. Was one of eleven children but only three are now living. Cause of deaths unknown. Woman states that she attended Brewer Normal School in Greenwood, South Carolina, where she completed the ninth grade. After the death of her father she stopped school so as to be at home with her mother. She soon became acquainted with Dawson, who used to call at the house, but as her mother did not like him on the ground that he was "not the kind of a boy a girl should bother with," she was compelled to have him stop calling. She, however, saw him occasionally at church. From these meetings they became very much interested in each other and finally eloped and got married. Dawson worked as a common laborer in the town of Laurens and they were very happy. Woman states her mother was very bitter for a while, but soon forgave them and had them to live at home with her. Children began coming which called for more money. Man was making very little if any actual cash so eventually he began his roving from one place to another.

Mrs. Dawson states that she tries to help her husband make ends meet by taking in sewing at home and cooking out. At her last job she started with $8.00 a week but was soon raised to $10.00 and then $12.00. But there have been weeks that she has made as much as $20.00 doing extra jobs at the house or working late. Woman states that when they are both working she tries to save a little money to help when in a "tight place." But her husband very often drinks up his money and she has to pay the bills.

Mrs. F., a very prominent white woman of Asheville, informed visitor that Mrs. Dawson is a good, hard working woman who is anxious to make progress and to secure an education for her children. Mrs. F. states that her own mother, who died a year ago, held an executive position in Brewer Normal School in South Carolina when woman was a student there. Knew her to be smart, neat, clean and from a good family.

(d) *Mother's Family.*—Mrs. Dawson's father died about 1907 and her mother died January, 1929. They were highly respected by people of both races. They owned 200 acres of land on which were located their own six room house and several tenant houses, always occupied by "share-croppers." Her father was the first colored man in the community to own a carriage and an organ. (Woman states that years ago in her community, these two things made one outstanding and considered "well off.") Her parents had cows, horses, chickens and other fowl. Her father very often acted in the capacity of a lawyer when a colored person was tried for some misdemeanor. After her father's death they lost their property gradually, never knowing how. White citizens took it without any explanation except that her father sold to them before his death. Both her parents could read and write, and were anxious for more learning. They were eager for their children to have the best, and at one time there were four children attending boarding school.

A brother who was a minister was a graduate of Benedict College. He died a few years ago. A sister who at one time lived in Asheville is now living in Knoxville, Tenn. Another brother, when last heard of was in Detroit, Michigan.

(e) *Children.*—"Ceil" (Lucille): born August, 1909—has never been to school. Woman states that when she was three years old she ran with some children to meet her one day and fell down on a "stone bar" which cut a very deep hole in her head. It healed quickly but left the child "unable to learn or act herself." "Ceil" appears strong and healthy, but one can tell at a glance that she is not right mentally.

Mrs. Dawson states that a few years ago before her own mother's death she took "Ceil" to a specialist who examined her head and told her that a bone was pressing against the brain.

When Mrs. Dawson is out working "Ceil" takes care of the house, cooks, washes, cleans and looks after Marion, the baby boy. "Ceil" can remember to do the things she does daily but can't remember to do a thing which her mother may send her into the next room to do. She is easy to handle and very obedient. Is kind to her sisters and brothers and very smart about the house.

Thama: born November, 1911—is serving a three year sentence on the county road for stealing. Stopped school in 4A. Was a hard working boy and good to his parents. He feels that his father is in a great way responsible, as he took him out of school to work. Made him do a man's work and when drinking would curse him and call him "terrible names." When Thama was out of work he would stand on the street corners with other boys and men who were idle.

Emery: born February, 1912,[1] is making $6.00 a week, washing dishes at a white school where lunches are served daily. He has lived at home until recently when he took a room with a fellow who works with him. He is very good to the family. On one or two occasions lately he has "paid on" the back rent without his mother's knowledge.

Daniel (subject): born August, 1913.

Thelma: born March, 1914—has just been promoted to 6A. Both her principal and her former teacher state that she is smart, but at times mischievous. The principal states that she feels the girl is passing a stage where she should have a great deal of her mother's care and attention, because of her interest in boys.

Everette: born May, 1917—has just been promoted to 5B. He is very dependable and looks out for many necessities about the house, such as wood, coal and kindling without being told to do so. He makes many nickles and dimes by selling baskets which he gets from stores. His teacher states that he is very smart in school. He gives no trouble whatever and is seldom absent or tardy.

Tom: born March, 1919—is in 3B. He did not pass this semester. His present teacher states that she has taught him before in the second grade. He always felt that there was no hope for him. He gives no trouble in the classroom but he has an exceedingly high temper. Tom makes pennies by selling coat hangers which people give or sell him. The pressing clubs which purchase them from him do so only on Monday.

Tom says he likes school all right but the teacher is so mean that a few of the boys decided not to go every day. Tom states that he does not like the idea of the teacher knocking his head against the wall. He also told of his gang. They are boys near his age who walk about gathering iron, bottles, boxes, coat hangers, etc., to sell. With the money they buy candy,

---

[1]There are obvious errors in the birth dates of several of the children, due to the absence of written records of birth and the consequent attempt of relatives to recall birth dates from memory.

fruit or cake and put a dime away for the moving picture serial on Friday. If there is enough money each takes a nickel or dime home. When the weather is warm they go fishing or swimming. Many times they have "swiped" fruit from wagons, but Tom states that he does not like "swiping" because he does not want to get in trouble.

Tom was very comical in his actions and expression. He promised to "try" to go to school every day and stop "swiping."

Ruby: born June, 1922—has just been promoted to 2A. She recited many poems and sang many songs which she learned at school and which her mother had taught her at home. Her teacher states that she is very bright in school and remembers exceedingly well.

Collier: born December, 1925—died a few years ago from croup.

Marion: born August, 1926.

2. Developmental History

Woman states that during her pregnancy she kept well, but at times was worried a great deal because of the actions of her husband. It was during these years that he drank heavily and ran around with women. At the time of confinement, she was attended by both physician and midwife. Daniel was a healthy, breast-fed baby. During his early childhood he had measles, whooping cough and mumps.

3. Home Influences and Neighborhood Conditions

Lincoln Avenue where the family has lived for the past two years is a narrow street, more of an alley, without sidewalks, a few blocks long, which runs off of a main street.

The house has no fence at the front. There is little front yard but there is a fairly large back yard where Mrs. Dawson has raised a few vegetables for the family's use. The house is a four room frame cottage, with a tiny hall which is badly in need of repairs and paint inside and out. The two rooms on the left are used as bed rooms. Both are completely furnished. The floors are bare and worn. The plastered walls are cracked, broken and very dirty. The front room on the right is the living room. The room back of it is the kitchen. The two small living room windows have gay flowered cretonne draperies to match the chair backs and covered pillows on a few of the chairs. There is a large cabinet victrola which woman states she bought so that "Ceil" could have some pleasure while at home during the day. She also had it in mind as something to entertain the whole family when at home in the evening. There is also a large fancy new style glass-front china closet. The other furniture is a trunk, a machine and a dresser. The dirty and broken walls display many of the old family pictures. There is a small coal stove which can also be used for cooking and ironing. This floor also is bare. The kitchen has a table covered with oil cloth, a kitchen cabinet and a large coal and wood range, trimmed in white and blue. Mrs. Dawson took pride in telling us that it cost $90.00 and gave splendid service.

At the time of the visit, about dinner time, the house was fairly clean. The meal consisted of fried fish, plain boiled potatoes and corn bread. There was no noise or scrapping among the children over the meal.

When gathered around the fireside at night the children discuss with their parents what went on in school during the day. Woman teaches them songs and speeches of her girlhood; they have a little concert or she hears the lessons. Mrs. Dawson says that once or twice during the week she goes to church and takes the oldest children with her. Mr. Dawson is seldom at home. If he is not away in the car with a bunch of "drunks" he is standing on some corner in West End talking.

The neighborhood is fairly quiet. There are no land owners on Lincoln Avenue, but the main street from which it branches off has several land owners whose homes are very attractive. All the streets in the neighborhood are very bad.

We saw the dilapidated house where the family lived before moving to Lincoln Avenue. There are two rooms and a kitchen. Every window pane is out and in their place are paste board, rags and sacks. The place looks as if it is about to topple over. Tom's teacher told us that Mrs. Dawson was ashamed

to live there but her husband said it was good enough. Mrs.
Dawson finally persuaded him to move.

4. Companions, Habits, Interests

Mrs. Dawson knows little about the bunch of boys to which
Daniel belonged. She had cautioned him several times because
neighbors had remarked that they were a "bad lot."

Mrs. Dawson has no idea what Daniel was doing or where
he was, but just before the last trouble he kept very late hours.
He would do better immediately after the scolding but would
repeat the same thing. One of his hangouts was "West End
where there is a grocery store on each corner." Many boys
and men "hang out" there after work hours for recreation.

His mother said that Daniel preferred above all things riding on trucks or wagons. Would go with any man to deliver
anything just to have the opportunity to ride about Asheville
or the suburbs.

5. School and Work History

Daniel stopped school in the fourth grade. From time to time
his father has kept him out of school to work.

Mrs. M., one of Daniel's former teachers, states that she
can't understand Daniel's trouble. He gave no trouble in
the classroom or on the yard. He could do well in class if he
studied. There were times when he felt inclined to be lazy. He
was good natured with temper, but much less than Tom.

According to his mother, Daniel had never had a permanent
job. He was always "lucky in picking up a job for a day or
two." For the most part he worked at a store, market or on a
delivery wagon.

6. History of Delinquencies and Court Record

Daniel's first appearance before the Buncombe County Juvenile Court, February 10, 1925, was for larceny. He was
placed on probation. Seven months later he appeared again
before the same court for larceny, and again was placed on
probation. A year later he was before the juvenile court for

store breaking. He was held in the County Home for several days.

Thama also has appeared before the juvenile court for larceny.

7. SUBSEQUENT RECORD

In October, 1931, after Daniel had been in Morrison Training School for about two and one-half years, the superintendent of that institution summarizes Daniel's record and prospects in the following report:

"Daniel in temperament was very bilious for some time. He is the same today to a limited degree. He will work hard all through with a smile if the person supervising or directing him exhibits kindly interest and tolerance. I think it was this method that has aided us most in bringing him around to that more sanguine temperament that best characterizes him today.

"Physically, he is not of the giant type but he certainly has developed.

"Some time ago he was placed in the laundry in charge of clothing for the boys. Prior to this he took but little stock in keeping himself tidy and clean. Since that time he has become one of our most particular boys in this respect. I note, too, that he is growing quite efficient in the students' dining room where the management is in the hands of the student officers. I noted in passing through the dining hall at meal time that he was serving as one of the monitors. The point of interest that attracted me was his care in seeing that new boys were getting their full share of milk. He was quite busy in this direction.

"His school work is slow and he is inclined to snap school at any and every opportunity, that he might do some interesting job instead. He is now in the fourth grade.

"It is quite difficult to say just what the future holds for. him, but I feel quite certain that full adjustment—within the range of one of his general abilities—is in full reach of him.

"He is prepared to do fairly well several things. As a farmer, he is quite efficient. As a washing machine operator, he can do good work. As a janitor under proper supervision he is capable of doing good work.

"This is the best I can predict for his future. He is now on the parole list. I hope to be able to dismiss him within the next sixty days."

II. Edward Thompson

1. Family

(a) *Father.*—David Thompson: About 50 years old, born in a small town in South Carolina. When about eleven or twelve years old, he came to Asheville with his father to live. He stopped school at the second or third grade to go to work because of his father's death. Before he was grown he started working around a baking shop, and after a number of years became assistant baker's helper, and was later promoted to position of one of the head bakers in a German bakery, where he made good money. A short while ago, man lost his job because the German owner of the bakery sold out to another man who hired all white help. At this time, man was making $40 a week.

In the latter part of 1918, Edward's mother died, leaving her husband and his own mother to care for the family of children. After two or three months, the father began to grow indifferent toward his family, and stopped coming home, although he bought food and paid the house rent. Later he got behind on the rent, and failed to supply enough food, so that his brothers and sisters had to come to the assistance of the children. At this point, the father's half-sister, Mrs. Charles Jenkins, took the man's mother, who was quite feeble, and all the children who remained at home to live with her. The father, thereupon, ceased all efforts to support his family, and began to live with another woman, Mary Smith. Man was a hard drinker, but never failed to support his family until after his wife's death. All who knew him, even Mary Smith, with whom he is still living, say that man is "indifferent, peculiar, and hard to understand." (The father himself was never interviewed, owing to inability to locate him, and such information as was

16

secured about his family history came from his half-sister, Mrs. Jenkins.)

(b) *Father's Family.*—Man's father was an illiterate tenant farmer in South Carolina, who moved with his family to Asheville and worked as a common laborer until his death. Man's mother did little work on the farm in South Carolina, but after coming to Asheville she sometimes did laundry work at home. After her husband's death she had to go out to work as cook or house cleaner and very often to make ends meet she also took in a little washing at home. This, together with what the children earned, enabled the family to live very well.

(c) *Mother.*—Mamie Thompson: Born in Greenville, S. C., when a small child, after her mother's death, she came with her only brother and her father to Asheville. Before her marriage she taught school for a while in the country. She was considered a good housekeeper and a good mother and wife. She died of influenza in November, 1918.

(d) *Mother's Family.*—Woman's mother died in South Carolina, shortly before the family moved to Asheville. The father, who was regarded as a "good gardener and tree trainer," lived for several years after Mamie's marriage to David Thompson. Mamie's only brother was an ex-service man who died "somewhere in the East." After his death some Government papers came referring to money left by him, but the matter was never followed up.

(e) *Children.*—David: Aged 31 years, lives with his aunt, Mrs. Charles Jenkins, at 90 Sycamore Street. He is deaf and dumb and for some years attended the Institute at Raleigh. He is working at Parker's Shoe Store, where he has been employed for the past eleven years.

Mattie: Age 29 years, stopped school in the 7th grade after her mother's death to assist with the house and children. Later she had some trouble with her father so she moved with a woman named Mary with whom she is now living in a neat three-room, well-furnished apartment. Both are maids at the white Y. M. C. A., where they have worked for a number of years. Mattie had an operation some months ago for "stomach trouble," but is now back on her old job and doing well. She states that her father has not bought her one thing or given her "a nickle" since her mother's death. Mattie's sister Annabelle, and others state that "Mary" is supposed to be "a woman lover" (homosexual) and is very jealous of Mattie.

Annabelle: Age 25, finished the 9th grade. At the time of her mother's death, Annabelle and the rest of the children were all in bed with the "flu." When her father refused to support the family afterwards, Annabelle got a place living with a colored school teacher. She continued to go to school but did the work around the house for which they fed and clothed her. After finishing school she got a job at the German baker's home through her father, earning $5.00 a week as general helper. She lived on the place and saved what she could until her father told her he would deposit her money in the bank for her. She did this until on one occasion, at Mattie's suggestion, she asked him to let her see the bank book and he refused. She states that she never did receive the money which she had given him. In 1924, she married Charles Wilson, whom she met 8 months before at a party. By this union there is a fine, healthy looking boy about 4 months old. For a little over four months they have been rooming with the Roberts family. Annabelle states that they kept house at one time but in order to be near the drug store where her husband is motorcycle delivery man, they had to move and could not find a small vacant house in the neighborhood. Mrs. Roberts is a very respectable woman who has two married daughters but only one living with her. The home is comfortable and clean. Before her marriage Annabelle was inclined to be "a bit wild," but she is now regarded by those who know the family as the most reliable, intelligent and stable of all the children. Her husband appears to be a steady, sensible young man.

Madaline: Age 21 years, stopped school at 6th grade; lives at 340 Valley Street in two rooms composing one side of a double tenement house. She has three illegitimate children, the oldest near five and the youngest 10 days. The father of the two oldest children is in California and the father of the baby is in South Carolina.

Madaline says that the baby's father when he is in Asheville lives with her but for some months he has worked in South Carolina where just before the birth of the baby he broke his back. At present her only means of support is the front room which she rented a week ago to a sixteen year old girl from Winston-Salem and a man who have been in Asheville two years. The former roomers stayed several weeks and paid her only for one week. She states that her aunt, Mrs. Jenkins, and Annabelle have been the most help, especially the latter, as she kept her in coal and staple food. She states further that until the birth of Annabelle's baby, she kept and bought clothing for her oldest child, Franklin. Madaline and her three children look very undernourished. She states that they keep well. Madaline, though pleasant, is very indifferent and seems to worry about nothing, not even the fact that she did washing when her baby was only 3 days old.

Nanie Mae: Age 19 years, stopped school in the 6th grade. She is now housekeeping with a divorced girl about her own age who has a child two and a half years old. Nanie Mae has not worked for eight months but is being taken care of by a "boy friend" about her own age.

Sallie: Age 15 years, stopped school in the 5th grade. She lives with her aunt, Mrs. Charles Jenkins, at 90 Sycamore Street. Sallie's first appearance in Juvenile Court was for truancy (April 2, 1924) and she was placed on probation. On Sept. 16, 1926, and again on March 5, 1927, she was before the Juvenile Court for fighting, being placed on probation each time. At present Sallie is in jail for stealing.

Edward (Subject): Age 12 years, stopped school in the 4th or 5th grade. Since the death of his grandmother he has lived with his aunt, Mrs. Charles Jenkins.

2. Developmental History

According to the aunt with whom Edward is now living, his mother kept well during the months of pregnancy. There was a normal birth with the attendance of a midwife. She can't remember if there was a doctor. Edward kept well except for "children's diseases."

3. Home Influences and Neighborhood Conditions

Mr. and Mrs. Charles Jenkins are middle aged people, living in a five room, two story house. Two of these rooms are usually rented out. The entire house shows lack of attention. Everything seems to be done in a shiftless sort of a way. The porch is littered with old chairs and other odds and ends. The yard about the house is unkept and gives the appearance of a catchall. Mrs. Jenkins is very untidy and dirty.

This end of Sycamore Street is fairly decent and quiet and there are few houses.

4. Habits and Companions

Edward has kept late hours because there was no one to "keep up" with his going. Very often he left home early in the morning with a group of neighborhood boys and his aunt did not see him again until he passed the house on a truck. He has always been interested in automobiles and trucks. His greatest delight was to ride on a delivery truck.

5. School and Work History

Edward stopped school in the 4th or 5th grade. His fourth grade teacher states that he did not miss one day while she was teaching him. He was very smart in school, and he gave absolutely no trouble in the classroom. He appeared to be a child who wanted affection and care.

6. Histories of Delinquencies and Court Record

According to the records of the Juvenile Court, Edward was born in 1917. On March 19, 1927, at the age of 10, Edward was brought into court for stealing chickens, and he was placed on probation. A year later, March 6, 1928, he was brought into court for larceny of a top, and was sent to the County Home. No note is made as to whether the order was carried out, and if so, how long he remained. In August, 1928, Edward and his chum, Daniel Dawson, stole a Chrysler motor car and drove to Hendersonville, N. C., where the gas gave out.

They abandoned this Chrysler and picked up a Chevrolet in which they made their return trip to Asheville. While riding around the city an officer picked them up and put them in jail, where they remained for five months before their trial.

7. INSTITUTIONAL RECORD

Edward's institutional record at Morrison Training School is presented by the superintendent of that institution as follows:

"Edward was very slow in confiding and talked when pumped. We felt that much of this was due to his undernourished body or to his natural physical frailness. But following special attention to his diet he took on a more cheerful attitude. I can't say that this was due wholly to his increased weight or assimilation or both. He grew more and more cheerful, with occasional spells of depression.

"His industrial efforts oscillated from thrift to indolence and back again. I kept him bolstered up through conferences from time to time, but on April 7, 1931 he escaped. He was returned to the school the next day. On April 25, 1931 he escaped during the early morning hours and made good his getaway. We have never been able to locate him. Edward reached the seventh grade. His class room record was fair. At times he showed a decided dislike for classroom work.

"While his progress did not measure up to our expectation, it is certain that real changes took place in his character. Time and again he expressed a wish to go back and prove to all that he could and would go straight."

CASE STUDIES OF TWO DELINQUENT NEGRO BOYS FROM CHARLOTTE, N. C.

Explanatory Note.—On August 29, 1929, the newly established Domestic Relations Court of the City of Charlotte and County of Mecklenburg (see *1929 Supplement of the N. C. Code of 1927*, pp. 41-42) which had assumed the power, authority and jurisdiction formerly vested in the juvenile court with the additional exclusive original jurisdiction in certain cases of adults, sentenced two Negro boys, Frank Jones, 14, and Isaac Park, about 15, to a term of one year in the State Prison for the offense of breaking and entering in the night time the office of the Parcel Delivery Company of Charlotte. When these boys were presented to the State Prison authorities, the question arose as to whether a Domestic Relations Court under its juvenile court jurisdiction could commit them to a penal institution, whereupon the matter was called to the attention of the Governor, who through the Executive Counsel, Mr. N. A. Townsend, held that the boys could not be legally committed to a penal institution except through the Superior Court of Mecklenburg County. In explaining his illegal commitment of these two boys to the State Prison, the Judge of the Charlotte Domestic Relations Court wrote to the Executive Counsel that the boys "are absolutely criminal in their conduct, and I have tried every other remedy available," offering in support of his statement a transcript of the juvenile court record in each case showing repeated failure of placement on probation. The boys accordingly were returned to the Mecklenburg County Jail. The State Commissioner of Public Welfare immediately secured permission from the Superintendent of Morrison Training School to receive both boys, and strongly urged the Mecklenburg authorities to send the boys to this correctional institution. The Judge of the Domestic Relations Court, however, refused to accede to this reasonable request, and kept both boys in jail until January when they were each placed in private homes for a twelve month period, although both boys had been placed in private homes previously by the juvenile court and had promptly run away. It was while the boys were in the Mecklenburg County jail after their return from the State's Prison, that they were interviewed by Miss Marshall, the case investigator for the Negro Child Welfare Study. From the following social case history of these boys, secured by Miss Marshall through talking with relatives and public officials who knew the boys, and by studying the type of home and the neighborhood from which the boys came, it is evident that the boys instead of being in-

herently criminal were but the natural products of their
social environment.

I. FRANK JONES

1. FAMILY

(a) *Father.*—Sam Jones; father's family unknown.

(b) *Mother.*—Minnie Jones. Woman states that she was
born in Belmont, Georgia, and reared in Gainesville, Georgia.
She stopped school in fourth grade to go to work. On December 3, 1911, she gave birth to an illegitimate child, Flora,
the father of whom is Sam Jones. On September 2, 1914,
she gave birth to Frank (subject), also an illegitimate child,
by the same man. Shortly afterward in Gillsville, Ga., she
married a man named Albert Keith, who died in 1917, cause
unknown. There were several children by this marriage, all
dying after living from a day to a month and a half. In
1918, Bennie, another illegitimate child, was born. After this
Minnie married a second time in Tallulah Falls, Georgia, in
1920, but her husband Prince was "so jealous and mean" that
she left him in 1921 in "less than a year's time" and came to
Charlotte, North Carolina "to work and get rid of him."

Since she has been in Charlotte she has tried to work to keep
the family together but she has found it very hard to feed,
clothe and provide shelter for three children.

The latter part of 1928 or the early part of 1929 she met
Willie Johnson who showed her some attention and "made
all kinds of promises to help her" if she would become his
friend. As a consequence Willie, Jr., was born October 3,
1929. During her confinement her expenses were going on
and there was no money to pay them. The landlord allowed
the rent to go on without troubling her, and Mrs. K. Harris
(white), who lives at 611 W. Seventh Street, for whom she
has worked for two years, came almost daily and brought
cooked and uncooked food. Bennie now about eleven years
old kept the house clean and did the cooking and attended her
needs. He also did the washing for the baby. Her daughter
Flora who came occasionally and the neighbors were of great

assistance. Willie Johnson came daily but offered very little financial aid.

At present Minnie is working for Mrs. K. Harris, earning $6.00 per week, hours are from 7:30 a.m. to 7:30 p.m. She cooks, cleans, nurses the three small Harris children and washes for them daily. One afternoon a week, Thursday, she is off at two p.m.

While Minnie is away from home working Mary White, a blind woman whose husband has been dead a year, and who has three children of her own, 18 months, 4, and 14 years of age, keeps house and cares for the baby, with Bennie's assistance.

Previous to her present job Minnie worked as presser at the Model Steam Laundry and the Glove Factory.

Church.—Minnie says that she is a member of Nazarene Baptist Church. Rev. Stanford, the pastor lives in Concord, North Carolina, and comes to hold service a night or two each month. Very often she attends Bishop Grace's Church with Mary White.

(c) *Mother's Family.*—Minnie's father died when she was such a small child that she can hardly remember him. Her mother married again but this husband has been dead a number of years.

Minnie's mother, who was born in Georgia, gave birth to nine children, and Minnie has no idea how many of them are still living. When last heard from her mother was in Florida with one of her daughters. A brother is in New York. An uncle, from last reports, was living in Gainesville, Georgia.

Minnie states that she does not keep in touch with her relatives, therefore, she is not in position to know if they are living or their exact whereabouts.

(d) *Children.*—Flora: born December 3, 1911, stopped school in the first grade. Minnie states Flora did not have the proper clothes and "the child got tired."

Frank: (Subject) born Sept. 2, 1914.

Bennie: born April 2, 1918, stopped school in second grade. Woman states that he is very smart at home and has never been in trouble. She would like to send him to school but is not able to get the necessary things for him, and Mary White is not capable of caring for the baby without Bennie's assistance.

Willie, Jr.: born October 3, 1929 in Charlotte, North Carolina.

2. DEVELOPMENTAL HISTORY

Minnie states that she had a mid-wife when Frank was born. There was no trouble. Frank has been healthy except for the diseases "which all chaps have," measles, whooping-cough and mumps.

3. HOME INFLUENCES AND NEIGHBORHOOD CONDITIONS

For the last year the family has lived at 123 West Twelfth Street. The house is a one story, six room double tenement, three rooms to a family. The front bedroom which serves as both bedroom and living room has two dirty windows which are hung with gay flowered cretonne. The floor is bare and dirty. The ceiling and wall show that at some time they were painted a dark grey. The three-quarter bed has two dirty worn mattresses which are partially covered with an old blanket. There is a dresser, wash-stand, small heater, a center table and three chairs which complete the furnishing of the room. Minnie occupies this room with the baby.

The middle room is even dirtier than the front room. It is occupied by Mary White, the blind woman, her children, and Minnie's children. There are two windows hung with soiled and worn, faded curtains. The two double beds, on opposite sides of the room, are covered with dirty and faded old quilts. Beside the old wash-stand there is a table and a few chairs. The small kitchen has only one window which allows little sun-light and fresh air to enter. There is a small wood stove, kitchen table, safe and an old ice box. This room is very dirty, and dirty dishes, pots and pans are piled on the stove and table. The back porch is small and shows an accumulation of old toys and many other things.

The front yard and the back yard are partly covered with grass. A dilapidated fence runs across the back, while a narrow, rough alley runs along the side of the house. On both sides of the alley are many two to four room houses built close together. The street in front of the house is hilly and has deep holes here and there. There is no side walk.

To the left of the house and across the alley there are a group of about five small stained houses which have wire fences and a few flowers in the yard. Most of those families have "a railroad man" as the man of the house.

Diagonally across the street are two houses which are sitting in water, caused by the rain of a few days previous. One house is occupied but the second one is not. In this yard the weeds have grown high and the fence is falling down.

4. Companions, Habits, and Interests

Since Minnie works all day she has never known many of Frank's companions. She thinks they were the neighborhood boys. On one or two occasions she has spoken to him about boys she heard were bad.

5. School and Work History

Frank stopped school in the second grade to go to work to help his mother make a living. Frank worked such a short while in each place that his mother "could not keep up with them." She does know that he was working at a pressing club when he first showed signs of being uncontrollable. It was while working there a boot-legger got him to work with him and Frank was caught. Minnie did "not know that the man was a boot-legger at the time."

6. History of Delinquencies and Court Record

The nature and extent of Frank's delinquencies are set forth officially in his juvenile court record, as follows:—

January 6, 1927. Before the Juvenile Court for larceny of pair of skates. Ordered to make restitution of $1.12, placed on probation.

October 11, 1928. Breaking and entering the apartment of B. F. Aiken, Standish Apartments, 101 N. Church St., and stealing several checks therefrom. Held in custody to be placed in a suitable private home.

October 19, 1928. Case reviewed, defendant committed to Brodie and Catherine Parker, colored people of excellent reputation and character, Rt. 3, Matthews, N. C. Ran away from this home immediately.

November 1, 1928. Case again reviewed, the defendant having been held at Separate Quarters County Jail since October 20, 1928. Again adjudged delinquent and ordered placed in a private home if possible.

December 20, 1928. Case again reviewed and boy released to the custody of his mother.

April 11, 1929. Before the Juvenile Court for breaking and entering cafe of Hattie Wilson, 18 N. Johnson Street, stealing and carrying away merchandise therefrom. Admitted his guilt, ordered committed to Morrison Industrial Training School at Hoffman, N. C., as soon as he can be admitted.

June 20, 1929. Case again reviewed and defendant ordered to be held until he can be placed in proper private home.

June 20, 1929. Case again reviewed and defendant ordered placed with John and Sallie Hampton, well recommended colored people living on route 14, Matthews, N. C. Refused to remain in said home.

August 22 and 29, 1929. Before the Juvenile Court for entering the place of business of Parcel Delivery Company and attempting to break and enter the safe of the said company, sentenced to one year in State's penitentiary.

The Juvenile Court Record also shows that Flora was at one time arrested for stealing. A good home was found for her in a nearby factory town with a white family.

In less than a year Flora was returned to Charlotte because of pregnancy. Minnie says that after the birth of the baby, Flora went to take care of Mrs. J. W. Maxwell (colored) in Burton Street Alley, who was sick. Since then she and her baby have remained with the family, coming to see Minnie occasionally.

7. CHILD'S OWN STORY

When the investigator talked with Frank at the Mecklenburg County jail in the presence of the jailer, Frank appeared to be full of mischief and he had the air of one who had had experience and responsibility.

The boy says "he just began getting into trouble" when he worked at a pressing club. He heard men tell jokes, curse and talk. A bootlegger who used to "hang around" asked him to work with him. Frank says that he did not know that he was to be used to help get the liquor. About the first or second time out in the country for the liquor the cops shot at them while at the still. The man ran and left him and he was arrested, but later that day was allowed to go. After this experience he became friendly with boys older than he was who used to "hang out" at stores or pressing clubs. The boys taught him how to break, enter and steal. He "tried it and continued to try it."

II. ISAAC PARK

1. FAMILY HISTORY

Since Isaac's mother and father are both dead, it was difficult to secure much information about the family history. According to an account given by Isaac's cousin, who is a trained nurse working for a prominent white physician in Charlotte, both Isaac's father and mother were born, raised and married in South Carolina, and Isaac's older brother, Arthur, was also born there. Isaac was born in Charlotte, Sept. 22, 1913, where his father had come to secure employment. The father died when Isaac was quite small, and the mother shortly thereafter married Logan Cook, a quiet, respected, middle aged Negro man employed at a large warehouse in Charlotte. When the mother died in 1925, Arthur and Isaac continued to live with their stepfather. Both boys were smart and obedient, and worked after school and on Sat-

urday. Things went well until the boys' companions insisted
on them staying out late at night, telling them that Logan
Cook was not their own father and they did not have to mind
him. After this the boys were no longer obedient, and stayed
out late at night in spite of their stepfather's protest. The
boys then left him and moved from place to place, but later
came back and lived with him until he married again in 1926.
For a while things went smoothly, then when the boys refused
to obey the new wife, Logan Cook told them they would have to
leave if they would not be obedient, and the boys left. Arthur
went to live with a paternal uncle who did wholesale stealing,
and had Arthur and his son to sell the stolen goods. This
uncle is now serving time on the county roads for stealing.
In November, 1928, Arthur was found guilty of larceny and
was sent to the State's Prison for five years. He was later
sent to an honor camp where he was caught selling liquor,
for which he was reduced in grade, and transferred to another
road camp in a distant part of the State.

2. CONDUCT RECORD

After leaving the home of his step-father, Isaac went to
live with a friend of his mother's. His delinquencies began soon
afterward, as may been seen from his Juvenile Court record
as follows:

August 11, 1927. Isaac Park before Juvenile Court, shooting
William T. Loggins, a colored boy of juvenile age. Ordered
to work and pay $16.00 restitution to Lattie Loggins, mother
of William T. Loggins.

April 4, 1929. Before the Juvenile Court for assault on the
person of Jeff Sawyer with a pistol with intent to kill. This
being the second offense for shooting, defendant sentenced to
six months at Separate Quarters County Jail, with provision
that he shall be placed in a private home provided home can
be found.

May 27, 1929. Placed in the custody of Bob Garland, well
recommended colored man living on a farm near Huntersville,
N. C. After a few weeks ran away from this home.

August 29, 1929. Before Juvenile Court for entering place
of business of Parcel Delivery Company and attempting to
break and enter the safe of the said company. Sentenced to
one year in State Penitentiary, upon its appearing from the
evidence that the defendant was on the outside watching while
the co-defendant, Frank P. Jones, was on the inside attempting
to break open the safe.

When interviewed in the county jail after his return from
the State's Prison, Isaac said that when Frank told him to
watch on the street and let him know if any one was coming,
he did not know Frank was going to try to open the safe of
the Parcel Delivery Company. He says he has learned his
lesson, and if he ever gets out of jail he will be a better boy.

CHAPTER XIII

CHILDREN IN THE STATE'S PRISON, RALEIGH, N. C., 1918-1931, WITH SPECIAL EMPHASIS UPON NEGRO CHILDREN

EVER SINCE the establishment of the North Carolina State's Prison in 1869, children have been found among its inmates. In the earliest list of pardons of penitentiary prisoners (1869) may be noted that of a boy from Wilmington sentenced for one year on a charge of assault. The reason for the pardon was, "Prisoner only ten years of age and was led into crime by bad company." Two or three years later at a hearing before a legislative committee on the penitentiary, a prison guard testified that he had known two boys from Wayne County "not more than twelve or fourteen years old to be kept in the (shower) bath[1] until they could not speak when they came out."

Children were committed to the State's Prison in the early days for even the most trivial offenses. A sixteen year old Negro boy from Caswell County, for example, was sentenced in 1875 to three years in the penitentiary for stealing an old worn plow point. "A weak-minded, almost idiotic boy of fourteen years," convicted in 1869 on circumstantial evidence of setting fire to a barn, was sentenced to five years' imprisonment. Another boy of fifteen "considered an idiot" was sen-

---

[1] The "shower bath" (not a method of promoting cleanliness, but a much dreaded form of punishment) consisted of a barrel of water (ice-cold in winter) on a ten-foot scaffold. The prisoner was placed in a coffin-like box underneath the barrel, with hands tied, and face upturned by placing a bayonet or pointed stick underneath the chin. The water from the barrel falling with terrific force upon the upturned face and eyes and open nostrils of the helpless prisoner caused strangling and intense suffering.

tenced to twenty-five years in the State's Prison for burglary. Other children were sent to the State's Prison for accidental homicide. A young white girl about sixteen years old, "of gentle retiring manners and reserved disposition, was brought in chains to the State Penitentiary under sentence of imprisonment for fifteen years for murder in the second degree—her crime being a blow inflicted with a pen knife upon a man who was accusing her of unchastity in the presence of her mother. Her surroundings had been bad, with a dissolute mother and a father of weak intellect." In 1889 a fourteen-year-old boy was sentenced on a charge of larceny to eighteen months in the penitentiary. When the sentence was pronounced the boy said in open court, "I don't give a damn for that!" whereupon the Judge changed the sentence to three years in the penitentiary, and the boy served two and a half years before he was pardoned.

It is impossible to learn from the Prison reports previous to 1883 the number of children confined in the State's Prison. In 1883, however, the reports began listing the number of children under fifteen years of age. The percentage of prisoners under fifteen years of age when admitted to the State's Prison is listed for the separate years as follows:

	Per Cent		Per Cent
1883	3.70	1889	6.17
1884	2.85	1890	4.98
1885	3.18	1891	6.34
1886	2.52	1892	3.90
1887	1.82	1893	2.95
1888	3.03		

Beginning in 1894, the prison reports list the number of prisoners under sixteen years of age upon admission, the percentages being as follows:

	Per Cent		Per Cent
1894	8.39	1905-1906 (2 yrs.)	8.04
1895	6.14	1907-1908 (2 yrs.)	2.46
1896	4.24	1909-1910 (2 yrs.)	3.22
——	——	1911-1912 (2 yrs.)	1.02

Per Cent		Per Cent
1899-1900 (2 yrs.) .. 9.03		1913-1914 (2 yrs.) .. 2.79
1901-1902 (2 yrs.) .. 3.39		1915-1916 (2 yrs.) .. 3.97
1903-1904 (2 yrs.) .. 5.01		1917-1918 (2 yrs.) .. 2.46

Unfortunately these earlier reports of the State's Prison failed to classify these children according to race, sex, charge, or length of sentence.

In the following tables are presented important social data from the Prison files secured by Lieutenant Oxley and Mr. Eugene Brown of the State Board of Charities and Public Welfare, regarding children sixteen years of age and under, committed to the State's Prison in Raleigh during the fourteen-year period, January 1, 1918-December 31, 1931. During this period, according to Table XXII, 349 children were admitted to the Prison, 139 white children and 210 Negro children. As pointed out elsewhere in this study, the white children make up approximately 69 per cent, and the Negro children compose about 31 per cent of all children in North Carolina of juvenile court age. It is apparent, therefore, that the proportion of Negro children in the State's Prison is almost twice as high as the proportion of Negro children in the state as a whole. It is significant also that the proportion of girls committed to the State's Prison is only about one-third as high as the proportion of girls handled by the juvenile courts of North Carolina.

In Table XXIII is presented the number of children of each specified year of age, from eleven years of age through sixteen years, by race and sex. Eight children, all Negro, under fourteen years of age, and hence belonging under the exclusive jurisdiction of the juvenile court, were committed illegally to the State's Prison.

Why are children sixteen years of age and under sent to a State's Prison anyway, in a state which boasts of a juvenile court in every county, and which is provided with five state training schools for juvenile delinquents? A glance at the charges (Tables XXIV and XXV) indicates that over 60 per cent of the children are committed to the State's Prison for offenses against property, namely, breaking and entering, 30.4 per cent, and larceny, 29.8 per cent. Rape is the most frequent of the offenses against the person, comprising 8.3 per cent of all charges, while murder makes up only 5.4 per cent, burglary 4.9 per cent, and arson 3.7 per cent of all cases. It is difficult to understand why any child should be committed to a State's Prison for crime against nature, yet 2.3 per cent of all children sent to the State's Prison are committed on this charge. As far as racial differences in charges is concerned, it may be of interest to note that white children lead in larceny, murder, arson, and robbery, while the Negro children lead in breaking and entering, rape, manslaughter, burglary, assault, and crime against nature. The number of girls is too small to draw any significant conclusions, but it may be pointed out that the most frequent charge of the white girls is arson, while the most frequent offense of Negro girls is larceny.

The last table (Table XXVI) is presented for the purpose of showing the difference in length of sentences of the white as compared with that of the Negro children. Over half of the white children, 55.4 per cent, were committed on sentences of less than two years, while only 28.5 per cent of the Negro children had sentences of this length. On the other hand, 31 per cent of the Negro children were sentenced for five years and over. The corresponding group of white children comprised only 17.2 per cent. It is quite evident that, comparing sentences of white and of Negro children for all charges, or by separate charges, the sentences of Negro children considerably exceeds those of the white children. Since, as already pointed out, there is no difference in the seriousness of offenses of whites as compared with Negro children, the difference in length of sentences of the two races is due apparently to race prejudice.

TABLE XXII

CHILDREN 16 YEARS OF AGE AND UNDER COMMITTED TO THE STATE'S PRISON, RALEIGH, N. C., JANUARY 1, 1918-DECEMBER 31, 1931, BY RACE AND SEX*

Race and Sex	Number	Per Cent Distribution
White...	139	39.8
Boys..	126	36.1
Girls..	13	3.7
Negro..	210	60.2
Boys..	193	55.3
Girls..	17	4.9
Total...................................	349	100.0

* In this and the following tables two Indians and one Cuban are not included.

TABLE XXIII

CHILDREN 16 YEARS OF AGE AND UNDER COMMITTED TO THE STATE'S PRISON, RALEIGH, N. C., JANUARY 1, 1918-DECEMBER 31, 1931, BY RACE, SEX AND AGE

Age	Total Cases	White Total	Male	Female	Negro Total	Male	Female
11	1	0	0	0	1	1	0
12	2	0	0	0	2	2	0
13	5	0	0	0	5	4	1
14	29	4	4	0	25	25	0
15	75	26	22	4	49	43	6
16	237	109	100	9	128	118	10
Total.............	349	139	126	13	210	193	17

TABLE XXIV

CASES OF CHILDREN 16 YEARS OF AGE AND UNDER COMMITTED TO THE STATE'S PRISON, RALEIGH, N. C., JANUARY, 1, 1918-DECEMBER 31, 1931, BY RACE, SEX, AND CHARGE

Charge	Grand Total	Total	White Male	Female	Total	Negro Male	Female
Breaking and Entering.	106	40	37	3	66	63	3
Larceny	104	54	54	0	50	41	9
Rape	29	3	3	0	26	26	0
Manslaughter	24	8	7	1	16	14	2
Murder	19	10	9	1	9	9	0
Burglary	17	2	2	0	15	14	1
Arson	13	10	3	7	3	2	1
Assault	14	4	4	0	10	9	1
Crime vs. Nature	8	0	0	0	8	8	0
Robbery	7	5	5	0	2	2	0
Miscellaneous	8	3	2	1	5	5	0
Total	349	139	126	13	210	193	17

TABLE XXV

PER CENT DISTRIBUTION OF CASES OF CHILDREN 16 YEARS OF AGE AND UNDER COMMITTED TO THE STATE'S PRISON, RALEIGH, N. C., JANUARY 1, 1918-DECEMBER 31, 1931, BY RACE, SEX, AND CHARGE

Charge	Grand Total	White Total	Negro Total
Breaking and Entering	30.4	28.8	31.4
Larceny	29.8	38.9	23.8
Rape	8.3	2.1	12.4
Manslaughter	6.9	5.8	7.6
Murder	5.4	7.2	4.3
Burglary	4.9	1.4	7.1
Arson	3.7	7.2	1.4
Assault	4.0	2.9	4.8
Crime vs. Nature	2.3	...	3.8
Robbery	2.0	3.6	1.0
Miscellaneous	2.3	2.1	2.4
Total	100.0	100.0	100.0

TABLE XXVI

Length of Sentence of Children 16 Years of Age and Under Committed to the State Prison, Raleigh, N. C., January 1, 1918-December 31, 1931, by Race

Sentence	All Offenses						Breaking and Entering				Larceny			
	Total		Negro		White		Negro		White		Negro		White	
	No.	Percent	No.	Percent	No.	Percent	No.	Percent	No.	Percent	No.	Percent	No.	Percent
6 mo. and under 12 mo.	21	6.0	7	3.3	14	10.0	4	6.1	4	10.0	2	4.0	8	14.8
12 mo. and under 18 mo.	87	24.9	42	20.0	45	32.4	18	27.3	19	47.5	15	30.0	19	35.2
18 mo. and under 2 yrs.	29	8.3	11	5.2	18	13.0	6	9.1	5	12.5	3	6.0	5	9.3
2 yrs. and under 3 yrs.	70	20.1	47	22.4	23	16.6	18	27.3	6	15.0	17	34.0	13	24.1
3 yrs. and under 4 yrs.	41	11.7	29	13.8	12	8.6	9	13.6	1	2.5	6	12.0	6	11.1
4 yrs. and under 5 yrs.	12	3.4	9	4.3	3	2.2	1	1.5	0	...	3	6.0	1	1.8
5 yrs. and under 10 yrs.	47	13.5	31	14.8	16	11.5	6	9.1	4	10.0	3	6.0	2	3.7
10 yrs. and under 15 yrs.	20	5.7	14	6.7	6	4.3	3	4.5	1	2.5	1	2.0	...	...
15 yrs. and under 20 yrs.	14	4.0	13	6.2	1	.7	1	1.5	...	...	...	...	...	...
20 yrs. and under 30 yrs.	5	1.4	4	1.9	1	.7	...	...	...	...	...	...	...	...
30 yrs. and under 50 yrs.	2	.7	2	.9	0	...	...	...	...	...	...	...	...	...
50 yrs. and over	1	.3	1	.5	0	...	...	...	...	...	...	...	...	...
Total	349	100.0	210	100.0	139	100.0	66	100.0	40	100.0	50	100.0	54	100.0

PART IV

NEGRO CHILDREN IN HOME AND SCHOOL

CHAPTER XIV

CARE OF DEPENDENT NEGRO CHILDREN THROUGH MOTHERS' AID AND IN FOSTER HOMES

MOTHERS' AID

THE NORTH CAROLINA General Assembly of 1923 passed "An Act to Aid Needy Orphan Children in the Homes of Worthy Mothers." This is known as the Mothers' Aid Law. This General Assembly likewise Appropriated an annual sum of $50,000 for the State Mothers' Aid Fund. This fund is distributed among the counties participating with the state in its administration on the basis of population and each county appropriates from county funds a sum equal to the amount it receives from the state fund. The combined state and county fund becomes the total fund available in a county for eligible applicants for aid residing in that county.

To be eligible "to apply for mothers' aid a woman must be the mother of a child or children under fourteen years of age, a resident of the state of North Carolina for three years, and a resident of the county for one year preceding, and possessed of sufficient mental, moral, and physical fitness to be capable of maintaining a home for herself and child or children and prevented only from lack of means. Such person must be either a widow, or divorced, or deserted, if it be found impossible to require the husband to support her, or the husband is found to be mentally or physically incapacitated to support his family, or if the husband be confined in any jail and assigned to work the roads of any county or in any penal or eleemosynary institution, provided no relative is able and willing to undertake sufficient aid."

The law further specifies "that the maximum amount to be allowed per month under this act shall not exceed fifteen dollars for one child, ten dollars additional for the second child, and five dollars additional for the third child, or any excess of three; provided, the total amount shall not exceed forty dollars, except in extraordinary circumstances in which it appears to the satisfaction of the board of county commissioners that a total of forty dollars a month would be insufficient to secure the purposes set forth." The grants actually made, however, are usually far under the maximum. This is especially true of rural sections where the family has a garden, pig, chickens, and cow, and can secure fuel from near-by woods. In the urban and textile centers, grants more frequently are for maximum amounts.

The average mothers' aid family consists of mother and four children under fourteen years of age. Average grant per month was $16.44 for 1929-1930 and $16.67 for 1930-1931. On December 31, 1931, there was a total of 419 families receiving this assistance from public funds. To that date 1,084 families had been aided through this fund since it first became available. Between 70 and 75 per cent of the cases discontinued (663), were discontinued because the mother had married again or the family had become self-supporting.

The majority of mothers' aid families live in the more rural sections of the state, as North Carolina is still predominantly agricultural. Even in the more populous counties having cities, more mothers' aid families are to be found in the country or in mill villages than in the city proper. In 1929-30 seventy-nine of the one hundred counties administered mothers' aid; in 1930-31, eighty-three counties; in 1931-32, eighty-seven counties.

A Negro Family Receiving Mothers' Aid.—The family of Ellen Abbott is that of a successful Negro mothers' aid case. The record is one among the very best of the total of 1,084 cases. In 1920 at the age of thirty-seven years, this mother was left a widow with six children, ages ranging from four to twelve years. Both the woman and her deceased husband were natives of county of residence. The woman was the daughter of a Negro school teacher, was well educated and highly respected by both white and Negro citizens. She owned her home, a four-room dwelling, and two acres of land located on the outskirts of the county-seat of a large cotton-growing county in the southeast section of the state. Taxes and insurance amounted to $28.00 per year. Kerosene lamps were used for lighting and water was secured from the well in the yard; so there were no light nor water bills. On the two acres the family planned to raise enough corn to feed the cow and "bread" themselves. They also raised potatoes and a good garden. There were pigs and chickens to provide meat and eggs for the family's use. Relatives assisted the family for almost four years and until the death of the maternal grandfather. In May, 1924 (ten months after the fund became available), a small monthly grant from the state and county mothers' aid fund was made to the mother. The children were now able to help not only with the work about the place but on neighboring farms during the summer and fall and in odd jobs about town on Saturdays and after school hours during the school term. They hoed and picked cotton and were paid in provisions. All the children consistently brought their earnings to the mother throughout the five-year period in which mothers' aid assisted the family. The mother earned by sewing as well as by work in cotton field and crops at home. She was a clever seamstress and not only altered worn garments most attractively for use of the family but she sold any surplus of altered garments to neighbors either for food or cash. She also was dressmaker for neighbors. This same skill was utilized in making the home attractive with draperies, covers, etc., from cheap material or old materials which had been dyed. As the children grew older and could earn more, the family invested in a suite of furniture for the living room, buying it on the instalment plan. But they were not able to exchange an ancient square piano and an organ, long family posessions, for a better, more tuneful piano which could be used, as they at one time hoped. Some music could be had, however, from the organ, and current magazines received as gifts from friends supplemented the small number of books. So cultural phases of family life were not neglected. The family was active in both Sunday School and church work. With the exception of dental work for the mother, there were no health conditions to be remedied. School records were excellent. In May, 1927, the oldest child, a daughter, graduated from high school and in the fall, with the help of an interested friend, was able to enter one of the grade A colleges for Negroes for the full four-year course. Her grades in this institution were A's and B's. The oldest boy graduated from high school in May, 1928, and went North, where he had secured a job with a white family with the privilege of attending college. In 1929 the third child finished high school. The baby of the family was now in her thirteenth year and the only child for whom the mothers' aid was available. Because of this fact and the fact that the family had steadily improved its condition, it was agreed it could be discontinued from mothers' aid as self-supporting, July 1, 1929. The last item of the record is a letter from the State Director of Mothers' Aid to the mother acknowledging receipt of her letter of appreciation and gratitude for mothers' aid. The last sentence of the letter reads, "I want to say that we are very proud of your record as a 'Mothers' Aider,' and are very glad that we could have been of any service to you and your children for the past few years."

Boarding or Foster Homes

The General Assembly of 1929 set aside the small sum of $2,500 from the annual mothers' aid appropriation to be used as an emergency fund for needy prisoners' families who were not eligible to assistance from the mothers' aid fund. By means of this fund a number of children of prisoners were cared for in boarding or foster homes.

But there were many other children in the state whose fathers were not prisoners who needed this care. They were children not eligible for help from mothers' aid, or for child-placing in a home for adoption or from a child-caring institution and who perhaps needed especial study because of behavior problems. For several years their peculiar needs had been realized by both private and public child-caring agencies in the state, and they were recognized as a truly neglected group.

Moreover, it was felt that their needs could best be met by a state boarding home fund sufficiently flexible to allow either temporary or long time care, according to the problem of the individual child.

So the General Assembly of 1931 made an annual appropriation of $5,000 for the biennium 1931-33 to be used for "Care of Dependent Children in Boarding Homes or with Foster Mothers" and to be administered under rules and regulations prescribed by the State Board of Charities and Public Welfare. The rules and regulations are as follows:

1. That county of legal residence of a child meet the state fund with an equal amount for relief given him pursuant to a constructive plan for child's welfare. Refund to be made to the county at the end of each quarter.

2. Only children of juvenile court age who have legal settlement in North Carolina and who have become charges of and remain under the supervision of the local juvenile court through official court action are eligible for assistance from this fund.

3. That a thorough investigation of each child needing such help including study of his home and relatives be made by the local superintendent of welfare (chief probation officer), or assistant, and submitted to the county boards of public welfare and commissioners for approval before application is sent to the State Board for action.

4. That a child receiving this aid continue under the supervision of the juvenile court and State Board of Charities and Public Welfare, or of the said State Board, during the period that aid is received.

5. That in an emergency situation where legal residence cannot be established in a county, full responsibility for the child's need be met from the State Fund.

6. That no child is to be made a Ward of the State Board of Charities and Public Welfare without consent of the said Board after it shall have reviewed the investigation of the case.

Every home used as a boarding home must be licensed by the State Board of Charities and Public Welfare for that purpose. To receive such license, the home must meet definite minimum requirements.

A Negro Child Placed in a Boarding Foster Home.—One
little Negro girl is maintained in a foster home in part from
this fund. She is now about seven or eight years old and has
been a state ward for several years. This child was found in
a so-called children's institution, undernourished and feeble.
This institution, which had been exploiting its inmates, was
closed; the other children had been placed and she had been
made a state ward by juvenile court order. At first she appeared to be deformed. She was unable to walk or talk, though
she was then about three or four years of age. So she was
admitted to the North Carolina Orthopedic Hospital for treatment. Here she remained for almost a year, during which time it
was found that she was not congenitally deformed but rachitic.
Slowly she gained strength and learned to walk and talk. When
released from the hospital, she was placed in a good Negro
home where she at first perhaps received too much attention
and was in danger of being spoiled. The foster mother gave
her excellent physical care and some kindergarten training;
so she has seemed to develop into a normal child mentally.
Unfortunately, she will always bear the scar of early neglect
in minor malformation of bone structure due to rickets. For
several years the foster parents supported the child without
financial assistance from the State Board. But following illness of the foster-father and unemployment due to financial
depression, a small monthly sum is now assisting the foster
parents in caring for her.

Children born to inmates of the State Prison have been
removed when six months of age from their mothers and placed
in foster homes, usually with relatives. These children, the
majority of whom are illegitimate, are charges of the juvenile
court of the county of the mother's settlement; when the mother
is released from prison she may be given custody of the child
if the juvenile court decides this is to the best interest of the
child. Necessary expenses for these children incidental to and
pending placement in foster homes have been met in the past
from the emergency prisoner's fund. Now assistance may be
given from the boarding or foster home fund.

In a few instances it has been necessary to place children born to inmates of state hospitals for the insane. When a home with relatives is not available, the child is placed in a boarding or foster home where every opportunity is given him for normal development.

Good homes for Negro children are not difficult to find. Several state wards of mixed parentage have been happily placed in excellent Negro foster homes.

Wholesome family life is the normal environment for development of a childhood, healthy mentally and physically. When the child's own family cannot assure this for him, society must provide some way. Whether a dependent child needing such care receives it in his own home with his own mother or in a home with a boarding or foster mother, depends on his individual situation. It is hoped that eventually there will be available in full measure through public funds either mothers' aid or a boarding or foster home for every child needing such care and protection.

CHAPTER XV

THE NEGRO UNMARRIED MOTHER AND HER CHILD

ILLEGITIMACY RATE, BY RACE, 1921-1930

ALTHOUGH NORTH CAROLINA was admitted into the birth registration area of the United States in 1916, it was not until 1921 that the rate of illegitimacy for the white and for the Negro population was made available in the published reports of the North Carolina State Board of Health. In the following table are presented the number and the percentage of illegitimate births, white and Negro, for each year of the ten year period, 1921-1930.[1]

TABLE XXVII

NUMBER AND PERCENTAGE OF ILLEGITIMATE BIRTHS, WHITE AND NEGRO, IN NORTH CAROLINA, 1921-1930, BY YEARS

	Negro		White	
	Number	Percent Illeg.	Number	Percent Illeg.
1921	3,403	12.88	927	1.53
1922	3,328	13.31	873	1.55
1923	3,188	12.49	907	1.55
1924	3,294	12.49	1,064	1.76
1925	2,687	10.62	867	1.49
1926	3,344	13.36	1,039	1.82
1927	3,585	14.24	1,037	1.79
1928	3,715	15.13	1,006	1.80
1929	3,783	16.17	1,063	1.99
1930	3,932	17.33	1,382	2.58

From this table it appears that in general the Negro illegitimacy rate is about eight times as great as that of the

---

[1] These figures are compiled from the annual reports of the Bureau of Vital Statistics of the N. C. State Board of Health.

whites, and that there has been a gradual increase in illegitimacy for both races throughout the ten year period. In 1930, however, the white illegitimacy rate had increased over the preceding year about 29 per cent, while the Negro rate had increased only about 7 per cent. The State Board of Health explained the increase in illegitimacy for the past few years as being due to "an increase in drinking indulged in by both sexes, and perhaps the depression which has caused a decrease in marriages."

A Survey of Rural Illegitimacy in Orange County, N. C. 1923-1927[1]

Many studies have been made of illegitimacy in urban areas, including both those mothers living in the city, and those who came to the city from other places in order to hide their pregnancy. This study, however, is an attempt to show the causes and results of illegitimacy in a rural county in the South—hitherto an unexplored field. Both white and Negro unmarried mothers are included, and in the tables presenting the social data, the races are listed separately for purpose of contrast.

One of the principal difficulties in making a study of rural illegitimacy is locating the unmarried mother. In the city she is most often discovered because she comes to some social agency seeking aid. In the country, owing to the lack of social agencies, the girl, both among the whites and the Negroes, is cared for in her own family. In the country too there is a stronger feeling of family solidarity than there is in a city. Even those people living in small towns have carried this feeling with them when they moved in from the country. This is due to the fact that in a rural, farming region, the family is the economic unit of production.

In a large city there is a higher rate of illegitimacy than

---

[1] A thesis submitted by Miss Janet Quinlan to the University of North Carolina for the degree of Master of Arts in the Department of Sociology, June, 1929. This study was made entirely independently of the Rosenwald study, but it throws such valuable light upon the Negro unmarried mother in the rural South, that the major results are presented here.

18

there is in the country. This is because so many girls go from the country to the city in order to hide their pregnancy from their friends and families. There are also more chance acquaintances in a city. In rural areas, if the girl stays at home, she keeps her child. The ratio of mothers keeping their children in the country is much higher than it is in the city. This may partially be accounted for by the fact that in the country even the labor of a child may be an asset, while in the city a child is a liability. In the former, the mother and child fit into the economic system while in urban regions this may not be the case. Then the fact that in the country there are few, if any, agencies through which the unmarried mother may dispose of her child would cause her to keep her child.

In both places the causes are about the same, although the paucity of rural recreation is an important factor. It is in the way the mothers are viewed that the differences show. In the city they lead an abnormal life, shut off, for a time at least, from their everyday existence. This applies to both whites and Negroes. Not the causes but the lack of treatment, either before, at the time of, or after the birth of the child, is the most outstanding difference between rural and urban illegitimacy. The city mother seeks assistance, the country mother must be found.

In making this study the registered illegitimate births occurring in the five-year period, 1923-1927, inclusive, were used. After the names of the unmarried mothers had been secured from the county register of deeds' office a personal visit was made to each of the mothers yet living in the county. The types of information desired had been organized in the form of a questionnaire, which was not shown to the mothers, but was filled out by the investigator after the interview. The factors secured in this way on questionnaire blanks form the basis for the tables presented in this report.

During this period, 1923-1927, 114 births were registered as illegitimate, 24 white and 90 Negro. Of these mothers, 31 had moved away, 4 had died, 7 had given birth to two or more illegitimate children during this period, and of 14 no trace could be found. This left 58 cases, or taking into account the

7 repeaters, 51 unmarried mothers, 11 white and 41 Negro.

Although the number of unmarried mothers which could be used was much smaller than had been expected, the explanation may be found in the transient population involved. There is a large amount of tenancy on farms in the county,[2] and tenancy ever carries with it a changing population. Cotton and tobacco are the two chief crops of the county, and where these are grown, there is a shifting population. The majority of the girls had moved from the northern part of the county, either to the adjoining counties of Caswell or Person, or over into Virginia. It is in the northern part of the county that most of the tobacco is grown. Cropper farmers drift in and out, leaving no trace. Then the fact that the Negro migration northward occurred during this time would account for a certain loss. At another period the change in population might not have been so great.

Orange County, selected for this survey, is located in the north central part of North Carolina—about midway between Greensboro and Raleigh. With the exception of three small towns, the county is entirely rural. The land is hilly and not very fertile except in the northern end. The entire population of the county is 17,870, of which 12,237, or 68 per cent, are whites, and 5,635, or 32 per cent, are Negroes.[3] Of this population 14,078, or 79 per cent, live in the rural regions, 64.7 per cent of the farms being operated by their owners. The Negroes are not grouped in the towns, but live throughout the county, either on farms or in small communities.

The total number of births occurring in Orange County for the five years taken for this study, 1923-1927, inclusive, was 2,927; of these, 1,838 were white and 1,089 Negro. As can be seen by Table XXVIII, out of this number 114 were definitely registered as illegitimate, 24 white and 90 Negro. Referring to Table XXIX, the percentage of the total illegitimate births was 3.9, giving a percentage of the white illegitimate births of 1.3 and for the Negro 8.3.

---

[2] The proportion of farm tenancy in Orange County is 35.3 per cent. U. S. Fourteenth Census, *North Carolina State Compendium*, 1925.

[3] *Ibid.*, p. 39.

Although five years is not a sufficient length of time to enable one to come to any definite conclusions concerning the birth rate, yet during this period both the legitimate and illegitimate birth rates show a slight tendency to decline. There is a marked decrease in the white illegitimacy rate, while the Negro rate is more variable. There is a higher rate in some townships than there is in others.

In all but two or three instances, when the unmarried mothers, along with their families, understood the purpose of the study they were quite willing to coöperate. Generally the visit, especially among the Negroes, was the occasion for the whole family to gather, all eager to help. This showed a strong family feeling, although it handicapped the investigator in her work. In this way a great deal of general information could be gathered.

Among the white mothers 11 lived in the two small mill villages. On the whole the white mothers were a little more difficult to approach than the Negroes. In three cases of white illegitimacy the girl had been in school at the time of her misfortune, and in others either working at home or in the mill. Unfortunately no mental tests were made. The story of the majority was that they had known the man, he had promised marriage, then later refused. Her family had cared for her, assisting her to get some aid from the father of the child. Generally this aid came through outside settlement. Since the birth of her child she has been living at home, either working on the farm or in the mill to help support her child.

The Negro mother lives either on a farm or in a small Negro community. As is characteristic of the whole race, they are most cheerful and friendly. The father of the child born out of wedlock was someone who had come to work nearby and then drifted on to another job. Promise of marriage among the Negroes was not a common cause. Mollie, or Josie, or Nancy goes on living at home, if she is not married, helping with the washing her mother takes in, or working on the farm. It is her aim to marry, but to find someone much "better 'count" than the father of her child. Her attitude is not bitter, for she says of the father, "Yes'm, he some good. He right smart, but he don't work." She accepts her lot philosophically and is very fond of her baby.

In the eyes of the whites there is nothing unusual in a Negro woman's having more than one illegitimate child. There is a different standard by which the two races are judged. A white person explains this by saying that the Negro has not yet grown up to the white people's moral standard. This explains the humorous sympathy shown in the South toward most Negroes, even to those women having as many as six illegitimate children. From an ethical viewpoint one can question such a standard, but in practice it works well. Illegitimacy on the part of a white house-maid would be the occasion for instant dismissal, but illegitimacy on the part of a Negro servant would not endanger her position. Several Negro cooks in the county had as many as three illegitimate children, and one had six.

TABLE XXVIII

COMPARISON BETWEEN ILLEGITIMATE BIRTHS AND THE TOTAL NUMBER OF BIRTHS FOR WHITES AND NEGROES IN ORANGE COUNTY, NORTH CAROLINA, BY YEARS, 1923-1927

Year	Illegitimate Births			All Births		
	White	Negro	Total	White	Negro	Total
1923	11	19	30	409	221	630
1924	5	17	22	377	219	596
1925	3	23	26	380	227	607
1926	3	20	23	335	206	541
1927	2	12	14	257	216	573
Total	24	90	114	1,858	1,089	2,947

TABLE XXIX

PERCENTAGE OF ILLEGITIMACY, WHITE AND NEGRO, IN ORANGE COUNTY,
NORTH CAROLINA, BY YEARS, 1923-1927

| Year | Percentage of Illegitimacy | | |
	White	Negro	Total
1923	2.7	8.6	4.8
1924	1.3	7.8	3.7
1925	.8	9.7	4.3
1926	.9	9.6	4.2
1927	.6	5.6	2.4
Total	1.3	8.3	3.9

Ages of the Unmarried Mothers.—The ages of the unmarried
mothers ranged from 14 to 42, as is shown by Table **XXX**.
Seventy-four girls were between the ages of 16 and 21,[4] and
in this group 13 girls gave 17 as their age at the time of the
birth of their illegitimate child. The white unmarried mothers
were younger than the Negroes, who were scattered over a
longer age period. There were two Negro mothers for whom
no age was given on the birth registration.

Only on 32 birth registrations was the name of the father
given.[5] On 10 of these, all Negro, his name, but no other information was found. On the other 72 birth registrations his
side of the page was left entirely blank. The most common
age for the men was between 21 and 26, with the greatest
number, 6, at 23. In nearly every instance the man and the
girl were near the same age. Only three times was there a
marked discrepancy. In one, the father was 36, the mother
21; in another the father 40, the mother 26; and there was
one case in which the man was 46 and the girl only 16. The
majority of cases in which both the mother's and father's

---

[4] These ages were given on the birth registration and authenticity cannot
be guaranteed.

[5] In North Carolina the name of the father is not required on the birth
registration. If placed there, it is done so with the consent of the mother.

names were given would show that there is no great difference in ages.

TABLE XXX

AGES OF UNMARRIED MOTHERS, WHITE AND NEGRO, IN ORANGE COUNTY, NORTH CAROLINA, 1923-1927

Age of Mother	White	Negro	Total Number	Percent
Under 15 years*......................	2	4	6	6.0
15 to 19 years........................	11	40	51	45.0
20 to 24 years........................	7	30	37	32.0
25 to 29 years........................	1	8	9	8.0
30 to 34 years........................	2	2	4	3.0
35 to 39 years........................	0	3	3	3.0
40 to 42 years........................	1	1	2	1.5
Age unknown	0	2	2	1.5
Total	24	90	114	100.0

* The 6 unmarried mothers under 15 were 14 years of age.

Home Conditions and Ownership.—Since the city limits of the towns, especially that of Hillsboro, do not include all the people who really make up the community, three divisions were made—those living in towns, those living in communities, and those living on farms. In the second division were included those who, in the case of the whites, worked in the mills at West Hillsboro, and, in the case of Negroes, those living in the Negro communities just outside the city limits. The fact that the majority of these Negroes were in domestic service in Hillsboro will enable one to judge how very close they really were. Then there are two well defined Negro communities in the county, that at Morrow's Store and that at Cheeks Crossing. Both of these are on the main highway, only two miles apart. As these settlements comprise more than 15 families, they are distinctly apart from the rural farms. In the last division are those living on farms, near and remote.

On the whole the housing conditions for the unmarried mothers were unsatisfactory, since the majority of them lived in houses far too small for the size of the family. This would prohibit privacy and home recreation, making the girls go elsewhere for their pleasures. The housing conditions of farmers in general, however, leave much to be desired, and the homes from which the unmarried mothers come are no worse than the average home in Orange County.

Referring to Table XXXI, one may see that the proportion of home-owning families was 49 per cent, and of renting families 51 per cent.[6] It was surprising to find that the number of home owners and renters was almost the same, although the number of owners was higher than expected. With such results one cannot say that the unmarried mothers come from a lower type of home than the majority of girls who do not have children born out of wedlock. In the cases in which the girls had married and were living in their own homes they showed great pride of ownership, and had made their homes quite attractive.

The six white mothers living in towns and communities lived in the mill villages of Carrboro and West Hillsboro (Table XXXI). The two unmarried mothers from home-owning fam-

TABLE XXXI

HOME-OWNERSHIP OF FAMILIES AND TYPES OF COMMUNITIES IN WHICH UNMARRIED MOTHERS, WHITE AND NEGRO, LIVED, IN ORANGE COUNTY, NORTH CAROLINA, 1923-1927

Type of Community	Owners			Renters		
	White	Negro	Total	White	Negro	Total
Town	2	3	5	1	7	8
Settlements*	0	9	9	3	2	5
Farm	3	8	11	2	11	13
Total	5	20	25	6	20	26

* A settlement includes the mill village of West Hillsboro, the two Negro communities near Hillsboro and the Negro communities in the county. For the purpose of this study a community includes 15 families, earning their living by other means than farming.

[6] The percentage of home ownership in Orange County is 57.0 U. S. Fourteenth Census, *North Carolina State Compendium* (1925), Table 23, p. 54.

ilies were sisters, and, accordingly, came from the same family.
This makes only one home-owning family among the whites in
any town or community.

School Record.—As is shown by Tables XXXII and
XXXIII, the grade completed in school, with only a few excep-
tions, was one of the grammar grades. Only four mothers had
gone beyond the seventh grade and one beyond the tenth. The
grade which the girl had finished, not the one she was in at the
time of leaving school, was the standard by which the school
attainment was judged. Eight, 4 whites and 4 Negroes, had
never been to school at all. One Negro girl stated that she
went to school only three days. Among the white unmarried
mothers two were of such low mentality that their parents
had never sent them to school. More unmarried mothers were
found who had completed the fifth grade than any other grade.
They best understood the limit of their education when asked
which "reader" they had completed. The white unmarried
mothers were more advanced educationally than the Negroes.
It must be remembered in this connection that the most of
the rural schools, especially those for Negroes, have been
inferior to the schools in towns and are only beginning to
improve. Even though the educational record for the unmarried
mother is low, it is probably no lower than the general average
in rural sections of the county.[7] No unmarried mother had a
high record of school attendance, although the number of white
unmarried mothers was too small to make an adequate
comparison.

---

[7] In order to give some idea of the nature and extent of the school
attendance in Orange County, it may be pointed out that the white enrollment for the four school years, 1924-1928 was 3,046, and the percentage of
attendance was 72.9. The Negro enrollment was 2,297, and the percentage
of attendance was 68.8. This makes the total percentage of attendance
70.8. In the four year period taken, 1924-1928, the Negroes showed more
gain in their percentage of attendance than the whites. *State School Facts*,
Vol. V, No. 8, Jan. 1, 1929. (Published semi-monthly by the State Superintendent of Public Instruction, Raleigh, North Carolina.)

TABLE XXXII

EDUCATIONAL STATUS (GRADES COMPLETED) OF UNMARRIED MOTHERS, WHITE
AND NEGRO, IN ORANGE COUNTY, NORTH CAROLINA, 1923-1927

| | Grade of School Completed | | | | | | | | | |
	1	2	3	4	5	6	7	8	9	10
White	0	0	1	0	1	1	2	1	0	1
Negro	2	2	3	8	12	6	1	1	0	1
Total	2	2	4	8	13	7	3	2	0	2

TABLE XXXIII

EDUCATIONAL STATUS (SCHOOL ATTENDANCE) OF UNMARRIED MOTHERS,
WHITE AND NEGRO, IN ORANGE COUNTY, NORTH CAROLINA, 1923-1927;
NUMBER AND PERCENTAGE ATTENDING SCHOOL

| | School Attendance | | | |
| | Never Attended | | Attended | |
	Number	Percent	Number	Percent
White	4	36	7	64
Negro	4	10	36	90
Total	8	16	43	84

Church Membership and Attendance.—As could have been
expected in a rural community where the church and church
activities have a large place in the people's lives, there was a
high percentage of church membership. As can be seen by
Table XXXIV, 37, or all but 14 of the unmarried mothers,
had church connections, either past or present, and in the
latter group four attended church services. Of the five white
mothers who were still church members, four had voluntarily
dropped out of the church since the birth of their illegitimate
child. Only one of the white mothers continued to attend
regularly.

With the Negroes, all but seven of whom were or had been
church members, conditions were more unusual. Of this number
14 were still faithful attendants at church, 11 went irregularly,

and seven had been put out of the church because of their misconduct. When one considers how much a Negro woman enjoys her church life, the severity of this measure can be better understood. However, the church doors had not closed irrevocably for the erring, for several who at one time had been put out of the church were now in good standing, and three others said, "When I'se ready I kin come back in." It appears that the Methodist Churches are more strict than those of other denominations in their treatment of the unmarried mother, for six of the mothers who had been put out of the church were members of this denomination. All who had been put out of the church spoke of it sadly, although several gave the impression that they would enjoy making their repentance.

TABLE XXXIV

CHURCH STATUS OF UNMARRIED MOTHERS, WHITE AND NEGRO, IN ORANGE COUNTY, NORTH CAROLINA, 1923-1927

Church Status	White		Negro		Total	
	No.	Percent	No.	Percent	No.	Percent
Members attending regularly...	1	9	14	35	15	29
Members attending irregularly..	4	36	11	27	15	29
Members expelled	0	0	7	18	7	14
Non-members	6	55	8	20	14	28
Total 11		100	40	100	51	100

Whereabouts of Illegitimate Children.—As can be seen by referring to Tables XXXV and XXXVI, of the 75 illegitimate children born during the five-year period studied, all except five were kept by the mother, and only one of these was definitely placed out. This mother gave her child to some people living in the northern end of the county. Now the mother sincerely regrets her action, and if she were able to pay the doctor's bill of $150 incurred,[8] she would take her child back. Some day she hopes to be able to save this amount,

---

[8] This bill was caused by the several illnesses of the child after he was placed out.

but it is unlikely that this will happen any time soon. Three mothers did not keep their children after marriage. All of these children are living at present with the parents of the girl. Two of these mothers are planning to take their children soon.

In all except one case of the mothers giving up their children the mother kept her child two or three years before giving it away. The only instance of a mother's giving her child away earlier was that of a Negro girl who told her mother that the latter might have the baby when it was two weeks old. This girl was only 16 at the time of the baby's birth. All three live together, and both mother and grandmother seem to consider the child theirs. Only nine per cent of the mothers gave their child away and these seem to feel that they have done something unusual.

Of the total of 51 mothers, 46, or 82 per cent (8 white and 38 Negro) had kept their children. Of the number 10 were married and 36 unmarried. Where the mothers had married, only two had married the fathers of their children. The other eight seemed to feel that they had done better by marrying another man. In only one home did the presence of the illegitimate child present a behavior problem, and in this the husband was unwilling to spend much money on the child. All of the unmarried mothers were anxious to show off their children, not differing in this respect from all other mothers.

In the cases of the girls who had not married, and were keeping their children at home, the parents of the girl were devoted to their grandchildren. One old woman said, "I feel like a hen with heaps of chickens, but I'm glad to have them all."

Six of the children, 9 per cent, had died, either at birth or so soon afterward that the cause could not be determined. The mothers of two of the children who had died were repeaters, having had two illegitimate children in close succession.

TABLE XXXV

DISPOSITION OF, AND PRESENT MARITAL STATUS OF MOTHERS OF ILLEGITIMATE
CHILDREN, WHITE AND NEGRO, BORN IN ORANGE COUNTY, NORTH
CAROLINA, 1923-1927

	Child With Mother		Child Not With Mother		Child Dead	
	No.	Percent	No.	Percent	No.	Percent
White—						
Mother married.........	0	0	1	50	0	0
Mother unmarried.......	8	100	1	50	1	100
Total	8	100	2	100	1	100
Negro—						
Mother married.........	11	27	2	67	2	40
Mother unmarried......	27	73	1	33	3	60
Total	38	100	3	100	5	100
Total—						
Mother married.........	11	24	3	60	2	33
Mother unmarried......	35	76	2	40	4	67
Total	46	100	5	100	6	100

NOTE. The number 57 is used in this table to account for all the illegitimate children born during the five-year period. Although there were only
51 unmarried mothers, there were six repeaters, and this makes the higher
figure used here.

TABLE XXXVI

DISPOSITION OF ILLEGITIMATE CHILDREN, WHITE AND NEGRO, BORN IN
ORANGE COUNTY, NORTH CAROLINA, 1923-1927

Disposition of Child	White		Negro		Total	
	No.	Percent	No.	Percent	No.	Percent
Child with mother........	8	73	38	82	46	82
Child not with mother....	2	18	3	7	5	9
Child dead..............	1	9	5	11	6	9
Total	11	100	46	100	57	100

NOTE. The number 57 is used in this table to account for all the illigiti-
mate children born during the five-year period. Although there were only
51 unmarried mothers, there were six repeaters, and this makes the higher
figure used here.

Number of Illegitimate Children Each Unmarried Mother Had.—Although among the 51 unmarried mothers used in this study there were only six repeaters (12 per cent) during the five-year period, yet, as is shown by Table XXXVII, many of the women had other illegitimate children previous to this time. In one instance the number went as high as six, and two mothers had four illegitimate children. While over one-half of the number, 30, had only one child, 14 mothers had two illegitimate children.

Several of the illegitimate children were born as long as 10 years ago. In the case of one woman, a cook in Chapel Hill, having as many as six illegitimate children, the same man was the father of them all. In all, the 51 mothers had 86 children born out of wedlock, although not all this number were living in the county.

TABLE XXXVII

NUMBER OF ILLEGITIMATE CHILDREN HAD BY EACH UNMARRIED MOTHER, WHITE AND NEGRO, IN ORANGE COUNTY, NORTH CAROLINA, 1923-1927

| No. of | | | Total | |
Children	White	Negro	Number	Percent
1	8	22	30	59
2	3	11	14	27
3	0	3	3	6
4	0	2	2	4
5	0	1	1	2
6	0	1	1	2
Total	11	40	51	100

Subsequent Marriages of Unmarried Mothers.—Upon referring to Table XXXVIII, it is seen that of the 51 mothers, 16, one white and 15 Negroes, or 31 per cent, had married at the time this survey was made. Nine of the mothers, two white and seven Negroes, or 18 per cent, had previously been married. In these cases the husbands were permanent deserters. One white woman said, "He was no good to me, I'm glad he's gone." The same reply was received many times, although few were as pessimistic as the white woman who, having been brought up in the country, was now living in a mill village. She said, "All men are bad, some are worse, and I've just known the last kind." The explanation of her viewpoint might lie in the fact that she had two daughters, both of whom had illegitimate children, and one of whom was a repeater. There were 26 mothers, 8 whites and 18 Negroes, 51 per cent, who were still unmarried. Since those who had married had done so two or three years after the birth of their illegitimate child, a survey made a few years later probably would show a higher marriage rate. In considering the question of marriage among Negroes, it must be remembered that the number of females exceeds the number of males.[9] This might be one of the causes of illegitimacy among Negroes.

TABLE XXXVIII

PAST AND PRESENT MARITAL STATUS OF MOTHERS OF ILLEGITIMATE CHILDREN, WHITE AND NEGRO, IN ORANGE COUNTY, NORTH CAROLINA, 1923-1927

Marital Status	White		Negro		Total	
	No.	Percent	No.	Percent	No.	Percent
Unmarried	8	73	18	45	26	51
Married before birth of child..........	2	18	7	18	9	18
Married after birth of child	1	9	15	37	16	31
To father of child.........	(1)	(9)	(13)	(32)	(14)	(27)
To another man..........	(0)	(0)	(2)	(5)	(2)	(4)
Total	11	100	40	100	51	100

Number of Mothers Receiving Aid from the Father of the Child.—One of the most effective means of telling whether the present illegitimacy law is a suitable one is by finding how many of the mothers received aid from the father of the child. The question of assistance was one that all the mothers had

[9] In Orange County there are 2,875 Negro females to 2,760 Negro males. Contrast this with the white population of 6,214 males and 6,023 females. U. S. Fourteenth Census, *North Carolina State Compendium*, 1925.

in common, and a subject upon which they were always ready to talk.

According to Table **XXXIX**, only 24 of the mothers, 5 white and 19 Negro, received any aid at all. In five cases, or 21 per cent, this aid was secured through court action, and in the remaining 19 cases, 79 per cent, it came through outside settlement. In the latter the Negroes have a higher percentage than the whites. The number of unmarried mothers who received no help whatsoever from the father of the child was 33, 6 whites and 27 Negroes. The fact that only 42 per cent of the mothers received assistance, when under the law all should have been aided, clearly indicates the failure of the present illegitimacy law in North Carolina to protect unmarried mothers and their children. In several instances the women said that they did not expect any assistance. The amounts secured ranged all the way from $2.00 in one case to the maximum amount of $200. The last came through court action, and the first through what might be called outside settlement.

In the five cases in which court action was taken, one white and four Negro, there was only one instance of the mother's receiving the $200 prescribed by law. The amounts gained were $150, two settlements of $70, one $50, and the $200 previously mentioned. Several mothers said that it took one-third of their money to pay the lawyer who represented them. In all these settlements the money was paid in a lump sum.

When the money was gained through outside settlement, the amounts went from $150 to the $2.00 mentioned before, with $25 as the most frequent sum. In many instances it is impossible to state correctly the aid received since the mothers were indefinite, and in several instances the aid was food and shelter. In 10 cases, including the four white mothers, the money was paid in a lump sum, in five it came in small installments, and in three it was on a weekly basis, the father of the child contributing part of his wages. One Negro girl said that the man bought her and the baby's food and clothes. Just how their food could be kept apart from the rest of the family's she did not explain. In this same case the man boarded with the family and they charged him for his washing. Marriage between this mother and father will probably ensue.

Since not quite half the unmarried mothers were receiving the aid due them, the illegitimacy law in North Carolina, as indicated above, seems to be as deficient in its administrative aspects as it is inadequate in its scope and content. The majority of the mothers said they did not like to take cases to court under the present system, and the parents of the girls said the whole proceeding was too painful for the girl. The publicity entailed by the court proceeding, with witnesses, lawyers, the cross examination, and the testimony, all make it a process which few girls wish to undergo.

TABLE XXXIX

FINANCIAL AID RECEIVED, AND THE WAY IN WHICH IT WAS OBTAINED, BY MOTHERS OF ILLEGITIMATE CHILDREN, WHITE AND NEGRO, IN ORANGE COUNTY, NORTH CAROLINA, 1923-1927

Financial Aid Received	White		Negro		Total	
	No.	Percent	No.	Percent	No.	Percent
Mothers receiving aid.....	5	45	19	41	24	42
Through court action.....	(1)	(9)	(4)	(9)	(5)	(9)
Through outside settlement	(4)	(36)	(15)	(32)	(19)	(33)
Mothers receiving no aid.	6	55	27	59	33	58
	—	—	—	—	—	—
Total	11	100	46	100	57*	100

* Since the number of illegitimate children born during the five-year period was used in this table, instead of the number of unmarried mothers, the total number is raised to 57 instead of the usual 51. The percentages have been worked out on this basis.

Occupations of the Unmarried Mothers.—In a study of illegitimacy taken in a city the various gainful occupations of the mothers throw a light on their manner and way of living, both social and economic. In the country there are only a few occupations given, such as farm and mill work. The white mothers gave these two occupations, although on two or three birth registrations "school girl" was put down. For the Negroes farm and domestic work were the two given. In a

19

few instances the nature of the domestic work was specified, as "cook," "washwoman," or "servant." The words "domestic work" include both the work in a girl's own home and her work elsewhere as servant. In like manner the term "field hand" means work on the home farm as well as another. Little could be gained from the occupation given, although it showed that the majority of the unmarried mothers had no regular wage earning occupation.

Causes of Illegitimacy.—As could have been expected promise of marriage was given as a frequent cause of illegitimacy, since 22, 2 whites and 20 Negroes, gave this reason. In some instances where promise of marriage was not expressly made, such an outcome was expected or assumed by the girl. All the following replies have this reason in common: "He say he going to marry me"; "I was getting ready to be married"; "I think I might be"; "We, I, was intending to."

There were at least 25 who said that there was neither promise nor intention of marriage. Their explanation was that they "were just having a good time," or "didn't know no better," or "was just fooling." In many cases the girl said that she did not care for the man. With such a situation a study of the moral conditions is needed before any conclusion can be reached.

In the cases in which the girl was very young her innocence and susceptibility may have been the causes. This would have been true when the man was older than she was. In the scarcity of rural recreation and the crowded home conditions lie two contributing factors to illegitimacy. Due to the size of the families the girl cannot see her friends at home and must go elsewhere for her pleasures.

Some of the older people in the communities said that they thought there was a breakdown in the moral reserve of the girls. "They just don't seem to care what they do; they seem proud of having a baby," was the way one old Negro woman put it. Undoubtedly, in many instances, the girl had just drifted into the relationship with the man. There were 10 or more cases in which the girl was not sure how it happened, or at least would not give any definite reason for her misconduct. In four cases the man was boarding in the home of the girl at the time of their misconduct. It is interesting to note that in the cases of the repeaters different reasons were given for each offense. Promise of marriage was the cause of the first child, and, "I just don't know how it happened" for the second.

The whites regard illegitimacy in Negroes as something to be expected. This attitude is not conducive toward raising the standard of Negro morality. Negro illegitimacy is not taken as seriously by the whites as illegitimacy among their own race. Thus there are two standards of conduct by which the Negro women are judged, by the standard of the whites and by the standards of their own race. With this double standard, coupled with their ignorance of birth control measures, it is not surprising that the Negroes have a higher ratio of illegitimacy than the whites.

One interesting phase of this study was discussing the question of the Negro children born out of wedlock with the Negro midwives. Although ignorant, they seemed to accept their responsibility and proudly spoke of themselves as "doctors." The homes of all the Negro midwives were spotlessly clean, except Aunt C—— W—— who lived in the most picturesque, if the worst type of Negro community. They were all interested in this survey, agreeing that it was needed. The majority of them seemed to think that the moral conditions, as shown by the number of illegitimate children among the Negro girls, were increasingly bad. They were much concerned with the situation, "but what kin you do? you raise 'em up right and then they go wrong," was the burden of their speech. One said, in summing up the situation, "At camp meeting dere'll be so many babies you won't hear de preaching for de crying." The Negro midwives agreed that a new illegitimacy law is needed, but more than that, "De girls needs to look out for themselves." Aunt C—— W—— came from her kitchen leaving her washing and her many grandchildren, to sit on her green "parlor suite" and talk. In spite of her two granddaughters having "woodcolt children," she thought "that girls was more

careful" now than formerly. This coming from one of the most
backward Negro settlements was a most hopeful sign. All the
Negro midwives discussed the matter in a calm and friendly
manner, and on the whole they were a better type than had
been expected. Ignorant they may be, but they accept their
responsibility toward "even the girls what has got no sense,"
as one Negro midwife characterized the unmarried mothers of
her race.

The results of this study indicate that illegitimacy is far
greater among the Negroes than among the whites; that the
ages of the white unmarried mothers are lower than the ages
of the Negroes; that, in the country, the unmarried mothers
come in equal numbers from home-owning and renting families;
that almost without exception they keep their children; that
very few of the mothers receive any aid, and that such aid
as is received is inadequate; that many of the mothers marry
in time, but not the father of the child; and that, although
the girl may lose her place in the community for a time, such
as her church membership (this is often the case with Negroes),
she is readmitted in about a year's time, and is soon in good
community standing. With such an attitude the girl does not
consider her life ruined completely since her family accept
her, and welcome the child. In the country there is a fatalistic
equanimity of mind not found in the city. This feeling prohibits
the supposition that marriage with the father of the illegitimate child will make everything right. Illegitimacy is regarded
as a passing phase and one that will not always be counted
against a girl.

The following brief case studies illustrate in a concrete
way some of the problems faced by Negro unmarried mothers
in Orange County:

Case I.—Following a complaint from a neighbor about the
misbehavior of Lou Morrow's children, several of whom were
illegitimate, the Superintendent of Welfare visited the Morrow
home. The family lived on the outskirts of town in a Negro
community. The three-room house, owned by Lou's mother,
was unspeakably dirty; the one bright feature was an old

church window, barbarically colorful, which, laid sidewise, was used in the house as a window.

The family consisted of Lou, aged 28, her mother, and Lou's 7 children, the oldest 14, the youngest a baby four weeks old. At one time Lou had been married but her husband developed the habit of wandering away for short periods of time. These periods lengthened, and at the time Lou had not heard of him for four years. It was impossible to tell which children were legitimate and which were illegitimate, for Lou called the children "just mine."

Lou was a slender, sprightly, pleasant faced woman, with a ready tongue. She said she was going to keep the children as long as she could give them "beans, bread, and a chance to get a little book learning." Although such was her intention, the children had not been attending school for some time. Since her husband's desertion Lou had become a cook, trying to earn money this way in order to support her ever increasing family. During this time she had also lived with several men, but she gave no details as to this part of her life. In spite of her having several illegitimate children she had made no plans other than those stated, and had received no aid from the father or fathers of the children.

This is an indeterminate case, for although the children were sent to school regularly, yet they did not receive what they really needed, some adequate support financially. Lou needed assistance so that she might bring up her family, and this she had not received. This record is just a statement of the events happening with no systematic treatment. Indeed Lou did not want any form of aid, and said that she expected no help. No effort was made on her part to work out her problem, if she called it that. With the happy carelessness of a Negro she let things go as they would, and made no effort to place her family upon a surer footing economically.

Case II.—The record in which Sue Jones, a Negro girl, appeared, was a record of the whole Jones family, a record of family maladjustment in which the inability of the mother to control the children had a large part. Jim, the only boy at home, was so incorrigible that his mother was unable to manage him, and she asked the Superintendent of Welfare to help her.

It was found that before Sudie Jones, the mother of Sue and Jim, and three older children, was married to Will Jones, she already had two illegitimate children, the father in both cases being white men. It was suspected strongly that the father of Sue was also a white man. Sudie's husband, Will, was a hard working Negro, and soon bought a house and small plot of ground in one of the Negro settlements in the county. The marriage was not a peaceful one, for Sudie was a most untidy housekeeper and had a high temper. After 12 years of married life, Will deserted her, going North. The other children had gone there previously, leaving only Sue and Jim at home.

The five-room house, although a comfortable one to begin with, was in a miserable condition; the porch sagging, the roof leaking, and stagnant water standing around. The rooms had little furniture, the floors being covered with tow sacks. Sue and her mother were both slatternly in appearance, although Sue, who was a mulatto, might have been pretty. Both of them were willing to talk, although it was hard to hold their attention. Neither had been to school more than three years.

At the time the case was opened, Sue had one illegitimate child, and in a few weeks another was born. Sue appeared very fond of her two children, and stated that one man, George Rogers, was the father of both. It seems that she and George had been intending to get married for some time, but kept putting it off. In the meantime two children were born. One result of this was that Sue had been put out of the church of which she had been a member. Sue said that George was a brick mason, earning $22.50 a week. He gave part of this money, $10 at least, toward the support of Sue and the children.

The only outcome in this case was the one asked by Sudie; that something be done about Jim. In spite of the family's having a bad reputation he was placed in a good farm home, where he is doing well. Concerning the rest of the family, Sue and her children, nothing was done.

Promise or intention of marriage, together with bad moral conditions within the home, were the causes of the illegitimacy. The whole case is the record of a broken home and a degenerate family. Sudie had more than one illegitimate child, and Sue is but following in her footsteps. Since Sue was already securing aid, no financial treatment was needed. This is one of the two cases found in the county in which weekly aid had been secured, both times through outside settlement. The problem had been worked out, and the outsome, that in time Sue and George will be married, is almost certain. What the outcome of that marriage will be one cannot say.

Case III.—Olive, Maude M.[10] September 15, 1931. L. T. Olive (Negro) ; Box 40, Route 4, Melton, in the office at Valeville. He was greatly concerned over his daughter, Maude M., 16 years old next April, who is now seven months pregnant. There are six children younger than Maude, 4 girls and 2 boys, and her parents are most desirous of making some arrangements for her so that she can leave home very shortly and not return until some time after the birth of her child. They feel that on account of all the younger children such procedure would be the thing to do. Maude has finished the seventh grade at Pine Tops Grove School and had planned to go on to high school. According to her father, she is intelligent and well behaved, but a young man who is a cousin of the girl took advantage of her.

It was explained that there are no maternity homes in this state for Negro girls and in view of this fact, aside from care at a regular hospital, about the only other procedure would be for the girl to make an extended visit to relatives or friends who might be interested in her. L. T. stated that practically all of his relatives and his wife's relatives live in the immediate neighborhood and he felt that that would not answer this purpose. None but the immediate family are aware of the girl's condition and he feels that if the matter can be

---

[10] This case record was taken from the files of the County Superintendent of Public Welfare of Orange County, N. C.

kept quiet the girl's reputation will not be terribly impaired. He will gladly stand for a considerable expense in order to make the best arrangements for Maude and said that he would go as high as $100.00. He feels that it would be for the best to have the baby placed and never brought home and he would like for the Welfare Officer to make some arrangements along this line.

L. T. was advised that a visit would be made to Lucy Jackson, Negro midwife who lives near Lost Hope Church. It is possible that some arrangements may be made through her for the girl to live with her and be cared for for some considerable length of time, before and after confinement. The law concerning separation of infants from mothers was explained but it was stated that there might be some possibility of placing the baby. L. T. will return to the Valeville Office on Tuesday, September 22d.

September 18, 1931. Visited Lucy Jackson, licensed midwife, at her home and explained the situation. She seemed to be very sympathetic and interested in the case and stated that she would be glad to take Maude with her. She said she would not state any definite sum of money to be paid her for these services but that she would take care of the situation and expect the girl's people "to do what was right about it." Welfare Officer asked if she thought $5.00 a week for a period of some three or four months would be satisfactory and Aunt Lucy indicated that she would be pleased enough with such a financial arrangement.

Welfare Officer will probably return with the girl's father late Tuesday, September 22d, to further discuss the situation.

September 22, 1931. L. T. Olive, father of Maude, did not meet Welfare Officer as agreed upon.

September 26, 1931. L. T., his wife Mandy, and Maude at office in Valeville in reference to letter which L. T. had just received that day. He explained that he was detained in York last Tuesday in connection with selling a load of tobacco until after dark and could not, therefore, see Welfare Officer.

The tentative arrangements made with Lucy Jackson were

explained and the family seemed considerably relieved to know that there was this possibility of handling the situation.

Took all three to Lucy Jackson's house and left Maude there. Her parents had anticipated this and the girl therefore, had a suit-case full of clothes and was prepared to stay. Aunt Lucy and the Olives discussed the situation at considerable length while Welfare Officer remained outside. Arrangements were made which seemed to be mutually satisfactory and L. T. promised to pay $5.00 a week, although probably a portion of this payment will be in provisions rather than in cash. He paid Aunt Lucy $5.00.

Maude seemed rather downcast over the whole situation and had almost nothing to say, although she seemed to be appreciative that arrangements were being made in her behalf. Her mother, Mandy, who is a sister of Bessie Groves, seemed to be very intelligent and accepted the situation philosophically. Both she and L. T. stated that they planned to do everything within their power for Maude.

Upon leaving Aunt Lucy's, L. T. cried rather profusely. On the return trip to Valeville, Welfare Officer mentioned to Mandy and L. T. the necessity of providing reasonable sex instruction to children, and expressed the hope that the other four girls in the family could be advised along this line.

October 26, 1931. Letter received from Aunt Lucy Jackson stating that Maude had "found a fine little baby boy."

Later. From previous acquaintance with Bettie Saylor, it was known that she and her husband who have no children of their own are interested in securing a child. Visited at the house where the Saylors lived at one time and found that they had moved to West Virginia, where they are both working.

Later. Saw a brother of Bettie Saylor's husband, who operates a Negro barber shop on East Jefferson Street. He said that he supposed Bettie and her husband would remain indefinitely in West Virginia since they both had reasonably good jobs. He doubted very much if under the present circumstances they would be in a position to take a child. However, he expects to write to his brother very shortly and he will mention that

Welfare Officer is on the lookout for a home for an infant boy.

October 27, 1931. Visited the home of Lucy Jackson. Maude and her baby seem to be in the best of condition. The child was born at 12:30 p.m. on October 21st. The birth of the child seemed to be normal in every respect. Aunt Lucy seems to be very much interested in Maude and the child. She explained that tomorrow she would probably allow Maude to sit up and that if she progresses as satisfactorily as she has already done, she will let her get out of bed next Saturday, October 31st. Maude's parents have not yet been notified of the birth of the boy. No letter was written because it was expected that they would visit Maude last Saturday, October 24th. As the situation now is, they are expecting her parents on October 31st and it is Maude's ambition to be out of bed when they come. They have made one visit since Maude was taken to Aunt Lucy, at which time they brought a considerable amount of food supplies. They have not paid Aunt Lucy anything more in cash.

Assisted Aunt Lucy in filling out birth certificate, which Welfare Officer will turn over to the Registrar of Vital Statistics in Davietown township.

No name has been given to the baby yet. He is very light colored but Aunt Lucy explained that all Negro babies are light in color when born and he likely will not get his color until he is a month or two old. She predicts that he will be a light brown—somewhat lighter than Maude herself. Aunt Lucy said that Maude had been very smart and had helped her in every way possible before confinement and since that time had been very good about taking instructions.

Aunt Lucy would like very much for Welfare Officer to bring her some clothes, since she has only a poor supply. She wants to have a sweater especially. An outfit of baby clothes provided by the Health Department of the Community Club was left for the baby.

November 7, 1931. Mr. Wilbur Hill said that Aunt Lucy had sent word that she was anxious for Welfare Officer to stop by her house the next time he is in the neighborhood.

November 18, 1931. With Welfare Officer went out to Aunt

Lucy Jackson's to see Maude and the baby. Found Maude at home but she said Aunt Lucy had gone to York.

Maude said that her parents had been down to see her a week or so ago. She does not think her father has paid Aunt Lucy any more money but he has brought supplies each time he has been there. She said that she did not want to keep the baby herself. Stated that Aunt Lucy has said she would like to keep it. Explained to her that Aunt Lucy is too old to have the complete care of such a small baby. She replied that she hoped she could stay with Aunt Lucy for six months or a year.

Left some groceries and also a coat for Aunt Lucy. Told Maude to tell her father to come by the Valeville office. (Virginia Earle, Office Secretary.)

December 2, 1931. While going out to see Mrs. Lily Gray, Welfare Officer requested student worker to stop by Jim Walton's house and ask if his wife is still interested in adopting a baby. A year or so ago the Waltons were most anxious to secure a child and at present Welfare Officer would like to find a suitable home for Maude Olive's baby. The Waltons live in the Little River neighborhood about three miles north of Harry Thurston, Melton, Route 3.

Found the place without any trouble. Jim was not at home but his wife was there—out in the barn curing tobacco. Explained to her about the baby. She said she really would hesitate to take so small a baby and that she is still anxious for a child but would like one about two years old. However, the more she talked the more evident it became that she would probably be willing to take the baby if he suited her. She said she would make no statement until she could see the baby and that she would like very much to see the baby. (Virginia Earle, Office Secretary.)

December 15, 1931. Saw L. T. in the office in Valeville. He is still anxious to have Maude's baby placed by Welfare Officer and hopes that arrangements may be made along this line within the next couple of months. He feels that there is no great hurry about having Maude return to her home but the family, including Maude, all wish to have the child placed. He also repeated the information previously secured from Maude to the effect that Aunt Lucy says she wants to keep the baby. It was explained to L. T. that Welfare Officer considers that this would be inadvisable.

(L. T. was questioned concerning a pig which is now in Aunt Lucy's possession and over which there is a dispute as to ownership. See case record of Lucy Jackson.)

December 16, 1931. Visited the home of Jim Walton. He was not at home but talked with his wife and explained in considerable detail the circumstances in regard to Maude Olive and the baby. However, no names were mentioned. She manifested considerable interest and stated that she would be glad to accompany Welfare Officer some time in the near future to go and see the child. She was advised that such trip would not be made until some time after the new year.

Later. Saw Mr. Chris Hunter at his store in Julien and requested him to advise Welfare Officer if he knew of any reliable Negroes who might be interested in taking a child into their home. Mr. Hunter has a wide acquaintance with Negroes in the southern part of Black County.

Later. In response to a message from Mr. Hunter, saw him at his store at night. He said that Lester Jones' wife was interested in taking a baby. Lester works for the University as a janitor; he and his wife are considered good, reliable Negroes. They have been married several years and have no children.

December 21, 1931. Mrs. S. T. Sawyer of the Davietown King's Daughters advised Welfare Officer that Lester Jones' wife had sent her messages that she was very much interested in the baby that Mr. Hunter had spoken of and to please have the Welfare Officer see her about it.

Letter.

December 25, 1931.

Dear Sir,

I will droop a lines to let hear from me this leave us well and I been looking for you a long time for I need help Maude father was here the 24 day and brough me some provision just like he said he would do but he was not able to pay me anything. I show was bad dissopoint when Christmas come I did

not have $1.00 for Christmas Maude father is $70.00 in my
debt and he said he thought you had been to see me he was
surprised to know you had seen me Maude father was not able
to come up in the money line and he was so sorry he was not
able to come up in the money lines.

Your Truly

LUCY JACKSON.

I am expect to hear from you some time Soon.

January 5, 1932. Saw Lester on the street. He said his wife
is very much interested and they both would like to have the
child. It was explained to him that the matter of taking this
particular child had already been discussed with another family
and that Welfare Officer could hardly do anything about the
situation as far as the Joneses are concerned unless the other
family did not take the child.

L. T. in the office in Valeville. He says that he and his wife
are now not sure exactly what they want done about Maude's
baby. His wife is inclined to favor bringing the baby home,
and he himself is not especially opposed. However, he is anxious
to do the best thing for Maude and the child and would like
to have Welfare Officer's advice. It was explained to him that
ordinarily if the mother of an illegitimate child was able to
care for the baby it is probably best for her to keep it. In the
present situation there seem to be several things to be considered and L. T. was advised to discuss the situation as thoroughly as possible with his wife and Maude from the various
standpoints of the welfare of the baby, the effect upon Maude,
and also the probable influence upon Maude's younger sisters,
and the general effect of the standing of the family in the
community.

L. T. will further consider the situation and will advise
Welfare Officer within the near future.

Letter, January 27, 1932.

Melton, N. C.
R. No. 4, Box 40

Dear Sur.

I have decided I would bring Maude and the baby home. I
think it would be better in the time to come.

She dont wont to part from it. and I am afraid to forest it. I guess I will bring her home the first week in Feb.

Yours Devotly,

L. T. OLIVE.

CHAPTER XVI

NEGRO SCHOOLS IN NORTH CAROLINA

ELEMENTARY SCHOOLS

THE TOTAL Negro school population in 1920-21 was 213,757 rural; 56,840 urban; 270,597 total. The enrollment in the schools for 1920-21 was 175,268 rural; 39,637 urban; 214,905 total. The average daily attendance for the year 1920-21 was 110,649 rural; 27,632 urban; 138,281 total. In 1928-29 the school population was 312,976 and the elementary school enrollment was 246,419. The total school enrollment in the 99 counties having Negro school population for 1928-29 was 189,191; the total enrollment in 41 counties having Jeanes workers was 132,288; and in the remaining 58 counties the enrollment was 56,903. The total average daily attendance in the rural schools of the 99 counties for 1928-29 was 126,832; total average daily attendance in the 41 counties having Jeanes workers was 87,569; and in the remaining 58 counties it was 39,263. In other words, the 41 counties having Jeanes teachers enrolled 75,385 more children than the 58 counties not having Jeanes workers; and the average daily attendance was 48,306 more than in the 58 unsupervised counties.

HIGH SCHOOLS

Beginning in 1919, ten high schools all connected with institutions of higher learning, both public and private, were given the accredited four-year rating. In 1923 the first distinctly public high schools were accredited, one rural and three special charter. Approximately 16,000 boys and girls were enrolled in the high schools during the year 1928-29, with an aggregate senior class enrollment of 2,000. Fifty-two per cent of the 1,800 graduates of 1928 entered institutions of higher learning in the fall. Of this group, 80.8 per cent were cared for in North Carolina institutions.

The close of the school year 1930-31 showed a total of 150 Negro schools in which some high school work was done. Of these schools, 98 were accredited, 10 having been added to the list in 1931. Eight of these 10 schools are operating in Rosenwald buildings, making a total of thirty of the thirty-six schools accredited in the last three years (1928-1931) Rosenwald schools.

Of the one hundred fifty high schools, one hundred thirty-one are public; seventy-four being rural and fifty-five special charter, with two being connected with state institutions.

Of the ninety-eight accredited high schools, eighty are public, thirty-four being rural and forty-four being special charter, and two connected with state institutions. Thirty-two of the thirty-four accredited rural schools and twenty-two of the forty-four accredited special charter schools are housed in Rosenwald buildings.

There were 14,657 children enrolled in the standard public high schools in 1931. Of this number, 8,025 were housed in Rosenwald buildings, 3,514 being in rural schools and 4,511 in special charter schools.

In 1931 there were 1,903 students graduated from public schools, 970 of these being from Rosenwald schools, 434 from rural schools and 536 from special charter schools.

The following table gives a summarizing picture of the educational progress in our Negro schools—five year intervals:

TABLE XL

	1918-19	1923-24	1928-29
Number schools	2,470	2,432	2,417
Average value of school......	$709.55	$2,705.91	$4,510.82
Average value per child enrolled......	9.83	26.44	41.91
Average annual salary................	197.08	436.32	510.07
Total school population..............	265,424	293,183	312,976
Total enrollment	178,252	248,904	260,135
Total average daily attendance........	107,181	164,698	180,339
Percentage of population enrolled.....	67.1	84.9	83.1
Percentage enrollment in average daily attendance	60.1	66.2	69.3
Number public high schools...........	......	58	114
Enrollment in public high school.......	......	4,715	13,218
Public H. S. graduates...............	......	380	1,522
Value of school property.............	$1,752,594	$6,580,770	$10,902,643

NORTH CAROLINA CONGRESS OF COLORED PARENTS AND TEACHERS

Since the organization of the State Parent-Teacher Association, its membership has grown from 10,117 in 1927 to 17,180 in 1929. This membership was taken from the reports of the 26 cities and 20 county units reporting in the organization meeting in 1927, and from the reports of delegates representing 38 cities and 36 county units in 1929. Total amount of money reported by delegates from 1927 to 1929 was $160,204.99.

This organization is now active in forty-two counties and thirty-eight cities with a total membership of 17,180; of this number, 14,720 are rural members. The total membership at the time of its organization meeting in 1927 was 784, and in 1930 it showed an increase of 16,396.

One of the main objectives of Parent-Teacher Associations is to improve school attendance, especially in the rural schools. There are so many handicaps, such as poverty, work, weather, and sickness and other causes, which keep the children out of school.

20

After working hard on this and school improvement, the Parent-Teacher Association decided to start a movement to do something definite in Health.

Three clinics were reported in 1930. Last year a county Parent-Teacher Association raised $100 through the efforts of the Jeanes Supervisor to have a dental clinic for the children of her county. The State Director of Dentistry was in sympathy with the movement and made special arrangement for them to have the clinic, giving as much as possible free.

The Jeanes worker is the leading spirit in the rural Parent-Teacher organization, and is an inspiration to the city organizations. Indeed, it is hardly possible to have an active county Parent-Teacher Association without a Jeanes supervisor.

INSTITUTIONS OF HIGHER LEARNING AND TRAINING OF TEACHERS

During the year 1930-31 there were enrolled in the thirteen accredited institutions of higher learning 2,631 students. Of this number, 1,360 were enrolled in public institutions and 1,271 were enrolled in private institutions. In June, 1931, there were graduated from these institutions 291 students planning to teach in the elementary schools (two year college level), and 195 students having been trained to teach in the secondary schools (four year college level).

TABLE XLI

EDUCATIONAL STATUS OF TEACHERS AS DETERMINED BY CERTIFICATES

	1921-22	1930-31
Less than four years of high school	2,306	887
Average of one year of college	1,578	2,117
Two and three years of college	519	1,911
Four or more years of college	141	1,128
Total	4,544	6,043

In 1921-22 less than one-half of the Negro teachers had training equivalent to high school graduation. For the year 1930-31, only about fourteen per cent of the teachers belonged to this class. Approximately, one-seventh of the Negro teachers for the year 1921-22 had training equal to two years or more of college training. In 1930-31 more than one-half of the teachers employed were of this standing.

OUTSIDE AGENCIES IN THE DEVELOPMENT OF NEGRO EDUCATION

1. THE JULIUS ROSENWALD FUND

Rural School Buildings.—It was in 1915 that our own state of North Carolina began building Rosenwald Schools. Up to July 1, 1931, the Rosenwald Fund aided on eighteen teachers' homes, seven shop buildings, and 783 schoolhouses,[1] which have 2,498 classrooms and can accommodate 112,410 pupils. On these 808 buildings which cost $5,070,356, the Rosenwald Fund gave $704,726; the Negroes gave $665,236; white friends contributed $75,140; and the public appropriation was $3,625,254.

Libraries.—By July 1, 1931, the Rosenwald Fund aided on 135 libraries, distributed to 120 schools in 59 counties. These libraries cost $18,656, of which amount the Rosenwald Fund gave $6,218.

Extension of Terms.—Up to July 1, 1931, the Rosenwald Fund aided on the extension of school term in fifty-five schools, located in seventeen counties, to the amount of $20,966.

Transportation.—During the school years 1929-30 and 1930-31 the Rosenwald Fund helped on the purchase of forty-three new busses and the operation of eighteen additional ones. These busses travel 1,629 miles daily, transporting children to thirty schools located in twenty-one counties. The Rosenwald Fund has contributed $29,245 on the purchase and operation of these busses.[2]

---

[1] In addition to the above buildings, the Rosenwald Fund made a special appropriation to the Atkins High School in Winston-Salem in the amount of $50,000. This building, which has sixty classrooms, together with the equipment and site, cost $350,000.

[2] In addition to the appropriations indicated under a, b, c, and d above, the Rosenwald Fund has contributed to: building programs at public and private colleges; library service for institutions, communities and counties;

2. GENERAL EDUCATION BOARD

The General Education Board is a Rockefeller Foundation of New York, which has for its general object "the promotion of education within the United States without distinction of race, sex or creed."

For Negro Public School Enterprises this Board has contributed the sum of $503,201.30. This money has been used in the following ways: For buildings and general equipment at the State Normal Schools at Fayetteville, Elizabeth City, Winston-Salem Teachers College, and the North Carolina College for Negroes at Durham, $240,099.81; for Fellowships in universities and colleges to assist worthy men and women to further prepare themselves for the teaching profession, $18,550; for the purchase of equipment and paying of salaries in county training, or high schools, in some instances thus enabling these schools to become standard high schools, $112,-100.07; for payment of salaries of instructors in state or approved summer schools, $25,724.42; for State Agents of Rural Schools, that is, for the salaries and traveling expenses of certain members of the State Department of Public Instruction for directing and supervising the work of the Division of Negro Education, $89,712.69; for Home Makers Clubs, $17,014.31. During the period from 1913-1918, the work of the Home Makers Clubs was carried on in this state. These clubs were organized in 26 counties under the supervision of well trained women, in most instances the Jeanes supervisors of the respective counties. The simple rudiments of home-making, gardening, canning of fruits, food values, and the like were stressed. The value of this work, no doubt, may be observed today by the better home conditions which obtain in practically every Negro rural school.

For Negro Private School Enterprises, the General Education Board has contributed the sum of $583,632.27. Of this

support of salary and expense of building agent for Rosenwald schools; scholarships to teachers in the secondary schools and colleges. In brief, the Rosenwald Fund has, therefore, contributed to all phases of work the sum of $1,056,907 in North Carolina.

amount, $576,973.97 has been used for the erection of new buildings and in equipping them at Livingstone College, Salisbury; St. Augustine College, Raleigh; Shaw University, Raleigh; Kittrell College, Kittrell; and Johnson C. Smith University, Charlotte. Then for special courses in teacher-training at Livingstone College and Waters Institute, the remaining $6,658.30 was used in paying the salaries of the instructors of this special course.

In brief, the General Education Board has, therefore, contributed to all phases of work the sum of $1,086,833.57.

3. The Anna T. Jeanes Fund

Since the beginning of the work in 1908, the Jeanes Fund has contributed $194,058 to the salaries of Jeanes teachers in North Carolina. During the school year 1930-31, forty supervisors were employed to do work in forty-two counties. These workers, by making 7,762 visits, supervised 1,405 schools with 2,873 teachers. In these counties thirty-five new school buildings were constructed and twenty-two buildings were enlarged at an approximate cost of $150,000. During the year the Negroes in these counties have raised funds for buildings, lengthening of terms, equipment and improvements of all kinds in the amount of $25,315.

4. The John F. Slater Fund

During the first thirty years of its existence, from 1882-1912, the Slater Fund gave practically all its aid to private and denominational schools. During this period the sum of $134,840 was appropriated for the general development of schools of this type in North Carolina.

During more recent years this Fund has been contributing more largely to the public schools, principally in the development of county training schools. The first schools of this type to be established in North Carolina were in Johnston, Pamlico and Wake counties (1914-15). There are this year 45 such schools operating in this state, 31 of which are standard four-year high schools.

For the year 1931-32 the Slater Fund appropriated $8,500

for salaries of teachers and for equipment in county training schools and other high schools. Previously, this Fund contributed for this purpose the sum of $175,655. For the development of private institutions this Fund has contributed $148,790. Thus the Slater Fund has contributed $325,020 to aid in the development of Negro schools in this state.

5. THE PHELPS-STOKES FUND

About fifteen years ago the director of this Fund and three assistants made a careful study of all Negro high schools, normal schools and colleges, both public and private, in North Carolina. This study and the recommendations made have been of great value in the development of all these types of schools. In addition to this service, this Fund has contributed in money to aid several school enterprises.

CHAPTER XVII

HEALTH WORK FOR NEGRO CHILDREN

In the more than fifty years existence of the State Board of Health in organized public health work in North Carolina, there has never been any distinction made between white and colored people. In short, the Negroes of North Carolina have always been regarded by health department officials as simply people, just like Indians or white people, and all public health questions have been settled on this principle. Naturally, owing to the poverty of a large proportion of the Negro population and to their lack of proper organization in their own communities, the Negro race has not received the benefits of the public health work to the same extent that the white people have. But the average health conditions among the Negro population is just about the same as the average health conditions among a majority of the white people of the state.

Organization of Negro Health Work in State and Counties

About fourteen years ago the Department of School Health Supervision in the State Board of Health inaugurated the plan of dental service to the school children of the State. This was confined to the ages between 6 and 13, inclusive. When the work was first inaugurated, in 1918, five white dentists and one colored dentist were employed. Since that time there has always been at least one colored dentist on the staff of the State Board of Health. At present two colored dentists are employed. Very frequently some of the counties, such as Durham, make provision for supplementary work for Negro children, and therefore the proportionate amount of work done by the state dentists in such counties is extended through these county appropriations and the work has therefore been more effective. In the earlier years of the dental service, the white dentists also treated Negro children on the same basis.

In 1919 the same division of the State Board of Health inaugurated a physical inspection service, employing seven nurses for this purpose. Until October first, 1931, these seven nurses had been constantly employed. On the first of October one of the nurses resigned and, owing to a decreased appropriation, her place has not been filled. The other six nurses are still at work. They have worked in more than eighty counties of the state and have held clinics in which emergency hospital equipment was set up, generally in the local school building, for the removal of tonsils and adenoids in about eighty of the state's one hundred counties. In sixty counties during these years having no whole time organized health departments, these nurses have worked in every school district in such counties, both white and colored. During this period a total of 23,211 children have been successfully operated upon in these clinics. The clinics have been conducted for four days each week during the summer months. Twenty-five children per day have been operated upon, and the fourth day of the clinic has always been assigned to Negro children. They have not always filled the clinic. When such is the case, the quota was filled out by white children. However, about 15 per cent of the foregoing number of operations have been for Negro children, almost totally free of cost to their families. They have had the same surgical attention and the same nursing care which has been extended to the white children.

There are forty-nine counties having whole time health workers at this time. Sixteen of these counties are working with standard unit health departments. That is, they have a full time physician as health officer, one or more full time public health nurses, and one or more full time sanitary inspectors, and a secretary. Thirteen county health departments have a whole time health officer and two additional employees. Two county health departments have a whole time physician and one additional employee. Four counties have only a full time health officer with no assistant. Six counties have one or more public health nurses on a whole time basis. Five counties have one sanitary inspector working all the time, and in one county there is a nurse and a sanitary inspector. Also in another county there is a nurse, a sanitary inspector, and a secretary. In two counties there is a part time county physician, but a whole time nurse. Of the seventy-four nurses employed in this county work a few of them are colored nurses. All of the counties, as well as the State Board of Health, are faced with inadequate funds for competently carrying on the work; but as there seems to be no way to avoid this at present, they are doing the best they can.

The State Board of Health encourages the organization of local county health service at all times. The objective of the State Board of Health in working toward a comprehensive plan for meeting the health needs of North Carolina is to try to provide for some type of organized whole time local health service in each one of the one hundred counties. For the counties that cannot have a standard unit of health work headed up by whole time health officers, it is hoped to work out some plan of district county work, combining two or more of the smaller counties, which would be supervised by a whole time health officer. This work is of equal importance to the Negroes and to whites. There is a division exclusively for Negro patients at the State Sanatorium for Tuberculosis. Provision is also made in the different county sanatoriums for tuberculosis for the treatment of Negro patients. In the immunization clinics conducted by the various county and city health departments, the Negroes enjoy the same facilities for protective immunity that is extended to the white people.

NEGRO INFANT MORTALITY RATE (CONTRASTED WITH WHITE RATE), 1920-1930

The following table of comparative rates indicates that the Negro infant mortality has made about the same decline in the ten-year period that the white rate has. The general average in North Carolina is entirely too high. Possibly a half dozen other states have a higher rate, but not many more than that. But as will be noted, the high rate is applicable to the whites as well as to the Negroes, although, of course, the Negro rate is higher. One reason is that the birth rate among the Negroes is a little higher.

TABLE XLII

Year	Infant Mortality White	Negro
1920	73.0	111.2
1921	64.9	92.1
1922	68.8	100.1
1923	69.8	108.0
1924	70.1	112.2
1925	66.6	106.2
1926	70.6	108.4
1927	65.4	109.9
1928	74.6	110.3
1929	66.5	107.9
1930	66.9	105.3

THE NEGRO MIDWIFE

No one knows the exact number of Negro midwives, or white midwives, at present at work in North Carolina. The State Board of Health has made diligent efforts during the last few years to have all midwives registered. At present there are 4,266 midwives whose names and addresses are known to the State Board of Health. We do not know just how many of these are Negro midwives, but it is presumed that a large proportion of them are Negroes. In about forty counties the local health departments have special rules and regulations governing the licensing of midwives. In these counties the midwives are given a course of instruction annually and advised as to their equipment and the necessity for cleanliness emphasized, and they are also urged to call a physician immediately upon the first indication of danger to a patient they are serving, regardless of whether white or colored. In the year 1930 there were 53,515 white babies born. This constitutes a rate of a little less than 24 per 1,000 of the population. In the same year there were 22,681 colored births. This constitutes a rate of a little more than 24 per 1,000 of the population, making the average birth rate for that year 24.1 per 1,000. Of the white women giving birth to babies in 1930, 80 per cent of them had the services of a physician; 12 per cent of them were delivered by midwives. Of the Negro women giving birth to babies in the same year, 31 per cent had the services of physicians; 69 per cent were attended by midwives.

MATERNITY AND INFANT HYGIENE WORK FOR NEGRO CHILDREN

As described in one of the foregoing paragraphs, the Negroes have the same benefits to a limited extent that are extended to the whites. In a number of the city health departments where colored nurses are employed, the maternity and infancy centers or clinics are extended to the Negro mothers and babies in the same manner it is to the whites. The work of immunization against such diseases as diphtheria and smallpox is extended equally to the Negroes. The parent-teacher association of the State has taken the lead in recent years in pre-school round-ups and the health departments, both State and local, have aided materially in this work, the parent-teacher association committee bearing the brunt of getting the children to the clinic for the examinations and then in getting them into the hands of competent physicians and dentists and specialists for treatment later on. In this work the Negro school children have not had the advantages that have been extended to the whites in the same proportion as practically all other health work for the simple reason that there are few, if any, parent-teacher organizations among the Negroes. Especially effective work has been done among the Negro midwives during the last few years by some of the county health department nurses and some of the nurses operating in the Department of Maternity and Infancy of the State Board of Health. The status of the Negro midwives as a whole in the state has been materially advanced through these efforts.

MEDICAL INSPECTION OF NEGRO SCHOOL CHILDREN

As described in the first paragraph of this chapter, the medical inspection of schools work carried on by the State

Board of Health and by the different city and county health departments has extended to the Negro children, especially in the piedmont and southeastern districts. In some few of the county organizations this service has not been extended to the Negroes, but this is the case in only a very few of the counties. The statement may be conservatively made that during the last thirteen years nurses working for the State Board of Health exclusively have examined more than one hundred and fifty thousand Negro school children. Dentists working for the State Board of Health exclusively have examined between fifty and seventy-five thousand Negro school children. The educational value of these two enterprises has probably accomplished more in improving the health of Negro school children on a state-wide scale than any other agency operating in the state during the period.

CHAPTER XVIII

CONCLUSIONS AND RECOMMENDATIONS

THE PRIMARY purpose of this study has been to secure and to present such information as would enable the public welfare system in all its branches to function more successfully in extending its services to the Negro population of the state. Additional objectives have been the improving of the standards of care in the Negro child-caring institutions, and the working out of a state-wide program for the care of the feebleminded Negro children of North Carolina. Many detailed suggestions and recommendations have been made throughout the study, especially in relation to institutional management. Instead of repeating here all these recommendations—many of a minor value—it probably would be more worth while to concentrate attention upon a few major recommendations of far-reaching significance, and state-wide in scope, which affect the welfare and happiness of the Negro children of North Carolina. The recommendations are as follows:

1. That institutional provision should be made to care for Negro feebleminded children. In the interest of economy, it probably would be advisable, instead of establishing an entirely new institution, to establish at the State Hospital in Goldsboro, or at Caswell Training School, a separate colony for this most neglected type of state wards.

2. That a Maternity Home for Negro unmarried mothers, with a capacity of fifty beds, and serving the entire state, should be established in the central Piedmont area, preferably under private auspices, such as the State Federation of Negro Women's Clubs.

3. That the Industrial School for (Delinquent) Negro Girls at Efland, now operated and chiefly supported by the

Federation of Negro Women's Clubs, should be taken over by the state, and the facilities of the institution so enlarged as to provide for an increased number of girls, with improved medical care, educational and social training.

4. That some state-wide facilities should be provided for the placement of Negro children in foster homes, comparable to the Greensboro Children's Home Society which serves white dependent children.

5. That in every county where the Negroes compose as much as one-third of the total population, and in other counties where the Negro population exceeds ten thousand, a Negro case worker should be added to the staff of the County Superintendent of Public Welfare.

6. That there should be added to the staff of the State Board of Charities and Public Welfare:

a. A consultant in juvenile court organization and procedure.

b. One or more Negro case workers to serve the child welfare field.

7. In view of the fact that 69 per cent of the Negro births in North Carolina in 1931 were attended by midwives, social workers, public health nurses, physicians, and leading women of both races in the various communities of North Carolina are urged to assist the maternity and infancy program of the State Board of Health, (1) in getting prenatal literature in the hands of all expectant Negro mothers, and (2) in arranging for midwife classes twice a year in the local communities.

8. The mortality rate for Negro babies in North Carolina is excessively high during the first year. If the free literature on the hygiene of maternity and infancy provided by the State Board of Health, which gives instruction as to the simple methods of feeding during the first year, could be more generally distributed among Negro mothers of infants, the mortality rate would be greatly reduced.

INDEX

low-up work, 10, 11; paroles and pardons, 10; purpose, 5, 6.

Dosher, Lois, field worker, ix.

Duke, B. N., gift of Negro ward for crippled, 9, 137. *See* Duke Memorial Ward.

Duke Foundation, gifts to Memorial Industrial School, 104.

Duke Memorial Ward, orthopedic hospital, Ch. VI, 137-148; diet, 140; diseases treated, 140; education of children, 138, 139; number treated, 140; religious instruction, 139.

Education, Negro, Ch. XVI, 307-314; aid, outside agencies, 311-314; elementary school attendance, 307; General Education Board, aid, 312, 313; high school attendance, 307, 308; higher institutions, 310, 311; Jeans fund, 313; Phelps-Stokes fund, 313, 314; educational status Julius Rosenwald fund, 311; Slater fund, 313, 314; educational status of teachers, 310.

Efland. *See* North Carolina Industrial School for Negro Girls.

Family life, Negro, 160, 257, 258; case studies, 217-221; 228-231; 236-242; 245, 246, 249; 252-255; mother's aid as preserver, Ch. XIV, 269-275.

Farm demonstration agents, work of, 13.

Feebleminded, care for. *See* State Hospital for Negro Insane.

Follow-up work, Division of Work, 10, 11.

Foster homes. *See* Boarding homes.

Health work for Negro children, Ch. XVII, 315-320; county service, 316, 317; infant mortality, 317, 318; maternity and infant hygiene, 319; medical inspection, schools, 319, 320; medical service at Colored Orphanage, 90-95; at Memorial Industrial School, 122-127; at Morrison Training School, 41-43; at N. C. Industrial School for Negro Girls, 56; nurses, work of, 13; or-

ganization work for Negroes, 315, 316; Parent-Teacher Association, 310; State Board, attitude toward Negroes, 315; extent of State Board work, 316, 317; tuberculosis tests, 147, 148. *See* Duke Memorial Ward *and* Sanatorium.

Home demonstration agents, work of, 13.

Housing, Negro, 220, 221, 231, 241, 242, 254, 255; case study, 270, 271, 297; unmarried mothers, 283, 284.

Illegitimacy, Negro, Ch. XV, 276-306; ages of mothers, 282, 283; attitude of churches, 286, 287; attitude of midwives, 295-297; attitude of whites, 282, 295; case studies, 296-306; causes, 278, 280, 294, 295; disposal of children, 287-289; financial aid to mothers, all sources, 293; financial aid from fathers, 291-293; home ownership, 284; marital status of mothers, 289-291; number births, five-year period, 287; occupations of mothers, 293, 294; Orange County, table, 281; rate by race, 276; school record of mothers, 285, 286; treatment at birth, 278.

Institutes of Public Welfare for Negroes, annual, 8.

Jeanes, Anna T., fund for Negro education, 313; supervisors, work of, 12, 13; effect on school enrollment, 307.

Johnson, Kate Burr, suggestions for research, vi.

Juvenile courts, cases classified, 200-202; cases by county, race, sex, 210-214; charges against children, 193-196; charges classified, 203; charges, distribution by race and sex, 204; effectiveness, 185-189; immorality charges, white and Negro, 194, 195; method of securing records of, 183, 184; municipal, 184; number and types of children handled, 189-192; purpose of law, 183; records, as sources of study, viii; records faulty, 185-189; whipping as punishment, 197-199.

www.ingramcontent.com/pod-product-compliance
Lightning Source LLC
Chambersburg PA
CBHW020335270326
41926CB00007B/186